THE LAW OF THE SEA: U.S. INTERESTS AND ALTERNATIVES

A conference sponsored by the
American Enterprise Institute for Public Policy Research
and the U.S. Department of the Treasury

THE LAW OF THE SEA:
U.S. INTERESTS
AND ALTERNATIVES

Edited by
Ryan C. Amacher and Richard James Sweeney

American Enterprise Institute for Public Policy Research
Washington, D. C.

ISBN 0-8447-2072-0 (Paper)
ISBN 0-8447-2073-9 (Cloth)

Library of Congress Catalog Card No. 76-1303

© 1976 by American Enterprise Institute for Public Policy Research
1150 Seventeenth Street, N.W., Washington, D. C. 20036

Printed in the United States of America

CONTRIBUTORS

Seyom Brown
Senior Fellow, The Brookings Institution

Kenneth W. Dam
Professor of Law, University of Chicago

Ross D. Eckert
Associate Professor of Economics, University of Southern California
and Fellow, The Hoover Institution, Stanford University

Northcutt Ely
Attorney, Washington, D. C.

Ann L. Hollick
Executive Director, Ocean Policy Project
Johns Hopkins School of Advanced International Studies

David B. Johnson
Professor of Economics, Louisiana State University

James L. Johnston
Standard Oil of New Jersey
Former member, U.S. delegation to UN Conference
on the Law of the Sea

H. Gary Knight
Campanile Charities Professor of Marine Resources Law
Sea Grant Legal Program, Louisiana State University

Dennis E. Logue
Associate Professor of Business, Amos Tuck School
of Business Administration, Dartmouth College

John Norton Moore
Chairman, U.S. Law of the Sea Task Force

Myres S. McDougal
Sterling Professor of Law, Emeritus, Yale University

CONTENTS

PART THREE
Epilogue

INTRODUCTION AND OVERVIEW OF THE CONFERENCE

Ryan C. Amacher and Richard James Sweeney

This volume presents the proceedings of a conference sponsored by the U.S. Treasury and the American Enterprise Institute to help focus attention on U.S. interests in the law of the sea negotiations and to discuss possible alternatives to a comprehensive treaty. This conference was held on 14 February 1975 and was attended by more than fifty private and government lawyers, economists, and political scientists. The participants were carefully chosen by the conference organizers to represent a broad spectrum of views of the law of the sea negotiations.

The morning session of the conference concentrated on U.S. interests. The session was chaired by Ronald Coase of the University of Chicago Law School.

The first paper, "U.S. Security Interests and the Law of the Sea," is written by Robert E. Osgood, dean of Johns Hopkins School of Advanced International Studies. Osgood, formerly of the National Security Council staff, points out that U.S. military security interests lie in the use of ocean space to achieve five goals: maintenance of a strategic nuclear capability, maintenance of adequate capacity to project American forces overseas, maintenance of access to vital resources, maintenance of adequate surveillance capabilities, and maintenance of peacetime naval functions. He then discusses the type of treaty or regime that would attain these objectives.

As far as the law of the sea is concerned, Osgood argues that U.S. strategic interests boil down to the problem of protecting only two straits, Gibraltar and the Indonesian straits. Most important from the standpoint of protecting American nuclear strategic interests in these two straits is simply to carry on the kinds of modi vivendi that we already have with Malaysia, Indonesia, and Spain. This does not require a universal law, but rather, favorable political relations with the few countries involved. The concessions that would have to be made in order to reach a compromise on straits for a law of the sea treaty are, by comparison, not worth making.

Osgood feels that the future environment within which we have to protect our military mobility, for various purposes concerning conventional force and the projection of conventional force to support far-flung commitments, is going to be rather inhospitable. It will be an environment in which coastal states will

1

be more assertive of their desire to control what goes on in waters a good way off their shores. Any ocean regime must, therefore, accommodate itself to the concerns and apprehensions of these states. Osgood's conclusion is that the United States is not so badly off in the present environment with a variety of ad hoc modi vivendi, however politically messy and difficult that may be. Osgood cites our relations with Iran as a case in point. U.S. ocean security interests, as they bear on our relations with Iran, are not defined by a law of the sea treaty, but rather by the overall estimate of what U.S. interests are in what is, in effect, Iran's assertion of a kind of hegemony in the Persian Gulf.

Osgood concludes by arguing that there are critical limits to the ability of the United States effectively and usefully to insist upon codifying into international law the protection of interests that appear to be the interests of a few great maritime states, without jeopardizing the working arrangements that can affect its security interests.

The second paper, "U.S. Economic Interests in Law of the Sea Issues," by David B. Johnson of Louisiana State University and Dennis E. Logue of Dartmouth College, is an attempt to reach some tentative conclusions concerning the value of resources on the outer continental shelf, in the deep seabed, in fisheries, in rights of transit, and in pollution control.

Johnson and Logue collect and analyze empirical evidence concerning the stakes involved in the law of the sea deliberations. They express the hope that the data will provide an adequate frame of reference for the formulation of nego-tiating priorities and will assist in the analysis of those trade-offs necessary to any successful negotiation. The authors also hope that these data and the implications drawn from them will stimulate the Departments of State and Defense to place some values on the strategic and political variables so that trade-offs can be examined. For example, how many divisions, tanks, or ships would Defense be willing to give up to obtain free transit? How many foreign service officers would State be willing to "sacrifice" to obtain various specific articles in the 1970 U.S. draft treaty?

Initially they examine the potential benefits to the United States of free access to the mineral resources of the deep sea. For example, by 1985 the deep sea could meet 85 percent of U.S. manganese needs, 6 percent of U.S. copper needs, 85 percent of U.S. nickel needs, and provide nearly four times the annual cobalt requirement. Their estimates show that in subsequent years even greater propor-tions of U.S. needs might be supplied by deep-sea resources. The U.S. acceptance of a rigid regulatory regime, which would hinder free access to the minerals and the free choice of timing of exploitation, could cost the United States, under very conservative assumptions, as much as $310 million in 1985 and more in subse-quent years. Considerably greater economic costs would be borne by the United States if hydrocarbon resources were discovered in the area controlled by such a

2

restrictive regime. They therefore conclude that it appears that the choice of regulatory regime is a critical aspect of the law of the sea negotiations.

Johnson and Logue then examine the costs of particular proposals for the delineation of the continental margins and for revenue sharing on the margins. Their estimates suggest that the cost to the United States of accepting a narrow margin or agreeing to very high revenue-sharing rates may range from $2 to $8 billion per year, depending on the specifics of the arrangements.

Next they turn to the issue of freedom of transit through straits. With respect to commercial navigation, achieving agreement on the U.S. position might be worth $140 to $180 million per year, but only if *all* straits are closed and the United States still insists on carrying out previously established trade with those trading partners who control and have closed the straits—an unlikely circumstance. Because the data supporting these estimates are, unfortunately, quite incomplete, a case study is performed measuring the cost of shipping oil from the Persian Gulf to the United States given the assumption that all states have 200-mile territorial seas that can not be transgressed, thus closing off many of the straits used by oil tankers en route to the United States. The increase in oil transport costs to the United States would be $91 million per year at current import levels. Since these imports are likely to decline within a few years as a result of federal policy (Project Independence), this is a high estimate. It is also high because it would be unlikely that every coastal state would prohibit the passage of oil tankers within 200 miles of shore. On the basis of this analysis, it appears that free transit may not be worth as much to the United States as some analysts originally thought, although the analysis is admittedly incomplete—largely, they argue, because no one with knowledge of U.S. strategic military capabilities has addressed the issue, or released the results of their studies if they have, so that these important considerations might be included in an overall assessment of the worth of moving from the current regime of "innocent passage" to one of "free transit."

Johnson and Logue also consider the question of international pollution standards. Once again, the analysis is incomplete, although this time because specific standards have yet to be proposed at the law of the sea negotiations. They do, however, present a case study based upon the kinds of international standards being discussed at the International Maritime Consultative Organization. The standard examined is the requirement for double-skin segregated-ballast oil tankers to prevent oil discharge in ballasting operations. The case study reveals that the cost-benefit ratio for such a requirement was approximately twenty to one, that is, the costs of the requirement exceed its benefits by a wide margin. They also argue that nations, for their own self-interest, will naturally move toward relatively compatible standards; hence there is no pressing need for this issue to be resolved within the law of the sea deliberations. Moreover, the costs to the United States of accepting standards internationally agreed upon could be quite high.

Finally, they analyze the issue of fisheries and conclude that the type of fisheries regulation likely to emanate from an international treaty may be far worse than no regulation at all.

Johnson and Logue conclude their paper with a call for more analytical work on law of the sea issues. They feel that not enough analytical sophistication and empirical investigation have been brought to bear on the relevant issues and that this lack of sophistication will undermine the negotiating astuteness of the delegation.

The third paper, "Institutional Mechanisms for Dealing with International Externalities: A Public Choice Perspective," by Robert D. Tollison of Texas A&M University and Thomas D. Willett of the U.S. Treasury, attempts to provide some theoretical perspective on the law of the sea negotiations. The general theme of their remarks is that, given the difficulty of reaching international agreement, it would seem wise to concentrate efforts on those areas in which agreements can make the greatest contribution. It would be necessary, of course, to determine the degrees of prospective difficulty of achieving agreement in the various areas.

Tollison and Willett begin by looking at the relevant trade-offs involved in designing policies and institutions to internalize international externalities. One example of a prominent externality in the law of the sea negotiations is ocean pollution, where shippers and consumers of products dependent upon ocean shipping for transportation constitute an externality to the quality of the marine environment. They stress that not every international externality should be internalized at the highest level of government possible. In particular, merely to show that the market is failing to perform perfectly, or that there is some possible gain from coordination of national policies, is not sufficient reason to establish a clear case for international action. The need for caution in taking market or national government failure as a prima facie case for international intervention is reinforced by the recognition, derived essentially from contributions to the theory of public choice, that "perfect intervention" by governments or international organizations is as rare in the real world as the "perfect competition" of economists' models. Likewise, even where some degree of externality is imposed upon the whole community of nations, if the large majority of the externality is concentrated on a smaller subset of countries, then in an imperfect world, it may be more desirable to concentrate attempts at international action on this smaller number of countries. The issues here correspond closely to those of desirable patterns of fiscal federalism within a nation state.

Tollison and Willett then apply this approach to issues in the current negotiations on the law of the sea. Specifically, they examine the potential externalities from the exploitation of ocean resources and conclude that there is no economic

4

rationale for the international regulation of deep-ocean economic activity, except for the specific case of fish that reside, to an economically significant extent, in international waters. Second, they examine oil pollution control, and consider the externalities that can arise from the harmonization of pollution standards. Their basic conclusion in this discussion is that the costs of not having internationally agreed upon pollution standards have been generally overstated relative to the benefits.

Finally, they extend their discussion of the law of the sea negotiations to consider questions bearing on the process of the negotiations as such. They argue that the prospective gains from international action must be weighed against the costs of securing international agreement and the potential diversion of scarce collective decision-making resources from other more important areas. They specifically examine the effect that the number and the complexity of issues can have on negotiations.

In particular, they stress the importance of not bringing too many issues before the same negotiating forum and relate this general point to the slowness of progress in the law of the sea negotiations. They point out the possibility that in the current comprehensive law of the sea negotiations the number of issues may well have been pushed past the optimum number.

The discussants in this morning session generally supported the broad conclusions expressed in the papers. Seyom Brown of the Brookings Institution agreed that unimpeded passage through straits is not essential to U.S. strategic nuclear capabilities. However, his opinion was that bilateral interactions between states would be the least efficient and least effective way to handle the problem. Joseph S. Nye of Harvard University felt that the law of the sea conference is a worst case of a trend that has been evident for some time, a trend toward larger and more unwieldy conferences. Ross D. Eckert of the Hoover Institution at Stanford University agreed with Johnson and Logue in stressing the importance of relatively open access to the deep seabed.

The discussion that followed, with open participation from the floor, was lengthy and far-ranging. The consensus that seemed to emerge was that there are substantial economic interests for the United States in the law of the sea negotiations and that these issues had heretofore received too little consideration in U.S. policy. Further, it was felt that the conference is too large and that it would perhaps be best to split the negotiations—for example, to separate the issue of unimpeded transit through straits from that of negotiations on the deep seabed.

The purpose of the afternoon session was to examine alternative approaches to the negotiations. The session was chaired by Louis Sohn of Harvard University. The first paper, "The Third United Nations Conference on the Law of the

Sea: Caracas Review," was given by Ann Hollick of Johns Hopkins School of Advanced International Studies.

Hollick examines the law of the sea negotiations at the important 1974 sessions in Caracas. She argues that the task of the Caracas and other sessions, at least as officially defined, may be impossible. That is not to say that there will not be a treaty emanating from some later session. Indeed, the negotiators' interests in achieving some tangible results from the prolonged negotiations almost rule out the possibility that nothing will emerge. The treaty, however, will probably be either a widely accepted partial treaty or a comprehensive treaty accepted by a simple majority. The question posed by this outcome is whether the substance of the agreement will be desirable—from the U.S. or the global perspective. She argues, when she turns to examine the outlook for Geneva, that no treaty at all may be preferable to the treaty that seems likely to emerge there. But as she indicated earlier, there are significant pressures to produce some treaty. She feels that the political nature of the forum and the diversity of the interests that are accommodated in the negotiation determine that what does emerge will be the lowest common denominator—enormous extensions of national jurisdiction over ocean resources. With the exception of the landlocked and shelf-locked, which will be either placated or ignored, every state should get something from this extension. The principal beneficiaries will be certain developed countries, and South American and island states.

In the second paper, "Alternatives to a Law of the Sea Treaty," H. Gary Knight of Louisiana State University argues that there are many alternatives to a comprehensive treaty. Among these alternatives Knight lists: acquiescence in other nations' acts of agreements, use of force, negotiation-purchase, limited international agreement, domestic legislation, and combinations of all of the preceding. Knight argues that there appears to be a number of alternatives to a law of the sea treaty which, used in concert and where most appropriate on the basis of subject matter, could provide the framework for a reasonably stable regime in the oceans in the absence of a widely accepted and comprehensive law of the sea treaty. In fact, it would appear that U.S. interests could be most adequately protected through a combination of domestic legislation, limited treaties, purchase of rights, and the occasional application of force. This being the case, a strong argument can be made for the United States not to sign or ratify any law of the sea treaty which fails to satisfy all of its major policy interests.

The discussants of these papers, and the view from the floor, generally supported the arguments in the papers. It was felt that there is a wide range of alternatives to a comprehensive law of the sea treaty and that failure to reach agreement in Geneva will not result in chaos.

A late appearance was made by John Norton Moore, chairman of the United States Law of the Sea Task Force. He expressed his optimistic belief that Caracas was a transition session and that it is now possible to go forward toward a treaty that will benefit all nations. He argued that the alternative to a treaty might be conflict and chaos in the ocean.

The conference ended with Moore's argument that we should not despair, because there is a good likelihood of a treaty, while much of the earlier argument had been concerned with the fear that a treaty might be reached.

Since publication lags are such that this volume is appearing after the Geneva session of the law of the sea negotiations, we asked James Johnston to prepare a review and progress report of that session, which appears as Part Three of this collection. We are grateful to Thomas F. Johnson of the American Enterprise Institute and Thomas D. Willett of the U.S. Treasury for cooperating in such a way as to make our task as organizers of the conference and editors of this volume proceed much more smoothly.

PART ONE

U.S. INTERESTS IN OCEAN POLICY

U.S. SECURITY INTERESTS
AND THE LAW OF THE SEA

Robert E. Osgood

U.S. Ocean Security Interests

U.S. security interests in the use of ocean space can be divided into the maintenance of military security (including the protection of allies and American citizens)
and the preservation of vital economic interests. If the United States maintains an
adequate balance of military power in the strategic nuclear realm, at key points
locally and at sea, and the constraints of detente moderate Soviet behavior, economic security may be the more critical concern in the next ten years. But economic
security is too large a subject and too ill defined to receive the examination it
deserves in this analysis. It is mentioned, therefore, only in its closest and most
critical connection with military security: the use of the sea-lanes to ship goods
and resources.

U.S. military security interests, broadly conceived, lie in the effective use
of four zones of ocean space—the seabed, the surface, the subsurface, and the
superjacent air—in order to: (1) maintain an adequate strategic nuclear capability; (2) maintain an adequate capacity to project American forces overseas
in local wars; (3) protect U.S. citizens, commerce, and access to vital resources
in peacetime; (4) maintain adequate intelligence and military surveillance capabilities; and (5) protect the sea-lanes, project forces abroad, maintain combat
capabilities, and perform other naval functions in a more-than-local war.

The question this paper addresses is, what kind of ocean regime—that is,
what set of norms, laws, and institutions governing the relations of states in the
use of the ocean—should the United States try to establish in order to attain
these security objectives through the use of the four zones of ocean space? Since
I assume that the nature of this regime would make no difference in a more-than-
local war, only the first four objectives are regarded as relevant to the question
posed.

The Political Context

Evidently, the U.S. government is determined to achieve its ocean security objectives in the context of a foreign policy that can be characterized as selective

11

retrenchment without political disengagement; that is, the reduction of the extent of U.S. foreign support and involvement, without the abandonment of existing commitments. The first concern of this policy is the orchestration of a global modus vivendi with the Soviet Union, undergirded by overall strategic parity. While reaffirming its pledge to shield allies and other states of vital interest from direct aggression by nuclear states, the United States has virtually ruled out direct participation in insurgent wars.

Even if the United States meets with a modicum of success in achieving these objectives over the next five or ten years, there will be local wars and crises. Various situations will jeopardize the security of friendly regimes and the unhindered supply of petroleum and possibly other resources, and in these situations American armed force may directly or indirectly make the difference between the loss and the protection of vital interests. And even if the actual employment of U.S. armed forces remains only an ambiguous possibility, the U.S. government will want to maintain the credibility of American military power and to manifest that power through military demonstrations and maneuvers. It requires little imagination to apply this generalization to the Middle East.[1] Only a lack of foresight prevents us from anticipating its relevance to other areas in a period in which nationalism, conflict, and warfare trouble so much of the developing world.

The world situations most likely to damage U.S. broad security interests, however, may be those which the United States cannot affect by military means, directly or indirectly, and over which it has little or no control by any means. These are situations in which American military mobility, military bases, access to oil, and less tangible security interests are damaged by the actions of the weaker and poorer countries, actions which the United States is inhibited from countering by force. Or they may be situations in which the conflicts among other states accidently impinge on American interests. (This latter type of situation arose in the "cod war" between Britain and Iceland, which threatened to lead to expulsion of the NATO base from Iceland.)

If the frustrations and resentments of the less-developed countries, no longer able to exploit cold war competition, should be directed against the developed countries in the form of harassment and pressure—whether for purposes of revenue, political influence, or just for nationalist self-assertion—the United States might find its security as threatened as it was at the height of cold war competition

---

[1] For example, one might recall a January 1975 incident in which the press reported Secretary of State Kissinger's carefully phrased interview with *Business Week*. While rejecting the use of armed force against members of the Organization of Petroleum Exporting Countries (OPEC) to bring down the price of oil, Kissinger conspicuously refrained from rejecting the use of force in case of "some actual strangulation of the industrialized world," and Secretary of Defense Schlesinger followed by stating that military action in the Middle East to prevent strangulation would be feasible. Subsequent assurances that the conditions under which the use of force might have to be contemplated were "absolutely hypothetical" and quite unlikely to exist did not offset the public impression that, at the least, drastic and overt actions, such as an embargo, could provoke U.S. armed action.

for influence in the third world. The rising dependence of the United States and its allies on oil and other natural resources of developing countries and on straits, seas, and the rights of overflight controlled by developing countries makes American commercial and military mobility particularly vulnerable. Thus, one of the primary U.S. security imperatives may become the formation of mutually advantageous and acceptable working relationships with coastal states in the third world. Success will depend on assuring developing countries generally that the ocean interests of the great maritime states are not inconsistent with their own newfound pride and independence, in a period in which the resource-rich countries of the third world are determined to redress the balance of wealth and power between themselves and the powerful resource-dependents.

Strategic Nuclear Interests

Turning to the specific ocean security interests that the United States must try to maintain in the international political environment of the next five or ten years, we must give priority to the preservation of an adequate strategic nuclear balance. Here the chief objective must be to maintain the effectiveness of U.S. nuclear-powered submarines carrying nuclear missiles (SSBNs)—currently the Polaris/Poseidon fleet—because the installation of many independently guided warheads on missiles (MIRVs) and improvements in missile accuracy increase the importance of concealing missiles under the ocean.

The U.S. government maintains that the invulnerability of SSBNs, and hence their indispensable role in an adequate second-strike force, depends upon their right to pass through international straits submerged and unannounced—a right initially called "free transit" but more recently called "unimpeded transit" as a concession to legitimate regulations to protect littoral states from the hazards of congested straits. Under existing law only innocent passage, which requires surfacing of all submarines, would be legal in straits that fall within territorial boundaries.[2] This distinction is considered very important, because under a twelve-mile territorial sea boundary more than a dozen straits of possible significance would be overlapped by foreign territorial waters.

To assess the validity and practical importance of this position, a number of questions must be answered:

---

[2] According to Article 14, par. 6 of the 1958 convention, submarines passing through territorial seas "are required to navigate on the surface, and to show their flag." But the official U.S. interpretation of innocent passage (in line with the International Court of Justice's report in the 1949 Corfu Channel case that "states in time of peace have a right to send their warships through straits used for international navigation between two parts of the high seas without the previous authorization of a coastal State, provided that the passage is innocent") does not concede that advance notice of passage through territorial waters is required. Advance notice of transit through straits, the United States holds, might lead to coastal state control of transit. In practice, however, the United States evidently provides advance notice of surface ships but not of submarines (except perhaps where secret bilateral arrangements have been agreed).

(1) Which of the world's international straits (there are 121, according to an unofficial chart devised by the Office of the Geographer in the U.S. Department of State) that would be overlapped by territorial waters if twelve-mile boundaries were agreed might also be important for the mobility of the U.S. Polaris and Poseidon fleet in reaching specified target areas?

The strategic importance of straits is a matter of opinion, but at a reasonable maximum this category would include, according to information provided by the same chart, sixteen straits: Gibraltar, two Middle Eastern straits (Bab el Mandeb and Hormuz), four Southeast Asian straits (Malacca, Lombok, Sunda, and Ombai-Wetar), Western Chosen strait (between South Korea and Japan), five Caribbean straits (Old Bahamas Channel, Dominica, Martinique, Saint Lucia Channel, and Saint Vincent Passage), Dover, Bering, and the Kennedy-Robeson Channels.[3] Nine of these straits, however, are not essential to America's strategic capability, and some would fall inside the territory of military allies. The five Caribbean straits are not needed for transit to Polaris/Poseidon patrol stations, because the Caribbean is not an essential launching area. They are not even essential for access to the Caribbean, which contains several passages over twenty-four miles wide (for example, Mona, Windward, Anegada, and Guadaloupe).

Western Chosen, the western half of the strait between Japan and the Korean peninsula, is only twenty-three miles wide; but Japan, if not South Korea, would presumably permit U.S. strategic warships routinely to pass through this strait to the Sea of Japan. In any event, the eastern half of the strait, Tsushima Strait, is twenty-five miles wide. The real victim of any closure of the Korean straits would be Soviet general purpose forces: they would have to travel more than twice as far from Vladivostok to the Senkakus by the La Perouse route (north of Hokkaido and south of Sakhalin), thereby affecting Indian Ocean operations, China coast patrols, or submarine deployments from Nakhodka.

Bab el Mandeb offers no significant targeting advantage over the eastern Mediterranean (and transit through the French side of the strait would probably be available anyway). If the Soviet antisubmarine warfare (ASW) presence became oppressive there, or if Gibraltar were closed, the Red Sea could be considered an alternative deployment area. But nearly all targets accessible from the Red Sea are also accessible from the Persian Gulf. Those in areas that could not be reached from the gulf (eastern Europe, the Baltic coast, and the Leningrad area) could be covered from the Atlantic. Passage through Hormuz is probably not necessary, now that the shorter-range Polaris A–1 (with a 1,200 nautical-mile range) and A–2 (1,750 nautical miles) have been phased out in favor of the A–3 (2,880 nautical miles). With Holy Loch available on the west coast of Scotland, there is no great need for SSBNs to use Dover in the English Channel.

---

[3] The chart, entitled "World Straits Affected by a 12-Mile Territorial Sea," capitalizes sixteen straits as "major." I have substituted Kennedy-Robeson for Juan de Fuca.

(2) In which of the remaining straits is submerged passage physically feasible but politically unobtainable on a reliable basis?

Malacca is too shallow (ten to twelve fathoms) and too busy for submerged passage. Sunda is barely deep enough (twenty fathoms in the approaches) but requires a passage of over 700 miles within a fifty-fathom depth. The Bering Straits, although about forty-five miles wide, are split by the Diomede and the Little Diomede islands, making each half of the straits less than twenty-four miles wide. But since Little Diomede belongs to the United States, submerged passage to the Arctic is not in question politically. Similarly, the narrow route to the Arctic through the Kennedy-Robeson Channels is presumably accessible by submerged passage, since it is in Canadian waters.

This leaves Gibraltar and two Indonesian straits, Ombai-Wetar and Lombok, as strategically important straits through which the submerged passage of U.S. SSBNs is now physically and politically feasible but which might be politically questionable if a twelve-mile territorial boundary were established. The two Indonesian straits are important to SSBN operation from the Indian Ocean to Guam. Without submerged passage through them, the United States would have to circumnavigate Australia (greatly reducing the number of days on active patrol), or double back to one of the entrances to the Timor Sea, 180 to 500 miles east of Ombai-Wetar (which would still require passage through Indonesian waters).

An additional hindrance to secret passage through Indonesian waters is Indonesia's interpretation of the archipelago principle of enclosed waters: the two strategically important straits are claimed to be internal rather than international waters.[4] Although the Indonesian government has argued that the archipelago principle does not infringe on innocent passage, it requires prior notification of transit by foreign warships and has begun to raise questions about the innocence of supertanker passage because of the danger of pollution. In April 1972, Chairman of the Joint Chiefs of Staff Admiral Thomas H. Moorer stated that the United States must have the freedom to go through, under, and over the Malacca Strait. Shortly thereafter, the chief of staff of the Indonesian navy reportedly warned, "Our armed forces will attack any foreign submarines entering territorial waters without permit, because it means a violation of Indonesia's sovereignty."[5] In spite of Indonesian jurisdictional claims, the United States maintains that the Indonesian straits are international. According to press accounts and Indonesian sources, however, the United States routinely provides prior notifi-

---

[4] In December 1957, the Indonesian government declared that "all waters surrounding, between, and linking the islands to the State of Indonesia . . . constitute natural parts of inland or national waters under the absolute jurisdiction of the State of Indonesia. . . . The 12 miles of territorial waters are measured from the line connecting the promontory point of the islands of the Indonesian state." Embassy of Indonesia, *Report on Indonesia*, vol. 8, no. 7 (Washington, D. C.: November-December 1957, January 1958).

[5] Captain Edward F. Oliver, "Malacca: Dire Straits," *U.S. Naval Institute Proceedings*, June 1973, p. 29.

cation of transit by surface ships and presumably (if only as a practical convenience) relies on some special bilateral navy-to-navy arrangement for submerged passage consistent with the requirements of concealing the details of SSBN passage from foreign intelligence.[6] Although this modus vivendi is rather contingent, it satisfies America's needs as long as an Indonesian government as friendly as that of Suharto is in power.

Gibraltar presents a more complicated situation. Although the strait is only 11.5 miles wide and Spain claims a 6-mile territorial sea, its international character has been preserved by historic tradition and by the treaties of 1904 and 1912 among Britain, France, and Spain that provide for secure free passage. In March 1971, however, foreign rights of transit became more restricted when Spain and Morocco agreed to cooperate to "promote the creation of Mediterranean awareness" and to consult on all matters of peace and security in the Mediterranean, particularly in the strait. In June 1972, the Spanish government announced at the United Nations that the freezing of naval forces and subsequent progressive reductions in the Mediterranean should be considered. At the same time, it indicated the necessity for some compromise between free transit and the rights of coastal states, such compromise to be achieved by a redefinition of the right of innocent passage.

Thus Spain may have prepared the way for asserting a unilateral right to force submarines passing through the Strait of Gibraltar to surface. On the other hand, the effect of such a claim on U.S. SSBNs will depend primarily on the political relations between the United States and Spain. As long as U.S. submarines are based at Rota, submerged transit of U.S. submarines will be permitted through the Strait of Gibraltar. However, even the closure of Gibraltar to unannounced submerged U.S. submarine passage would not be disastrous to America's strategic capability. After all, the Polaris/Poseidon system can target the entire Soviet Union from the Atlantic and Pacific oceans and the Arabian Sea. Although there has apparently been no need for SSBN patrols in the Indian Ocean, an Indian Ocean base—say, Diego Garcia—would obviate the need to use Gibraltar or the Indonesian straits altogether.

(3) To what extent would surface transit of U.S. SSBNs through straits impair their invulnerability to Soviet detection, identification, and—in the event of war—destruction?

This question really subsumes several others:

(a) Is it more difficult for the Soviets to detect and identify submerged U.S. SSBNs coming through straits than it is for them to detect surfaced SSBNs?

The answer is surely "yes" (assuming, of course, that submerged transit is not announced in advance to the straits state, thus alerting Soviet intelligence).

---

[6] The U.S. government officially denies that it has any agreement with any country to provide advance notice of the passage of warships through international straits.

It is relatively easy to detect surface passage through straits by means of surface vessels, land observers, or satellites. By far the most effective and practicable means of electronic surveillance of submerged vessels is a series of hydrophones (or sonars) connected by undersea cables anchored to the continental shelf, like the U.S. CAESAR and COLOSSUS system. However, this device has to be hooked up to a listening station on the shore, which would seem to preclude installation of it by the Soviet Union at Gibraltar or in Indonesia for the foreseeable future.[7] Moreover, in the high traffic-density straits of Gibraltar and Lombok, the high level of background noise would make it very difficult to single out transiting nuclear submarines. Even in the less-traveled Ombai-Wetar, possible Soviet hydrophone arrays would have to be supplemented by "trawlers" or towed arrays to be effective. The United States and the Soviet Union have developed ocean surveillance satellites, but U.S. efforts to use them to detect submerged vessels have proved impractical for basic physical reasons that technology probably will be unable to overcome in the near future. The Soviets would enhance their submerged detection capability if they were willing to assign nuclear-powered antisubmarine submarines (SSNs) to monitor the critical straits; but the difficulty that Soviet nuclear antisubmarines have had in shadowing American SSBNs from bases indicates that SSNs would be no substitute for fixed hydrophone arrays.

(b) To what extent and how consistently can the Soviet Union locate American SSBNs after passage through straits, assuming that Soviet surveillance detects and identifies these SSBNs?

It is now extremely difficult, and promises to remain so for the indefinite future, to track submarines that submerge after passing through straits, even if passage has been observed. It is virtually impossible to track all SSBNs on patrol (that is, in position to fire).[8] Open-area surveillance from aircraft, surface ships, and satellites will continue to have limited effectiveness unless and until large parts of the ocean floor are covered with a network of bottom detection systems in

---

[7] Hydrophone arrays towed by surface ships can be almost as effective as implanted systems, but the cost is much greater. Moreover, it is unlikely that towed arrays could avoid extended territorial seas off straits any better than implanted arrays can. It is technically possible to deploy implanted arrays at great distances from shore stations, but the need for amplifiers and the problem of breaks and maintenance make this option unattractive.

[8] Thus Secretary of Defense Laird stated on 20 February 1970, "according to our best estimates, we believe that our Polaris and Poseidon submarines at sea can be considered virtually invulnerable today. With a highly concentrated effort, the Soviet Navy might be able to localize and destroy at sea one or two Polaris submarines. But the massive and expensive undertaking that would be required to extend such a capability using currently known techniques would take time and would certainly be evident." He added, however, "A combination of technological developments and the decision by the Soviets to undertake a worldwide antisubmarine warfare effort might result in some increased degree of Polaris/Poseidon vulnerability beyond the mid-1970s. But, as a defense planner, I would never guarantee the invulnerability of *any* strategic system beyond the reasonably foreseeable future, say 5-7 years." Statement before joint session of Senate Armed Services and Appropriations Committees, cited in Stockholm International Peace Research Institute (SIPRI), *Yearbook of World Armaments and Disarmament, 1970-71,* p. 122.

communication with surface ships and aircraft. The most effective antisubmarine method in wartime is a forward barrier-control system, utilizing coordinated bottom detection devices, other sensors, attack submarines, and antisubmarine aircraft. In peacetime, however, this system cannot prevent SSBNs from passing through the barrier and disappearing.

(c) Would the Soviet capacity to destroy American SSBNs tracked and located after detected passage through straits significantly affect the U.S. second-strike capacity?

This is unlikely, unless one estimates the requirements of an adequate second-strike capability to be very low. To reduce the U.S. second-strike capability significantly, the Soviets would have to simultaneously knock out most of the twenty to twenty-five American SSBNs on station. Merely a few Poseidon-carrying submarines (eventually thirty-one of the forty-one U.S. SSBNs will carry Poseidons), each carrying sixteen missiles with ten MIRVs on each missile, could overwhelm the Soviet ABM system. Moreover, this situation will last at least as long as the initial Strategic Arms Limitation Treaty limiting deployment of ABMs is in effect.

(4) How will the prospective new Trident SSBN system affect the need to use the critical straits in question?

Although the amount of congressional funding and the outcome of efforts in the Strategic Arms Limitation Talks to limit SSBNs are uncertain, the development of a new Underwater Long-Range Missile System (ULMS) for the Trident SSBN system may produce a successor to Polaris/Poseidon in the 1980s. The Trident submarine would carry twenty-four missiles with MIRV warheads having a range of between 4,500 and 6,500 nautical miles. It would be quieter, dive deeper, and remain on station for longer periods. Deployment of the Trident system—or deployment of ULMS on Poseidon submarines, planned for fiscal 1978—would virtually obviate the dependence of the U.S. underwater nuclear force on transit of straits.

Given these considerations, a law of the sea treaty sanctioning twelve-mile territorial boundaries but excluding free transit of international straits would not seriously weaken nuclear deterrence, although it would make operation of the American SSBN fleet more difficult. From an operational standpoint, having to surface would be more difficult for nuclear antisubmarines, which play an important role in the strategic nuclear equation. Even though surface transit of SSNs would give Soviet intelligence more information, it would neither increase the willingness of the Soviet Union to launch a nuclear first-strike nor greatly enhance the efficacy of Soviet salvos after an initial nuclear exchange. In any event, the same requirements of surfacing imposed on Soviet SSNs would offset the disadvantage to the U.S. underwater deterrent.

18

Aside from the problem of detection, however, there are other operational disadvantages to surfacing nuclear submarines in straits. Where high-density traffic occurs, as in narrow straits and around headlands, the nuclear submarine is safer itself and less hazardous to surface shipping when it is below the surface. One reason is its huge size. An advanced model, such as the *Lafayette*, is 425 feet in length, has a beam of 33 feet and a submerged displacement of 8,750 tons, which means that it is longer than World War II destroyers and heavier than some World War II light cruisers. The nuclear submarine is designed to operate best underwater, where it has greatest maneuverability and its sensors work most efficiently. With a low conning tower and very little superstructure, the submarine must waive some construction standards in order to comply with requirements for light reduction for night navigation. Merchantmen find a submarine hard to detect both because of the minimal lighting and because much of its hull is below the surface and not visible to electronic searchers (radar). Moreover, a submarine's ability to travel under the surface frees it from the limitation of surface weather and wave motion, and any submarine is particularly vulnerable to collision because of its small reservoir of buoyancy.

The operational disadvantages of surface transit could be avoided, of course, if the United States would give littoral states advance notification of underwater transit, providing that the critical states in question would regard underwater transit on these terms as a satisfactory arrangement. However, this hypothesis only illustrates that the first issue is the importance of secret passage.

When pressed to explain the necessity for free transit of straits, U.S. officials have referred not only to the security of secret passage and to the safety of submerged passage, but also to the prospect that, without an international treaty prescribing free transit, straits states might resort to "subjective" (that is, politically inspired) interpretations of innocent passage to restrict the passage of U.S. warships. Thus John R. Stevenson, chief of the U.S. delegation to the UN Seabed Committee, testified before Congress that "we would not contemplate notifying [littoral states of an intention to transit straits] because if such a requirement is introduced, there is of course ultimately a risk of this leading to control of transit through straits." This danger, Stevenson said, lies mostly in the future, and he cited no case in which the requirement of advance notification had been used to restrict naval transit.[9]

---

[9] Testimony presented 10 April 1973 before the Subcommittee on International Organizations and Movements, House Committee on Foreign Affairs, 92d Cong., 2d sess., p. 12. Stevenson and Jared Carter, of the Department of Defense, substantiated the risk by citing Egypt's denial of passage to a commercial vessel in the straits leading to the Gulf of Aqaba before the June 1967 Arab-Israeli war, on the grounds that the cargo bound to Israel was not innocent. (Egypt, however, based its contention on the position that there had been a state of war since 1948.) Carter added that there were other examples of states claiming that warships do not have the right of innocent passage.

The risk of restrictive interpretations of innocent passage, however, applies largely to commercial vessels on grounds of navigational safety and pollution control. This point has recently received considerable attention, after years of neglect, because of the oil industry's heightened interest in unencumbered shipping. Safety and pollution control would seem to be objectively important grounds for controlling the passage of ships offshore. But assuming that there is a real danger that littoral states will interpret innocent passage and the requirement of advance notification in order to deny transit of straits to American warships for purely political reasons, why would these states sign a treaty prescribing unimpeded passage or be deterred by such a treaty?

Aside from SSBNs, there are other components of the U.S. strategic capability that deserve our attention. In the controversy over free transit through straits, the issue of overflight has been virtually ignored in public statements, although the U.S. position on the law of the sea treaty, presumably for strategic reasons, prescribes free transit over straits for military aircraft. (International law does not recognize innocent passage for overflight.) According to the prevailing official Triad nuclear deterrent system, the U.S. strategic nuclear capability requires manned aircraft as well as SSBNs and land-based missiles. The U.S. strategic bombing force is still a significant weapons system, with some distinct advantage of mobility and of control responsive to political guidance. One might suppose that effective denial of military overflight over key straits would seriously impair the utility of the U.S. strategic bombing force as a deterrent. In practice, however, the right to fly over twenty-four-mile straits has not proved critical to the U.S. strategic bomber force (as distinguished from the U.S. military airlift capability). Overflight of straits is only a small part of the pattern of overflight, managed by special arrangements where necessary; denial of overflight rights is physically infeasible for most states in any case.[10]

The emphasis in American ocean policy on free transit under, through, or over international straits has somewhat overshadowed another official concern: that the U.S. strategic capability may be hampered by territorial or continental-shelf jurisdictions claimed or established by coastal states.

The breadth of the continental shelf under national jurisdiction might have some effect on the freedom of the United States to place passive antisubmarine listening devices (SOSUS) on the shelf, particularly off the shores of foreign

---

[10] For those nations in which the United States has its own bases or regular access to foreign bases, the United States has interpreted overflight rights to be implicit in permission to use the bases. If there are no such base rights, permission for overflight is supposed to depend on diplomatic clearances (received by filing one-time transit requests with the defense attachés three or four days in advance of the flights). In emergencies the U.S. practice has been to get clearance, go around, or, infrequently, fly over without clearance. In practice, the distribution of American bases has obviated serious overflight restrictions. In the Middle East crisis of November 1973, however, only Portugal granted the United States overflight, thereby making it necessary to fly over the Strait of Gibraltar.

countries.[11] Apparently, these devices are most effective beyond the 200-meter depth and part way down the slope of the shelf,[12] although their effectiveness also depends on the peculiar acoustic properties of the ocean at various temperatures, depths, and degrees of salinity, and particularly on the depth of the sound channel that focuses sound energy in deep water. Presumably, the United States would not place SOSUS on shelf areas restricted by existing international law or protected by a new international treaty. Therefore, if SOSUS is vital to America's strategic capability, any ocean regime that extended territorial sovereignty over the whole continental margin would adversely affect U.S. military security.

Whatever the strategic or other military importance of antisubmarine warfare,[13] hydrophone arrays on the ocean bottom are (and will remain for the next five to ten years) critically important to the U.S. antisubmarine warfare capability. These acoustic devices may be vulnerable to Soviet interference, but it is safe to assume that the Soviet Union is installing many of the same kinds of devices and therefore has a vested interest in not interfering with those of the United States. Most developing countries do not have the capability to locate and destroy the arrays. In any case, the United States denies that it has placed them off their shores.

---

[11] See, particularly, the proceedings of 1969-70 in the Eighteen Nation Disarmament Committee (ENDC), renamed the Conference of the Committee on Disarmament (CCD) in August 1969, which led to the 1971 publication of Edward Duncan Brown's *Treaty on the Prohibition of the Emplacement of Nuclear Weapons and Other Weapons of Mass Destruction on the Seabed and the Ocean Floor and in the Subsoil Thereof*. Brown draws principally from CCD and other UN documents, such as the proceedings of the Seabed Committee, in examining the legal status of passive listening devices on the continental shelf in *Arms Control in Hydrospace: Legal Aspects* (Woodrow Wilson International Center for Scholars, Ocean Series 301, June 1971), pp. 22-35. See also SIPRI, *Yearbook of World Armaments and Disarmament*, 1969-70, pp. 154-79; Captain L. E. Zeni, "Defense Needs in Accommodations among Ocean Users," in Lewis M. Alexander, ed., *Law of the Sea: International Rules and Organization for the Sea* (Kingston, R. I.: University of Rhode Island, 1969), p. 33; John A. Knauss, "The Military Role in the Ocean and its Relation to the Law of the Sea," in Lewis M. Alexander, ed., *The Law of the Sea: A New Geneva Conference* (Kingston, R. I.: University of Rhode Island, 1972).

[12] One can infer this from the fact that the original U.S. position on the prospective law of the sea treaty implicitly protected the legal right of the United States to emplace such devices on the continental shelf beyond the 200-meter depth. See also, Knauss, "The Military Role in the Ocean," p. 79. Article 3 of the U.S. draft seabed treaty provides that the area beyond this depth "shall be open to use by all States, without discrimination, except as otherwise provided in this Convention." The only exception pertains to the exploration and exploitation of certain natural resources. In tabling the treaty, U.S. representatives, in a studied reference to military uses of the seabed, pointed out that it expressly protected the rights of states to conduct activities other than exploration and exploitation of certain natural resources in the area beyond the 200-meter isobath.

[13] The utility of antisubmarine warfare as a deterrent to a nuclear attack would seem to be negligible since its contribution to the U.S. second-strike capability by protecting SSBNs is insignificant as compared with that of the other components of this capability. Antisubmarine warfare would play a major role, as a part of the U.S. strategic war-fighting capability, particularly in protecting convoys. But the utility of protecting convoys in any reasonably imaginable war with the Soviet Union is highly questionable. Moreover, the efficacy of antisubmarine warfare against SSNs is probably declining. For a balanced and skeptical analysis of the role of naval forces in general war, see Laurence W. Martin, *The Sea in Modern Strategy* (London: Institute for Strategic Studies, 1967), chap. 2.

These facts notwithstanding, the utility of SOSUS would not be critically affected even by the broadest boundary of coastal state sovereignty on the continental shelf. The crucial monitoring areas where SOSUS needs to be emplaced, and the submarine passageways in which the devices are most useful, are the Greenland-Iceland-United Kingdom gap, the Arctic, the North Pacific, and the Caribbean. With the possible exception of Iceland, enough of the northern European countries are concerned about the Soviet SSBN force to permit U.S. listening devices in the area. Considering the width of the shelf off Alaska and Canada, the emplacement of hydrophone arrays in the Arctic would not be severely restricted by a shelf convention. With Guam, Midway, Hawaii, Alaska, and the Aleutians, the United States owns a significant amount of underwater real estate on which to emplace listening devices in the North Pacific. Whatever gaps may exist in this coverage would not seem to be affected one way or another by extended claims to the continental shelf. Only in the Caribbean and the Gulf of Mexico would a broad national shelf be likely to restrict U.S. coverage. In these areas U.S. coverage is limited anyway, because Cuba blocks it from the continental United States, while the Dominican Republic lies in the way of coverage from Puerto Rico.

In any case, as noted above, hydrophones have to be connected to shore stations (or, at great expense, to surface ships). Therefore, the United States generally needs the permission of coastal states to emplace SOSUS on their continental shelves, whether within or beyond the territorial boundaries claimed by these states. It should also be noted that an extension of national claims to the shelf edge probably would do more damage to Soviet than to American acoustic installations. It probably would be difficult to find a government beyond the Norwegian Sea that would consent to Soviet devices on its shelf—and Canada and Japan, of course, would object (although the effect of their objections would be limited by Soviet ownership of the Kuriles). The implications for SOSUS are the same even if national regimes encompass the continental margin. However, the bottom topography near Iceland makes it difficult to determine the precise limits of the shelf, margin, rise, and so on.

There is yet a third possibility if no international regime is agreed upon. The 1958 Continental Shelf Convention states in part that "the term 'continental shelf' is used as referring . . . to the seabed and subsoil of the submarine areas adjacent to the coast to where the depth of the superjacent water admits of exploitation of the natural resources of said areas." Since the technology for exploiting all but the deepest trenches soon will be available, this could eventually lead to a delimitation of the seabed on the basis of median lines. In this event, the United States would own most of the North Pacific seabed (although it probably would not be useful for more listening stations); the United States, Canada, and the Soviet Union would divide the Arctic; the situation in the

Caribbean would not be greatly altered; and Norway would own much of the seabed beneath the entrance to the North Atlantic.

Finally, in estimating the impact of alternative ocean regimes on America's military strategic capability, one must take into account the effects of extended territorial sea boundaries and other kinds of offshore zones. These effects, of course, depend in part upon what sort of restrictions coastal states choose to claim and are able to secure by consent or force. Added to the proliferation of extensive offshore territorial claims, coastal states are looking increasingly to pollution control, security, and other functional zones to restrict both military and civilian foreign navigation. Moreover, in the absence of a comprehensive and near-universal law of the sea treaty such as the United States has proposed, coastal states may resort to regional or local treaties, on the model of the Montreux Convention, or a version of the Soviet doctrine of "closed seas," that will severely restrict the numbers, types, and transit methods of warships belonging to nonsignatories. Assuming, then, for the sake of analysis, that more and more coastal states will be trying to apply more and more restrictions on foreign military passage within 50- to 200-mile offshore zones and adjacent seas, what are the implications for America's strategic capability?

If one were to select a 200-mile region to impede American naval passage and have the greatest effect on America's strategic capability, it would be the Arctic, given the premise presented here that the Mediterranean is not indispensable to America's strategic nuclear capability. But even with 200-mile sea boundaries, access to the Arctic would be possible through the Eastern Bering Strait and the Kennedy-Robeson Channels (given Canadian compliance). In the Atlantic, patrols could still go far north within the 200-mile boundary around the Shetlands. In Indonesian waters, a 200-mile boundary would not be much more restrictive than a 12-mile boundary, since Indonesia defines its boundary according to a broad archipelago doctrine. In any case, Poseidon missiles could still target all of the Soviet Union from points 200 miles off Bangladesh and Japan and in the southern Norwegian Sea.

More important than the impact of restrictive territorial zones and special seas on SSBNs may be their impact on the integrated operation of fleets—such as the Sixth Fleet in the Mediterranean—which have strategic functions beyond providing launching platforms for missiles. It should be noted, however, that the strategic function of surface ships, apart from their political and psychological uses, has been drastically eroded by technological advances in attack submarines, surface ships, and aircraft.

Moreover, it is worth noting that coastal state restrictions would have a much more adverse impact on Soviet than on American strategic mobility. If, for example, the restrictions applied to the current narrow sea boundaries were applied to 200-mile boundaries, Soviet SSBNs would be restricted to half of the

Arctic and to operations from Petropavlovsk. Submerged passage to the Atlantic would be prohibited. The Caribbean and the southern exits from the Sea of Japan would be closed. Soviet fleet maneuvers would be correspondingly more impeded than are American maneuvers by the proliferation of extensive restricted seas, pollution-free zones, and the like.

What, then, are the implications of all these considerations for the protection of American strategic interests under alternative ocean regimes? Unquestionably, America's strategic capability with respect to the Soviet Union would be better off under an effective, universally applicable law of the sea treaty that provided free transit through international straits, established a narrow continental shelf boundary, limited territorial sea boundaries to twelve miles, and protected military passage through pollution control and other zones, than under the more restrictive regimes we have postulated. But even the *most* restrictive of these regimes would not undermine America's strategic capability on the ocean, particularly if the Trident system were in operation. Moreover, the adverse impact of restrictive regimes on Soviet ocean-based strategic capabilities would be far more severe than their impact on American capabilities, although considering America's greater strategic dependence on the sea, U.S. naval leaders cannot be expected to gain much consolation from this comparison.

There is still the question of the most realistic alternative to the postulated proliferation of restrictive regimes. Is it advisable to insist on free transit through international straits and the maximum freedom of the seas against coastal state restrictions, at the risk of failing to get any agreed rules and regulations for navigation? Or is the best alternative the concession to coastal states of somewhat more extensive control of straits, sea bottoms, and sea boundaries, calculating that protection of essential strategic needs must depend, in the final analysis, on the political agreement of key states, with or without a universal law of the sea treaty? We shall return to this question after considering America's other security interests on the ocean.

Other Security Interests

If my assumptions about the political context of American security interests are correct, the United States must be prepared, for an indefinite period, to maintain a global, if pared down, overseas military capability that can respond quickly to a variety of possible crises and local conflicts in the third world. This kind of capability presupposes great military mobility in ocean space. The question is, what are the implications of this requirement of mobility for the kind of ocean regime the United States needs in order to protect its security interests?

If a local crisis or conflict were sufficiently serious to involve the deployment of American naval and air forces, would either the claims of sovereignty and control imposed by coastal and straits states, or the willingness of the United States to respect such claims, be affected critically by the legal status of territorial boundaries and straits? Presumably, it would depend on the seriousness of the crisis and the total political context. One can readily imagine local contingencies in which the United States would not be prepared to take major risks of war and in which it would feel compelled to honor proscriptions against passage of U.S. warships and aircraft applied by nonbelligerents. The denial of American over-flight by a number of friendly nonbelligerents during the Middle East war of 1973 illustrates this point, although denial of staging bases was even more critical in that instance.

In situations short of local wars and crises, too, local claims of jurisdiction and sovereignty could seriously restrict U.S. naval mobility, not to mention the shipment of oil. Six or seven of the world's international straits of major economic significance could be affected by states that might impose costly, inconvenient, and perhaps politically inspired restrictions on the passage of goods and resources valuable to the United States.[14]

The situation that occurred in the Strait of Malacca in 1969 suggests the potential trouble such restrictions might cause. Concerned about the ecological disaster that could follow an accident to supertankers in the hazardous channels of this strait, Malaysia claimed a territorial sea of twelve miles. Indonesia, which had proclaimed its archipelago doctrine of sovereignty in 1957, encompassing its 13,000 islands, joined Malaysia in 1970 in a treaty dividing the Strait of Malacca down the middle. When the carrier U.S.S. *Enterprise* and accompanying ships passed through the strait en route to the Bay of Bengal during the Bangladesh crisis of 1972, Indonesian spokesmen reaffirmed the right of the littoral states to control such passage but reconciled this right with the American action by stating that the Command of the Seventh Fleet had given advance notice.[15] The United States thus avoided one dispute, but more troublesome encounters had been fore-shadowed.

As some of the developing states become significant local and regional military powers (with the indispensable help of arms sales from the developed countries), they are likely to become more concerned with the security of their territorial waters, especially if they are rich in scarce resources. But quite apart from this security motive, coastal states have compelling reasons to increase restrictions on commercial and naval shipping off their shores. One reason, already manifest, is the desire to control the exploitation of newly discovered sources of wealth

---

[14] The following straits could be included in the category of major economic significance. Those that might be adversely affected by local restrictions, depending on political circumstances, are italicized: Florida, Dover, Skagerrak, Mozambique, *Gibraltar, Hormuz, Bab el Mandeb, Malacca, Lombok, Luzon,* and *Bosporus-Dardanelles.*

[15] Captain Edward F. Oliver, "Malacca: Dire Straits," *U.S. Naval Institute Proceedings,* June 1973, pp. 27-33.

recoverable from the oceans. This desire is leading to wider jurisdictional claims and more conflicts over the allocation of ocean resources. Some of these—Greek and Turkish differences over the Dodecanese, disputes between India and Sri Lanka, actions like China's occupation of the Paracel group, or Iran's occupation of Abu Musa—could result in violence. Even if such claims and conflicts do not directly impinge on mobility and shipping, they may create a turbulent political environment on the oceans that is uncongenial to the general American maritime interest in an ocean regime as unimpeded and peaceful as possible.

The extension of territorial claims to undersea areas will be reinforced by the desire of countries to police and regulate their coastal areas and their offshore economic activities. In this era of supertankers and expanding oil shipping one does not need to assume special political or nationalistic motives to explain the concern of countries about protection of their coasts and increasingly congested straits from shipping collisions, accidents, and pollution. The extension of offshore oil and gas extraction will add another reason for policing and regulating waters that used to be considered areas of free navigation—note the United Kingdom's claim to jurisdiction in a 500-meter safety zone around its North Sea oil rigs.

If offshore petroleum installations and supertankers should become targets for terrorists—and in this period of history one must assume that this is not unlikely—coastal states will have an additional incentive to maintain order in offshore jurisdictions, and other states will have more cause to object to coastal state restrictions and regulations. Then, too, in future local wars, which in the third world are likely to increase in number and perhaps in intensity, there may be assertions of blockade (as in the Indo-Pakistani war of 1971) and other restrictions on neutral shipping, including sabotage and terrorism.

Clearly, these trends could impair freedom of oil shipments, the mobility of general purpose naval forces, and military overflight in ways that would seriously jeopardize American security interests. The United States, therefore, needs new laws and regulations that are relevant to the new conditions and that will permit it to conduct essential military and commercial activity on the ocean without getting into political conflicts and resorting to arms. Given the force of the political and material reasons for growing restrictions on the use of the ocean, it is unrealistic to expect these new laws and regulations to correspond to the official American insistence on unimpeded passage and free navigation. It may also be unrealistic to expect any useful new laws and regulations to emerge from law of the sea negotiations in which these issues are inextricably tied to a whole range of other ocean issues and over 140 nations are expected to sign a comprehensive treaty.

Indeed, although new laws and regulations would be very valuable, formal agreements do not exhaust the remedies for protecting U.S. ocean security interests in the uncongenial environment postulated here. There are also more informal modi vivendi with key states. Thus, after the *Enterprise* incident the United States government proposed that a provision for "free passage" of straits in a law of the sea treaty be qualified by international standards for safety which would be established by the Inter-Governmental Maritime Consultative Organization (IMCO) or some other international organization, and enforced, beyond the coastal state's territorial sea boundary, by the flag state or port state.[16] But Malaysia and Indonesia, while willing to grant controlled transit through straits and waters near their shores at their discretion (although the United States evidently does not give either Malaysia or Singapore the advance notification Indonesia claims to receive), are not willing to relinquish such control to an international organization dominated by the United States. They are even less willing to entrust enforcement of pollution and safety standards to the great maritime states that continue to congest straits with huge tankers and other commercial vessels.

Therefore, the question arises: if countries athwart vital sea-lanes are inclined for basic ecological and political reasons to restrict U.S. naval mobility and over-flight to our disadvantage, why should we suppose that they will accept international agreements and regulations designed to prevent such action? It is doubtful that they will bargain away their right to impose such regulations in order to gain favors on other issues. Moreover, even if they are not inclined to impose unacceptable restrictions, they may nevertheless be reluctant to sign away their right to do so in an international legal agreement. There is evidence, on the other hand, that some kinds of arrangements that accommodate U.S. and coastal or straits states' interests can more readily be reached if they are not made the subject of inter-national legal agreements.

For example, there now seems to be a modus vivendi between the United States and Indonesia that works fairly well, although (and perhaps because) jurisdictional differences are not formally resolved. Judging from this case, basic political factors, such as Indonesia's determination to become the dominant South-east Asian power, its uneasiness about expanding Soviet naval activity and Soviet alignment with India, its latent fear of Japan and reluctance to become dependent on Japan's naval power, and its dependence on an American presence in Southeast Asia, together with American economic assistance and military sales, will have more of an effect on U.S. and Indonesian ocean interests than any law of the sea treaty.

Similarly, the protection of American naval and economic interests in the Persian (or Arabian) Gulf seems far more dependent on good relations with Iran than on a new law of the sea treaty. Iran's drive for control of shipping in the

---

[16] Within an undefined coastal seabed economic area, the U.S. position would give each coastal state complete authority to enforce both its own and international standards against pollution from seabed activities. With respect to vessels, however, the flag state would continue to have enforcement responsibility beyond the coastal state's territorial boundary, subject to the right of other states to resort to compulsory dispute settlement. The port state could enforce pollution control standards against vessels using its ports, regardless of where violations occurred.

gulf, through which two-thirds of the non-Communist world's oil imports pass, tends to conflict with the U.S. proposal for free navigation. Thus in March 1973, Iran was reported to be exploring an agreement with Oman to inspect all ships passing through the Straits of Hormuz at the entrance of the gulf.[17] Observers of gulf politics regard Iran's announced concern about the threat of pollution as secondary to its concern about other Arab governments supplying arms to Iranian rebels. Iran's inclination to seek control of shipping in the gulf may run counter to an ideal law of the sea treaty, but, considering the more than $2 billion in arms the United States has provided Iran to bolster its supremacy in the gulf, we cannot deny that Iran's policy is consistent with the official definition of American security interests in the gulf. Indeed, if the United States does rely on Iran as a surrogate for U.S. naval power in the area, Iranian control of the gulf may be a prerequisite for protecting American interests in the gulf.

Restrictions on overflight in the gulf and Mediterranean regions have a more serious effect on the mobility of general purpose forces in limited wars and crises than on the U.S. strategic capability. In these areas the United States cannot rely on military overflight being granted, even by allied and other countries in which it has air bases. As in the case of surface navigation, it would be a great asset to secure unimpeded passage over straits. In practice, however, securing essential mobility by overflight is not a general problem. It is politically and geographically confined. In this case, it is essentially confined to gaining passage over the Strait of Gibraltar. Resolving this kind of problem will depend primarily on political relations with a few key states. If they do not favor unimpeded passage, the key states are not likely to sign a free-transit provision because of bargaining at a law of the sea treaty conference. If they are not unreservedly opposed to passage, the United States might have a better chance of arranging a satisfactory modus vivendi outside an international conference than through either a multilateral or bilateral treaty.

Needless to say, if this general conclusion is valid with respect to naval and air deployments related to local crises in the Middle East or elsewhere, it certainly applies to possible direct encounters with indigenous states, as in the event of a strangulating blockade against vital oil shipments to the United States and its allies. For this kind of contingency an international law of the sea treaty would be irrelevant.

Unilateral Force

In the absence of adequate protection for ocean security interests by a universal law of the sea treaty sanctioning the kind of free navigation and unimpeded passage the U.S. government seeks, the United States faces the troublesome prospect

---

[17] *Washington Post,* 23 March 1973, p. A-1. Iran and Oman later denied the report. Iran subsequently announced that it was preparing a bill that would extend pollution controls to fifty miles from shore or the limit of the continental shelf.

of protecting American ocean security interests through ad hoc deals with local and regional powers. Understandably, U.S. ocean policy makers prefer to base the protection of American ocean interests on treaty-made laws that apply as generally and unambiguously as possible, rather than on less binding arrangements based on fragile political alignments and customary law. This policy preference is reinforced by their inclination to define both the threat to American ocean interests and the solution to the threat in abstract terms. This is consistent with the American tendency to identify national interests with a universal order. According to this outlook, the more coastal countries assert control over straits, claim 50- or 200-mile territorial boundaries, demand special restrictions on innocent passage, or otherwise constrain the use of ocean space, the more likely it is that these nations will clash with the major maritime states. Consequently, American security interests will face greater danger and the United States will have growing difficulties in moving air and naval units to the sites of crises that affect these interests. Bearing this in mind, government officials conclude that without a new universal law of the sea treaty the United States must either acquiesce to claims by coastal states of jurisdictional rights that constrict American ocean mobility, or forcibly contest such assertions.

The specter of resorting to force is used to point up the urgency of an international law of the sea treaty, as though force—at least when imposed by the strong against the weak—were either obsolete or too terrible to contemplate. But this generalization, too, is overdrawn. The great powers' constraint in enforcing their interests against the will of the less developed countries depends on a calculus of material gain (and, one can argue, long-run political gain) and political loss that may change with changing conditions.

Thus, the political costs of the United States forcibly protecting American tuna fishermen against Peru's claims of sovereignty have always seemed excessive in the light of what could be gained by such drastic measures and what would be lost without them. It is misleading, however, to infer from this situation that the United States would be equally passive in the face of some threat to a more serious economic interest or to a military security interest. Likewise, British resistance to Iceland's fifty-mile exclusive fishing zone claim, which led to a number of clashes between Icelandic naval ships and British escorts, demonstrates considerable British self-restraint, but it also shows—despite Britain's withdrawal of its warships in pursuit of a settlement—that a maritime state will not necessarily passively accept a small state's allegiance to a conflicting ocean regime when important economic interests are at stake and cannot be secured by other means.

Where military security, rather than fishing rights, is involved, the maritime states have been bolder in backing their interests. The most frequent examples of this have occurred in intelligence gathering. Despite North Vietnam's claim to a 12-mile boundary, the United States acknowledged that the U.S. destroyer *Maddox* was only 11 miles off North Vietnam shortly before the first Gulf of Tonkin incident. In other cases the United States has not been reluctant to fly aerial intelligence missions that contravene jurisdictional claims over coastal state waters.

In the past decade there have been several cases (excluding fishing rights interventions and cold war crises) in which maritime powers have exercised their naval superiority to support their definition of freedom of the seas. In July 1951, when an Egyptian corvette intercepted and damaged a British merchantman in the Gulf of Aqaba during an attempted blockade of Israel, a British destroyer flotilla was deployed to the Red Sea. Two weeks later Britain and Egypt reached an agreement on procedures for British shipping in the gulf. In February 1957, American destroyers patrolled the Straits of Tiran and the Gulf of Aqaba to prevent Egyptian interference with American merchant shipping en route to Israel. On 13 December 1957, President Sukarno's government enunciated Indonesia's archipelago doctrine. Less than a month later, Destroyer Division 31 passed through the Lombok and Makassar straits to reaffirm the U.S. right of innocent passage. On 21 July 1961, following a bombardment by French naval aircraft, a French cruiser-destroyer group forced the entrance to the Lake of Bizerta, thereby lifting a Tunisian blockade of the naval base and reestablishing French control. Following Egyptian closing of the Straits of Tiran in May 1967, the U.S. Sixth Fleet concentrated in the eastern Mediterranean, while the British admiralty announced that the carrier H.M.S. *Victorious* and other units were being kept in the Mediterranean "in readiness against any eventuality," although the threat was not carried further. On 22 April 1969, Iranian warships escorted an Iranian merchant ship from Khorrasmshahr (at the junction of the Tigris and Karun rivers just inside the Iranian border) to the Persian Gulf in defiance of Iraqi threats. Apparently a similar incident had occurred in 1961, but Iran had been forced to yield for lack of naval forces.

On other occasions maritime powers simply ignore or reject coastal state claims against their activities. The People's Republic of China routinely challenges U.S. vessels in the Lema Channel en route to Hong Kong, and the U.S. vessels routinely disregard these challenges. Despite protests from other nations, France enforces restricted zones around its nuclear testing site at Mururoa atoll. During the Algerian war, France undertook visit and search of the flagships of more than a dozen nations, on some occasions as far away as the English Channel.

Thus, if the jurisdictional claims of coastal states jeopardized American economic or security interests in the third world, the United States would not necessarily be deterred by immediate political costs from supporting its ocean interests with force. This would be true especially if the clash occurred out of the context of U.S.-Soviet competition, which is increasingly likely. If such clashes were to become regular features of the international environment, one can even imagine some of the maritime powers at least tacitly cooperating to enforce their conception of freedom of navigation. New laws of the sea would eventually result from the kind of military and diplomatic process, punctuated by test encounters, that created the traditional laws.

It is neither desirable nor necessary, however, that the new laws of the sea be made in this way. Coastal states and maritime powers have important common interests in preserving the flow of commerce, and neither group is yet united in opposition to the other. Nevertheless, the *prospect* of armed encounters may moderate the process of resolving conflicts of national interests. Short of armed force, the protection of American security interests in the ocean will depend on four factors: (1) the configuration of political interests and military power among the states that are in a position to affect vital American military and resource interests; (2) the balance of U.S.-Soviet interests and influence as it affects the actions of these states; (3) the perceived and actual disposition of the United States to back its ocean interests with force and only in this total context; and only finally on (4) the process of asserting, contesting, accommodating, and negotiating the modalities of the rights of navigation through and over offshore waters and international straits.

With or without a satisfactory law of the sea treaty, the United States, in keeping with the revised view of American power and interests underlying the Nixon doctrine, must depend more and more on the favorable configuration of interests and power among local states rather than on direct American intervention to protect its security interests in the use of ocean space. Insofar as the United States can affect such configurations at all, it must depend primarily on skill and tact in playing the politics of trade and investment, economic and military assistance, and on traditional diplomacy in its dealings with the major oil-producing states and the states astride commercially and militarily vital straits.

Implications for Law of the Sea

So far, coastal states show little inclination to comply with the insistence of the United States upon a law of the sea treaty embodying unimpeded transit and navigation through territorial waters or even through 200-mile zones of economic jurisdiction. Some coastal states—especially those with their own interest in unimpeded shipping—might change their mind when the international bargaining reaches the final stage, negotiating a treaty. But it is doubtful that the few key littoral states that have raised the major objection to free transit—notably, Indonesia, Malaysia, and Spain—will sign such a provision. Why, then, insist on such a treaty? Might not America's essential security interests be more likely to be protected by laws and regulations that made more concession to the coastal states' legitimate apprehensions about security, safety, and pollution? Might not such laws and regulations be more likely to emerge outside the context of negotiations on a comprehensive, universal law of the sea treaty? Why do U.S. ocean policy makers believe that adoption of a comprehensive treaty with a provision for unimpeded passage is overwhelmingly preferable to seeking a separate agreement for unimpeded transit or settling for either no treaty, a treaty satisfying coastal state definitions of residual sovereignty, or bilateral and regional arrangements short of a treaty?

One reason is the purported advantage of *uniformity*. American ocean officials feel that it would be excessively time-consuming, inconvenient, and disorderly to make differing ad hoc arrangements with all the littoral states involved. This point is compelling as it applies to jurisdictional zones and other ocean issues affecting commercial activities—whether fishing, petroleum and mineral exploration and exploitation, or merchant shipping. Having to adapt these activities to a diversity of local claims, regulations, and laws could impede commerce, while leaving unresolved many sources of international litigation and conflict. If, for example, littoral states continue to impose an increasing number of more stringent requirements on the type and construction of merchant ships, on insurance, and on navigational taxes and tolls for shipping, the result might be a chaos of claims and arrangements. This danger, however, is not nearly so serious as it applies to naval and air navigation for security purposes, because the critical problems of military use are not so numerous or diverse as to be beyond satisfactory resolution on an ad hoc basis, if necessary.

Of course, as U.S. representatives now emphasize, if a universal law of the sea treaty incorporating free transit could be obtained, it would benefit not only American military mobility but also merchant shipping, in which national commercial and security interests now merge. There would still be a need, however, for special international agreements applicable to merchant shipping. Hence, the U.S. government has (1) stressed that the "free" in "free transit" applies only to unrestricted passage through international straits rather than to all activities on the high seas, and (2) expressly stated that the problems of navigational safety and pollution risks in international straits should be resolved by separate international agreements and organizations.[18] If the right of transit must be qualified by recognition of the legitimate concerns of littoral states about the hazards of merchant shipping off their shores and in adjacent straits, it may be unwise to combine the protection of this right with the right of submarines to go through straits submerged and unannounced. It may be unwise to insist on the strict meaning of "unimpeded" passage if the substance of the right can be as readily protected in practice—and with less injury to the political sensitivities of postcolonial states—under the rubric of "innocent" passage.

A second avowed reason for the comprehensive treaty approach to ocean

---

[18] See the statement of John R. Stevenson to Subcommittee II of the UN Seabed Committee, 28 July 1972, UN Doc. A/AC.138/SC.II/SR.37 at 2; and to the U.S. Congress, House, Committee on Foreign Affairs, Subcommittee on International Organizations and Movements, "Law of the Sea and Peaceful Uses of the Seabeds," 92d Cong., 2d sess., 10 and 11 April 1972, p. 12.

lawmaking is that the United States gains a *bargaining* advantage in law of the sea negotiations by combining the free-transit straits provision with resource provisions, such as 200-mile resource zones and revenue. Concessions to broad economic jurisdictional zones would supposedly give coastal states otherwise opposed or indifferent to free transit an incentive to make concessions to U.S. security interests. The only trouble with this argument is that, in practice, this linkage strategy may not work. Indeed, it may work best for the states that, observing the great importance that the United States attaches to free transit, calculate that they can extract concessions on their control of resource zones and the like as the price of accommodating maritime interests. Judging from the concessions to coastal state control of resource zones that the United States has already made, the advantage seems to lie with the coastal states. Even where these states (as in Latin America) have evidently made concessions to the position on free navigation, they have done so in accordance with the Latin doctrine of "patrimonial seas" [19] at the price of American abandonment of opposition to exclusive resource zones.

A third reason for seeking a comprehensive law of the sea treaty is the alleged *political advantage* to negotiating the resolution of conflicting interests in a treaty applicable to *all* states. One supposition underlying this point seems to be that weaker states will find a general multilateral agreement less damaging to their national pride than bilateral or regional arrangements with the United States. The smaller states can explain their accommodations as concessions to the general international community. The United States can avoid the stigma of hegemony and limit the price for compliance the smaller states may exact.

A related supposition may be that in trying to reach bilateral or regional deals the United States must suffer the political embarrassment and the tactical disadvantage of having to satisfy the special interests of weaker states. However, if the United States can generalize its positions and its modes of influence in the United Nations, it will be less vulnerable to such pressure for concessions, and concessions made to one country or regional grouping are less apt to embarrass the United States in dealing with others.

These kinds of political considerations are, of course, valid in some cases of diplomacy; but since they are not always valid, only an exploration of the comprehensive law of the sea treaty approach and its alternatives could indicate whether it applies to the diplomacy intended to protect U.S. ocean security interests. Here the evidence is likely to remain quite incomplete. Although several key coastal states have not yet conceded free transit in return for international controls intended to prevent accidents and pollution, the United States has nevertheless managed to protect its essential security interests. There is no reason,

---

[19] A 200-mile area of coastal state jurisdiction and supervision over the exploration and exploitation of natural resources.

however, to think that the United States would come any closer to gaining acceptance of its position through bilateral or regional agreements.

Therefore, it would seem that the case for including the provisions of special security concern in a law of the sea treaty depends not so much on the alleged advantage of comprehensiveness and universality as on the feasibility of persuading a large number of states, including the key straits states, to accept particular provisions like free transit as consistent with their basic interests and sovereignty. If these states agree to free transit, it will not be because of any advantages of political accommodation and bargaining power inherent in the negotiating forum, but because of the particular balance of interests that emerges in the total context of their relations with the United States and other maritime states. If they regard free transit as inconsistent with their interests, the United States need not make free transit the condition for accepting a treaty to resolve jurisdictional issues in merchant shipping and commercial activity. American security interests will suffer far more if unresolved jurisdictional issues concerning resource and pollution control zones engender chronic conflicts and if coastal states impose regulations and restrictions on commercial shipping than if no additional formal agreements on straits are made at all.

American Law of the Sea Task Force officials stoutly insist that, in the end, when a treaty is ready for final negotiation, the coastal states will generally accept free transit as compatible with their national interests, and a few countries with maritime interests will see this as a positive advantage. Although there are many skeptics, this estimate may turn out to be correct if the United States makes enough concessions to the pride and interests of enough developing countries. If official optimism about free transit is unwarranted, however, or if the price is exorbitant, the United States might best serve its security and ocean interests by confining the law of the sea treaty's international-straits provisions to general principles of mutual maritime and coastal state interest, leaving the precise conditions of transit legally ambiguous. If these conditions need to be made more precise, the United States can delay their formulation until the United States and the key straits states reach an accommodation *outside* an international conference. Indeed, this may be the only course it can afford. In any event, the best alternative to protecting U.S. security interests in a comprehensive international treaty is probably not seeking protection through bilateral or regional treaties but simply through informal arrangements under existing law, leavened by international agreements that littoral states, along with the great maritime users, should have a fair share of control over the increasingly congested commercial ocean lanes.

The weakness of this alternative has been exaggerated by the official assumption that there is some great advantage to getting many countries to sign an international treaty embodying free transit even if the key straits states refuse to sign it (which U.S. Law of the Sea Task Force officials concede is likely). The most important objective of a treaty provision on free transit is to gain full legal recognition of the principle of unimpeded passage through straits from the few states that might impede passage—for military purposes, perhaps only Spain and Indonesia. It is unlikely that key straits states will grant such recognition, because they would thereby subordinate their special interests to "world opinion." Are we to assume, therefore, that, in the event of a showdown, the United States will be in a better position to resist assertions of control by these states, forcibly if necessary, if it can bolster its resistance with the sanction of a nearly universal treaty? There may be an element of truth in this calculation insofar as it applies to the moral courage of American statesmen; but it does seem naive to think that even a multitude of signatures to an international treaty would in itself induce the key opponents of free transit to sign, or to comply with a provision they had refused to sign.

The assumption of an international treaty's favorable effect on the behavior of reluctant states would be more convincing if there were more reason to share the official U.S. confidence in the eventual "rationality" of the large bloc of coastal and less-developed countries that now oppose a free-transit provision. Against this hopeful prospect one must weigh the danger that the United States will only aggravate the problem of reconciling its interests in unencumbered navigation with the interests and pride of a large number of coastal states in controlling the use of "their" waters by insisting on the maximum guarantees for its interests through international law. By elevating a set of political accommodations between the interests of the great maritime states and those of many coastal states into a matter of legal rights and national sovereignty, the United States may only polarize the issues. On the other hand, by asking for less in law, it may get more protection for its interests in fact. For on the practical basis of day-to-day dealings, most coastal states, including the key ones, are not necessarily opposed to granting what they may refuse to accept as a legal principle. And if the less-developed coastal states do not see themselves and the great maritime states in a contest of power (a contest in which they must rely on their superior voting strength in the United Nations), many of these states, whose shipping can be hampered by regional rivals, may conclude that they have as much interest as the developed states in unencumbered navigation.

In this "era of negotiation" and of American "retrenchment without disengagement" it behooves the United States to deal with all states—but particularly with the sensitive, less-developed states of the third world, who are undergoing an overdue redefinition of their interests—on terms of practical, mutual benefit and respect, as free as possible from ideological and nationalistic preoccupations. There are critical limits to the ability of the United States to insist upon codifying in international law the protection of the interests of a few great maritime states without jeopardizing the political accommodations upon which law rests.

U.S. ECONOMIC INTERESTS IN LAW OF THE SEA ISSUES

David B. Johnson and Dennis E. Logue

Introduction

The ongoing law of the sea negotiations have received considerable attention from political scientists, economists, lawyers, and members of the diplomatic corps.[1] Most analyses, however, have focused upon conceptual issues, methods, values, and the development of theoretical arguments. Our contribution to an understanding of the various issues involved in the law of the sea negotiations is the collection and analysis, from the perspective of the United States, of empirical evidence concerning the stakes involved in these deliberations. Hopefully, the data presented in the first section will provide an adequate frame of reference for the formulation of nego- tiating priorities and will assist in the analysis of those trade-offs necessary to any successful negotiation. Although we realize that economic efficiency is not the sole criterion that should be used in evaluating the law of the sea negotiations, we occasionally suggest certain policy implications derived from the data and the accompanying analyses. These policy recommendations should be regarded as tentative ones based solely on our preliminary estimates. However, we do not believe that they should be disregarded simply because they ignore certain political or strategic variables. Hopefully, these data and the implications drawn from them will stimulate the Departments of Defense and State, among others, to place some values on the strategic and political variables so that policy makers can consider the trade-offs. For example, how many divisions, tanks, or ships would the Department of Defense be willing to forego to obtain free transit through straits? How many foreign service officers would the Department of State be willing to "sacrifice" to obtain an internationally agreed upon document affirming ocean order?

In the second section of this paper, the potential benefits to the United States of free access to the mineral resources of the deep sea are examined. By 1985

---

[1] See, for example, A. Hollick, "Seabeds Make Strange Politics," *Foreign Policy*, no. 9 (Winter 1972-73), pp. 148-70; D. E. Logue, R. J. Sweeney, and B. A. Petrou, "The Economics of Alternative Deep Sea Bed Regimes," *Marine Technology Society Journal*, March 1975; D. E. Logue and R. J. Sweeney, "An Economic Analysis of the Law of the Sea Negotiations," OASIA/Research Discussion Paper, U.S. Treasury; and John R. Stevenson, "Who Is to Control the Oceans: U.S. Policy and the 1973 Law of the Sea Conference," *International Lawyer*, vol. 6 (July 1972), pp. 465-77.

the deep sea could meet 85 percent of U.S. manganese needs, 6 percent of U.S. copper needs, 85 percent of U.S. nickel needs, as well as providing nearly four times the annual cobalt requirement. In subsequent years, even greater proportions of U.S. needs might be supplied by deep-sea resources. The cost to the United States of accepting a rigid regulatory regime that would hinder free access to minerals and free choice of timing of exploitation could be as much as $310 million in 1985 and more in subsequent years, even basing cost projections upon very conservative assumptions. Considerably greater economic costs would be borne by the United States if hydrocarbon resources were discovered in the area controlled by the regime. Accordingly, it appears that the choice of regulatory regime is a critical aspect of the law of the sea negotiations.

The costs of particular proposals for the delineation of the continental margins and revenue sharing on the margins are explored in the third section. Our estimates suggest that the cost to the United States of accepting a narrow margin or agreeing to very high revenue-sharing rates may range from $2 to $8 billion per year, depending on the specifics of the arrangements.

The issue of freedom of transit through straits is considered in the fourth section. With respect to commercial navigation, achieving agreement on the U.S. position might be worth $140 to $180 million per year, but this is only if *all* straits were closed, and at the same time our trading partners who control those straits still insisted upon trading with us—an unlikely circumstance. The data supporting these estimates are, unfortunately, quite incomplete, so a case study was also performed. It measured the cost of shipping oil from the Persian Gulf to the United States based on the assumption that all states had 200-mile territorial seas that could not be transgressed. The increase in oil-transport costs to the United States would be $91 million per year at current import levels. Given the fact that these imports are likely to decline as a result of federal policy (Project Independence), this is a high estimate. It is also high because it would be unlikely that every coastal state would prohibit passage of oil tankers within 200 miles of shore. On the basis of this analysis, it appears that free transit may not be worth as much as originally thought, although the analysis is admittedly incomplete—largely, we might add, because no one with knowledge of U.S. strategic military capabilities has addressed the issue, or released the results of whatever studies have been completed, of the costs to the United States of failure to achieve agreement on free transit through straits for military purposes.

The fifth section considers the question of international pollution standards. Once again, the analysis is incomplete, though this time because specific standards have yet to be proposed at the law of the sea negotiations. A case study based upon the kinds of international standards being discussed at the International Maritime Consultative Organization is, however, reported. The standard examined was the requirement for double-skin segregated-ballast oil tankers to prevent oily discharge in ballasting operations. The case study revealed that the cost/benefit ratio for such a requirement was approximately twenty to one, that is, the costs of the requirement exceeded its benefits by a wide margin. This section also argues that nations, for their own self-interest, will naturally move towards relatively compatible standards; hence there is no pressing need for this issue to be resolved within the law of the sea deliberations. Moreover, the costs to the United States of accepting standards agreed upon internationally could be quite high.

The sixth section analyzes the issue of fisheries and concludes that the type of fisheries regulation likely to emanate from an international treaty may be far worse than no regulation at all.

The seventh section concludes the paper with a discussion of the need for sound economic analysis of law of the sea issues.

Economic Use of the Deep Seabed

The deep seabed contains a potentially rich stock of mineral wealth. Gold, silver, uranium, hydrocarbons, and numerous other mineral resources may some day be taken from the seas' bottoms. For the foreseeable future, however, the chief commercial interest in the ocean pertains to the recovery of manganese nodules from the oceans' floors.

Manganese nodules were first discovered in 1873 during the scientific research expedition of H. M. S. *Challenger*. Records kept on that voyage noted the presence of appreciable quantities of nickel and copper, but the grades were still too low to be considered of commercial quality in the 1800s. In 1975, however, price rises and advanced technology have made possible and profitable the commercial development of these resources.

Manganese nodules are rounded masses of manganese oxide which have developed through the gradual accretion of minerals chemically precipitated around some minute nucleus—perhaps a tooth, a bit of bone, a grain of sand. Some are substantially larger than basketballs while others are as small as grains of sand. There is generally no standard size in any location where the nodules are found, although an important element in site selection is the size distribution based on mean and standard deviation.

Five minerals are found in reasonable proportions in manganese nodules. Prime nodules tend to be composed of the following economically relevant minerals: 1 to 1.5 percent nickel, 25 to 30 percent manganese, 0.5 to 1 percent copper, 0.25 percent cobalt, and 0.05 percent molybdenum. The remainder is made up of silica, thirty other minerals, and water. Present commercial interest is concentrated on the nickel, manganese, copper, and cobalt contained in the nodules.

Manganese nodules are located generally at great ocean depths, 15,000 to

20,000 feet, and usually far from land. The largest concentration is in a belt in the northern portion of the Pacific Ocean between about 6°N and 20°N and extending from about 110°W to 180°W, but some concentrations have been found in the South Pacific, Atlantic, and Indian oceans.

To be economically exploitable, nodules must be of high grade and abundant. Generally, a density of at least two pounds (wet weight) per square foot (which corresponds to about 6,500 tons of dry nodules per square kilometer) is thought to be necessary before commercial exploitation is worthwhile, at least at prevailing prices and with existing technology. A typical mine is likely to be planned to yield approximately 3 million tons (dry weight) of nodules per year. After processing, such a mine might, very conservatively, yield approximately 35,000 tons of nickel, 30,000 tons of copper, 750,000 tons of manganese, and 6,750 tons of cobalt. Making the assumption that between 20 and 25 percent of nodules lying on the ocean floor will ultimately be recovered (in a first-generation mine), a mine yielding 3 million dry tons a year would require an area of roughly 42,000 square kilometers, where nodule density is two pounds per square foot, in order to have a working life of twenty years.[2]

There appears to be substantial agreement among geologists that there are likely to be 400 to 500 prime first-generation mine sites, that is, areas of sufficient size where nodules are of adequate density and quality. Accordingly, there is a great likelihood that a substantial portion of the world's needs, and particularly those of the United States, for copper, cobalt, nickel, and manganese can be satisfied by the economically efficient exploitation of the deep seabed. The efficiency of exploitation could, however, be severely hampered by the choice of an inappropriate deep-sea regulatory regime by the law of the sea convention. But before examining the implications for the United States of such a choice, we turn to a brief analysis of world and U.S. demand for the chief minerals contained in manganese nodules, and contrast these with the potential productive capacity of the deep seabeds.

Mineral Consumption and the Short-Term Potential of the Deep Sea. Projections concerning the future demand for copper, cobalt, nickel, and manganese abound. Most, however, are economically flawed in one way or another. For example, many projections assume that the current growth rate in demand will remain roughly constant, paying no heed to changes in the price of these minerals relative to that of other minerals,[3] nor to the rate of growth in income in the consuming

---

[2] Adapted from A. A. Archer, "The Importance of the Sea Bed as a Source of Minerals," Paper presented at the Financial Times Law of the Sea Conference, London, February 1974, pp. 5 and 6.

[3] All of the minerals in nodules have relatively good substitutes. For example, aluminum can be substituted for copper in many uses, so the demand for copper at a given price will depend on the price of aluminum.

Table 1
HIGH AND LOW DEMAND GROWTH RATES FOR NODULE MINERALS, THE UNITED STATES AND THE WORLD
(yearly percentage)

Mineral	United States		World	
	High	Low	High	Low
Manganese	2.5	1.5	5.0	2.5
Copper	5.2	3.7	6.0	3.4
Cobalt	2.4	1.0	6.0	1.5
Nickel	6.0	2.8	6.0	2.8

Source: See footnote 5, below.

countries.[4] Many other forecasts make ad hoc adjustments in these growth rates, reflecting subjective judgments. In spite of the range of methods used in making forecasts, the final results tend to cluster. We first consider the range in growth rates in the world and U.S. primary demand for nickel, cobalt, copper, and manganese.

Table 1 shows the high and low estimated growth rates in demand for nickel, cobalt, manganese, and copper for both the United States and the world. The growth-rate estimates, which were obtained from a variety of sources, include the highest of the high and the lowest of the low estimates.[5] The application of these growth rates to a base-period consumption yields forecasts of demand for these mineral resources in the years 1985 and 2000, as shown in Table 2. Base-year consumption was taken to be that of 1971.

Table 3 provides a summary of Table 2 and represents the midpoint of estimates in the case of world demand, but for the United States Morgan's estimates are used because these are likely to be the best estimates, being based on explicit assumptions concerning U.S. population and income. More precisely, Morgan bases his projections on a U.S. population of 250 million in 1985 and a gross

[4] For example, the growth in demand for oil, at a given price, is quite sensitive to income growth—the elasticity may be approximately unity. The recession that began in 1974 has had a significant impact on oil use. Other minerals are similarly sensitive.

[5] Estimated growth rates are derived from the following sources: United Nations, "Economic Implications of Sea Bed Mineral Development in the International Area: Report of the Secretary-General," A/CONF. 62/65, May 1974; Interagency Committee on Economic Implications of Seabed Mineral Resource Development, memoranda, July 1971; Richard James Sweeney, "Importance of U.S. Access to the Minerals of the Deep Seabed," unpub. memorandum, U.S. Treasury Department, November 1973; Conrad G. Welling, "Ocean Resources," Paper presented at National Materials Policy Forum, Washington, D. C., June 1972; John D. Morgan, Jr., "The Future Use of Minerals: The Question of Demand," in *The Mineral Position of the United States, 1975-2000,* ed. Eugene N. Cameron (Madison: The University of Wisconsin Press, 1973); and U.S. Department of Interior, "Importance to the United States of Access to Manganese Nodules," 1973.

Table 2

PROJECTIONS OF HIGH AND LOW CONSUMPTION OF NODULE MINERALS IN THE UNITED STATES AND THE WORLD, 1985 AND 2000

Mineral	1985				2000			
	United States		World		United States		World	
	High	Low	High	Low	High	Low	High	Low
Manganese (thousands of short tons)	1,770	1,439	19,796	13,700	2,360	1,802	41,153	20,700
Copper (thousands of short tons)	3,303	2,701	14,778	10,462	7,054	4,669	35,441	17,263
Cobalt (thousands of pounds)	18,651	15,431	122,533	66,688	26,702	17,846	293,862	83,496
Nickel (millions of pounds)	638	414	2,600	1,700	1,528	628	6,231	2,600

Table 3
MOST PROBABLE DEMAND FORECASTS FOR NODULE MINERALS, 1985 AND 2000

Mineral	1985		2000	
	United States	World	United States	World
Manganese (thousands of short tons)	1,770	16,748	2,360	30,926
Copper (thousands of short tons)	2,900	12,620	5,400	26,352
Cobalt (thousands of pounds)	20,000	94,610	24,700	188,679
Nickel (millions of pounds)	492	2,150	770	4,415

Table 4
PROJECTED PROCESSED OUTPUT FROM NODULE MINING, 1985 AND 2000

Mineral	1985	2000
Manganese (thousands of short tons)	1,500[a]	15,000[a]
Copper (thousands of short tons)	180	900
Cobalt (thousands of pounds)	79,500	405,000
Nickel (millions of pounds)	420	2,100

[a] This projection assumes that only one-third of the operations extract manganese.

national product of $1.8 trillion (in 1970 dollars). For 2000, his projections are based on the assumptions that population will be 300 million and gross national product $3.4 trillion (in 1970 dollars).[6]

The contribution that deep-sea mining can make in meeting this demand is substantial. Even at the mineral prices which prevailed in 1970, deep-sea mining

[6] Morgan, "The Future Use of Minerals," pp. 55 and 56.

was very nearly profitable, given the technological developments and forecasted costs of such mining, including substantial profit to compensate for risk.[7] Indeed, since that time the prices of those minerals have risen sharply, while the estimated costs have not kept pace. Thus, it is very likely that deep-sea mining could be profitable today.

Although the estimated initial investment in deep-sea mining is likely to range from $150 to $300 million, with annual operating costs in the range of $40 to $70 million per 3 million dry tons per year operation, there should be at least six mining operations by 1985.[8] Moreover, because of the technological advances made in recent years, each of these mining operations should be capable of dredging up and processing 3 million dry tons of nodules per year. In addition, it is not improbable that as many as twenty to thirty or more such operations will be active by 2000. Applying the proportions of minerals found in nodules which were cited above, multiplying by the number of tons per year, and by the number of operations, six in 1985 and thirty in 2000, gives a rough and very conservative estimate of the volume of minerals that may be obtained from the deep sea in the future.

Table 4 summarizes these estimates. (There are estimates which show much higher potential, but these were eliminated because of their greater tenuousness.) Note that the indicated volume of manganese is substantially less than the potential volume. This is because, of the six firms which will be in operation in 1985, only two have indicated serious interest in extracting four minerals from nodules.[9] The remainder, at least at the present time, have reported that they intend to extract only copper, cobalt, and nickel. This same proportion of four-metal processors to three-metal processors was applied to the possible thirty operations in 2000.

The Value of Deep-Sea Mining. For an appreciation of the potential significance of deep-sea mining, it is important to examine the contribution of deep-sea mining to potential world demand and U.S. demand. Moreover, experience with the OPEC cartel has shown that from the U.S. perspective it is also useful to consider the relationship of the output of minerals from deep-sea mining to U.S. import

[7] See, for example, Alvin Kaufman, "The Economics of Ocean Mining," *Marine Technology Society Journal,* July/August 1970, and Wayne J. Smith, "International Control of Deep Sea Mineral Resources," *Naval War College Review,* June 1971.

[8] United Nations, "Economic Implications," p. 30, and "Manganese Nodules (II): Prospects for Deep Sea Mining," in U.S. Congress, Senate, Subcommittee on Minerals, Materials, and Fuels of the Committee on Interior and Insular Affairs, *Mineral Resources of the Deep Seabed,* 93d Cong., 2d sess., March 1974, pp. 884-86.

[9] Marne Dubs, letter dated 6 April 1974, in Senate, Subcommittee on Minerals, Materials, and Fuels of the Committee on Interior and Insular Affairs, *Mineral Resources of the Deep Seabed,* p. 1033.

Table 5

DEEP-SEA PRODUCTION OF SELECTED MINERALS RELATIVE TO TOTAL U.S. DEMAND, U.S. IMPORT DEMAND, AND WORLD DEMAND, 1985 AND 2000
(percent)

Mineral	1985			2000		
	Total U.S. demand	U.S. import demand	World demand	Total U.S. demand	U.S. import demand	World demand
Manganese	85.0	85.0	9.0	636.0	636.0	49.0
Copper	6.0	18.0	1.0	17.0	30.0	3.0
Cobalt	398.0	398.0	83.0	1600.0	1600.0	215.0
Nickel	85.0	97.0	20.0	273.0	307.0	48.0

demand for such minerals. Table 5 offers such comparisons, with U.S. import demand being taken from the study by Morgan.[10]

Table 5 is quite revealing; it shows, among other things, that a significant portion of total U.S. demand and U.S. import demand for manganese, copper, cobalt, and nickel can be supplied from deep-sea sources. In fact, with respect to cobalt, 398 percent of U.S. needs can come from deep-sea sources. Indeed, by 1985, deep-sea sources can supply a large portion of world demand of each of the minerals in question, except copper, of which sea production will account for only 1 percent in 1985.

By the year 2000, all U.S. consumption requirements for manganese, cobalt, and nickel, and one-sixth of U.S. demand for copper, and also almost one-third of U.S. import demand for these minerals can be supplied by deep-sea resources, assuming thirty mining operations. The qualitative results apply to the rest of the world; the deep seabed can provide a substantial portion of the world demand for these mineral resources.[11]

Noteworthy, too, is the fact that if an institutional framework is adopted that does not impede ocean mining, of the six operating firms in 1985, at least three

---

[10] United Nations, "Economic Implications," p. 32.

[11] Another estimate for 1985 is given by the report "The Economic Value of Ocean Resources to the United States" prepared for the Committee on Commerce, U.S. Senate, December 1974:

	Tons	Dollar Value (1973 Prices)
Nickel	72	220
Copper	66	79
Cobalt	9.6	55
Manganese	270	180

will be U.S. firms, with headquarters and processing plants located within the United States. These three are Summa Corporation, Deep Sea Ventures, Inc., and Kennecott Copper Co. Moreover, there are reasonable possibilities that other U.S. firms will, before actual production is begun, form part of the consortia owning the three other firms. So on this basis, the United States should be assured of a reasonable share of these minerals, irrespective of potential developments in other parts of the globe. Similarly, a pleasant side effect will be that the U.S. balance of payments will improve as a result of this economically efficient reduction in dependence on foreign sources of supply.

Bergsten has argued that many of the traditional exporters of those mineral resources that the United States requires are threatening to form, and are capable of forming, cartels similar to that of the Organization of Petroleum Exporting Countries (OPEC), which succeeded in quadrupling the world price of oil in a period of little more than a year.[12] The United States would be particularly vulnerable to cartels formed in copper, cobalt, manganese, and nickel, among other minerals, because of our very high import dependence. However, as Amacher and Sweeney point out, deep-sea mining undercuts the viability of such cartels, and even if deep-sea mining produces too little to keep the world price of these minerals from skyrocketing in the short run as a result of cartelization, the productive potential of the deep seabed can certainly prevent long-run cartelization, for its sets a fairly low limit on prices in the long run.[13] Moreover, because of economical resource availability in the deep sea, self-sufficiency in many minerals can be achieved by many countries with little or no sacrifice in economic efficiency. Thus, the presence of known deposits and the necessary technology can serve as a quite powerful deterrent to prospective cartels.

Given the vast potential output of deep-sea mining, prices for the minerals produced are likely to be considerably lower than they would be otherwise, although it is impossible to predict with any precision price levels in 1985 or 2000, either absolute or relative to prices prevailing today. However, it should be noted that because of the different proportions of total world demand which seabed production can supply, there may be some rather dramatic shifts in the relative prices of the four minerals and their substitutes and complements, depending, of course, on the future development of land-based production and the extent to which the minerals become substitutable. Accordingly, the ratios offered under the year 2000 portion might be misleading.

Because of the security of supply afforded by deep-sea mining, and because of the beneficial price impact, the United States, as well as the rest of the world, stands to gain a great deal from the development of deep-sea mining. More

---

[12] C. Fred Bergsten, "The Threat from the Third World," *Foreign Policy,* vol. 11 (Summer 1973), pp. 103-24.

[13] Ryan Amacher and Richard James Sweeney, "International Commodity Cartels and the Threat of New Entry: Some Implications of Ocean Mineral Resources," *Kyklos,* forthcoming.

expensive land-based mines may be shut down, or with a view to the future, not opened at all, thus freeing resources for more highly valued uses. It should also be noted that deep-sea mining is likely to cause far less environmental damage than is done by land-based mines. Hence, it is attractive on environmental grounds as well. At the depths at which nodules are found, there are virtually no living organisms and dredging only stirs up relatively small amounts of bottom sedimentation; by contrast, land-based mining, especially the economically more attractive strip-mining, imposes heavy environmental costs. Indeed, increasingly severe environmental regulations on land-based production may increase the relative attractiveness of ocean mining.

These prospective benefits will accrue to the United States and the world only if the resources of the deep seabed are exploited efficiently. But in the law of the sea negotiations, there is much scope for imposing requirements and regulatory procedures which would unnecessarily and seriously hinder the development of deep-sea mineral resources.

Selection of a Regulatory Regime. Since there seems to be little environmental danger, the only economically satisfactory argument for regulation of the deep-sea mining industry's activity is the protection and enforcement of property rights. But given the large number of prime first-generation mine sites, perhaps 400 to 500, it is unlikely that any firm would risk endangering its nearly $300 million investment by claim-jumping. Since only six firms will be operating in 1985, and perhaps as few as thirty in 2000, there seems to be little justification for an international regulatory authority to prevent chaotic claim-jumping by other private firms. A slightly more relevant argument is the one which warns of politically motivated interference by the governments of less-developed countries. However, the rich nodule deposits are located a considerable distance (at least 1,000 miles) from any likely belligerent and, as pointed out above, are concentrated in a few areas. Both of these factors would tend to make it relatively easy for the United States and other mining countries to patrol. Second, because revenue sharing is possible with unilateral action or with an international claims registry, the government of any less-developed country which attempted to interfere with deep-sea mining would have to suffer a loss of revenues and possibly reduce revenues of other less-developed countries.

There are two extremes of the type of international organization that might be set up to govern deep-sea mining: first, a free-access, free-timing type of claims registry system; and second, a powerful International Seabed Regulatory Authority (ISRA) which, in its most extreme form, might reserve for itself all exploration and exploitation rights to the deep seabed. The first type would do nothing more than establish property rights and would, from the point of view of efficient exploitation of deep-sea minerals, be virtually costless. The second type could severely hinder resource availability and in so doing cause prices to be substantially higher than they otherwise would be. Perhaps more importantly, it could reduce the security of supply which a free-access, free-timing system would tend to ensure. The type of system envisaged in the U.S. draft treaty of 1970 comes close to the free-access, free-timing ideal, although a number of its features (for example, work requirements and relinquishment requirements) could wisely be abandoned. The important broad principles embodied in this draft are:

(1) When a producer thinks that exploiting a certain block is worthwhile, he can claim it; if no one else claims it, he can proceed with exploitation.

(2) If more than one producer claims a block, it goes to the highest bidder. Producers control the timing of exploitation, and the system is essentially a claims registry that sometimes performs the function of settling conflicting claims through auction.

Economic efficiency requires that lowest cost producers have access to exploitation rights, that lowest cost sites be exploited first, and that exploitation continue until the cost of raising one more ton of nodules equals its value. There is nothing in the spirit of the U.S. draft treaty that violates these principles, though there are a number of particulars which undercut their achievement.

In contrast, many less-developed countries support an international authority which, in fact, governs a monopoly enterprise and which in turn makes all decisions on exploration and exploitation of the deep seabed. The first consideration regarding such an enterprise is the goals it will pursue. It may be taken for granted that the bureaucracies of the proposed ISRA and its decision-making subsidiary will sometimes pursue goals opposed to each other's interests and to the interests of the various member states and blocs of member states of the establishing convention. This tendency, inherent in the operation of administrative and quasi-policy bodies, is by no means unambiguously or uniquely evil: such groups simply do tend to develop internal loyalties and goals.

In contrast to a system aimed at the efficient exploitation of deep-sea resources, an ISRA with a monopoly enterprise would be likely to pursue policies which would either maximize revenues for competing less-developed country producers, attempting the cartelization of the minerals contained in manganese nodules, or maximize its own revenues, a portion of which would be distributed among all less-developed countries. Any goal other than efficient exploitation will lead to higher prices for *all* consumers of these resources. Moreover, there is a strong likelihood that importing less-developed country consumers would receive substantially less in grants from the ISRA than they would pay in higher prices, particularly if the ISRA is captured by land-based mineral producers whose goal is to protect their income rather than maximize the revenue the ISRA has available for sharing. The United States would be particularly affected by production restrictions designed to keep prices high.

As noted in Table 5, deep-seabed production in 1985 could supply 85 percent of the total U.S. demand for manganese, 6 percent of the total U.S. demand for copper, substantially more than 100 percent of the U.S. demand for cobalt, and 85 percent of the U.S. demand for nickel. With respect to U.S. import demand, the corresponding figures are 85 percent, 18 percent, 398 percent, and 97 percent. Given the low price elasticities of demand for each of these mineral resources, and given the potential level of U.S. dependence on imports or deep-sea production, prices only slightly higher than those that would otherwise prevail could result in substantial costs (see the following section). Recall also that of the six probable producers in 1985, three will be U.S.-based. Hence other things being equal, the United States can virtually rely upon access to 50 percent of all seabed production, at least in 1985, and possibly in 2000. This magnifies U.S. concern over the type of regime to be organized and its goals.

One of the more persuasive arguments for a rigid regulatory regime with power to control world mineral production and prices is that less-developed countries will suffer if prices fall, because less-developed countries produce and developed countries consume. While in general terms this is not greatly misleading, the truth of the matter is that the mineral exports of only a small minority of less-developed nations will suffer either in potential quantity terms and/or in dollar terms [14] as a result of deep-sea mining.

For example, three less-developed countries accounted for 67 percent of all cobalt production over the period 1967–69, and only five accounted for 57 percent of total copper exports over the same period.[15] Other mineral production is also heavily concentrated among a small group of producers, though it is not as concentrated as the production of these two minerals. Indeed, if seabed mining were to depress prices, only a small minority of less-developed countries would suffer, whereas the great majority would gain because they could buy these minerals more cheaply than they could otherwise and, perhaps more important, they could buy goods produced with these minerals more cheaply.[16]

From the perspective of U.S. economic interests, it is quite clear that the best deep-seabed regime is one which will interfere minimally, and ideally not at all, with the efficient exploitation of the deep seabed. Restrictions of any kind will result in higher prices, hence higher costs for the United States, given our

[14] Producer-exporter less-developed countries may suffer because prices may be lower than they would be otherwise, as well as because formerly profitable operations may have to be shut down with the advent of a large number of deep-sea miners, say in the year 2000.

[15] Derived from United Nations Statistical Office, *Yearbook of International Trade Statistics, 1969* (New York, 1971), and United Kingdom Geological Sciences, *Statistical Summary of the Mineral Industry, 1964-1969* (London: Her Majesty's Stationery Office, 1964-69).

[16] For a more traditional, and opposing, argument of the effects of deep-sea mining on developing countries see the Report by the UNCTAD Secretariat, "The Effects of Production of Manganese from the Sea-bed, with Particular Reference to Effects on Developing Country Producers of Manganese Ore," TD/B/483, 23 April 1974.

potential dependence on seabed minerals. The greater the restrictions (at the limit, an all-powerful ISRA *cum* monopoly enterprise), the higher such costs.

Our final general argument against the establishment of a rigid regulatory authority rests upon the fact that, aside from those contained in manganese nodules, there are other minerals that are perhaps not known to occur in the ocean or are uneconomical to exploit at the present time. Establishment of an authority could quite easily hinder, or possibly prevent, the exploitation of these minerals because of nodule-oriented regulations or simply intransigence on the part of the ISRA. This may be too high a price to pay, for it could involve far higher world welfare costs than even the potentially quite costly restrictions on nodule mining.

We now turn to a case study of the potential cost to the United States of a highly restrictive deep-sea regulatory agency.

The Potential Damage of a Restrictive Regime: A Case Study. To assess the potential costs of a restrictive regulatory regime governing activities in the seabed, we must first determine the possible impact on prices if a restrictive regime is agreed upon in the law of the sea negotiations. More specifically, we must identify the costs of having few or no artificial, as opposed to technical or economic, restrictions on the use of the seabed.

As a starting point, note that most demand and supply forecasts for the minerals contained in manganese nodules suggest that there is a gap between the rate of growth in consumption and the rate of growth in land-based production at current prices. That is, at today's prices, the potential world demand for nickel, copper, manganese, and cobalt cannot be satisfied in 1985. Hence, unless a worldwide system of nonprice-rationing is in effect by 1985, the prices of these commodities will have to rise substantially so that supply can meet demand; that is, the gap which most forecasts currently envision must be closed. This will occur because higher prices will dampen demand and stimulate supply.

The magnitude of these price rises depends upon (1) the magnitude of the gap between growth rates of demand and land-based production and (2) the elasticity of demand for each natural resource.

For illustrative purposes, we consider possible gaps of .5, 1.0, 2.0, and 3.0 percent in 1985, but a zero gap in 1973. That is, four possible cases are reviewed in which demand will grow faster than land-based supply. The magnitudes of these gaps, it should be noted, are on the conservative side of most estimates; many studies suggest gaps of at least 2 or 3 percent. Similarly, we consider only two of the relevant minerals—nickel and copper. These were chosen because they appear to be the most economically relevant. Finally, we treat two cases for each mineral: (1) the case in which the elasticity of excess demand would be -1.0 at 1973 prices, and (2) the case in which it would be -2.0. These elasticities are assumed to be constant for the demand schedule and,

50

Table 6

POTENTIAL CONSUMPTION RELATIVE TO PRODUCTION OF NICKEL AND COPPER ASSUMING ALTERNATIVE GROWTH-RATE GAPS AT CURRENT PRICES

Mineral	Potential World Demand	.5 Percent Gap	1.0 Percent Gap	2.0 Percent Gap	3.0 Percent Gap
Nickel (thousands of tons)	1,075	1,018	966	865	778
Copper (thousands of tons)	12,620	11,946	11,312	10,150	9,117

Table 7

NICKEL AND COPPER PRICES THAT WOULD PREVAIL ASSUMING ALTERNATIVE GAPS

Mineral	Elasticity Assumption	Price per Ton (U.S. $) Assuming Selected Percentage Gaps of:			
		.5 percent	1.0 percent	2.0 percent	3.0 percent
Nickel	−1.0	$3,217	$3,370	$3,654	$3,910
	−2.0	$3,136	$3,213	$3,353	$3,483
Copper	−1.0	$1,260	$1,320	$1,432	$1,532
	−2.0	$1,229	$1,258	$1,314	$1,364

Note: Prices per ton are rounded to nearest dollar.

more important, are likely to be in the relevant range of elasticities for these minerals.

To sum up our method, we compute prices expected to prevail in 1985, assuming possible demand-production gaps of four different sizes and for two different excess demand elasticities, for two economically relevant minerals.

Table 6 shows the first stage of our examination. It shows the worldwide demand (from Table 3) which would obtain at 1973 prices in 1985. It also shows the amount of land-based production in 1985 under alternative possibilities concerning the size of the demand-production gap.

Prices prevailing in 1973 are taken as base prices. For nickel, the average 1973 price was $3,055 per ton; for copper $1,197 per ton. Table 7 shows the prices (in constant 1973 dollars) that would have to prevail in 1985 under the four alternative demand-production gaps and the two elasticity estimates if markets are to clear. As is readily seen, prices would have to be considerably higher in 1985 than they are currently under all alternatives. At these prices, the quantities demanded and supplied would be as shown in Table 6. We are now in a position to assess the effect of a restrictive regulatory regime on world economic welfare.

As previously indicated, a restrictive regulatory regime can control deep-sea output. By controlling output, it can control the size of the gap between consumption and total production growth rates. And the magnitude of the gap will depend upon the degree of restrictiveness of the regime. Making the not-implausible assumption that seabed production can fill large portions of the nickel gap and a not-negligible portion of the copper gap (see Table 4), the potential price rises that would occur in the absence of seabed mining could be eliminated. For example, nickel production for the deep seabed could lead to the elimination of a gap as great as 2 percent, and copper production could eliminate a gap of roughly .25 percent between demand and land-based production growth rates. A restrictive regulatory regime could prevent this gap from closing.

For the remainder of this analysis, we focus upon nickel, because the seabed production of this mineral is likely to have the greatest relative price impact, though not necessarily the most significant economic consequences in terms of total costs.

The costs to consumers of a very restrictive regime will vary with the size of the gap which results from its practices, and these costs have two components. First, consumers must pay higher prices for the amount that they do get. These costs may be estimated by simply multiplying the price differential—the difference between the prices which would obtain under alternative gaps and 1973 prices— by the quantity supplied at gap prices. This cost represents a transfer to producers from consumers and, in effect, encourages the inefficient use of productive resources by producers. Second, there is a net welfare loss to the world that economists call a deadweight loss. It represents consumer surplus forgone as a result of the higher prices, but it is not a transfer to any other party; it is a nonrecoverable loss in the economy due to the inefficient allocation of resources. Computationally, this is the price differential (as before) multiplied by the quantity differential (the difference between the quantity taken at the "gap" price and the quantity that would be taken at the 1973 price) divided by two.

Table 8 shows the first component of consumer costs—transfers to producers under various gaps, of .5, 1.0, and 2.0, and the two alternative elasticity assumptions for nickel. As shown in Table 8, the transfer costs are substantial. Depending upon assumptions, the transfer ranges from $82.6 to $518.3 million *per year* at 1985 output. It should again be emphasized that this is a conservative output estimate and that these transfers will *grow* over time, as gaps (in quantity terms) widen and as technology enabling greater seabed production becomes available, though if a restrictive regime exists it cannot be utilized.

52

Table 8
CONSUMER TRANSFER AND WELFARE COSTS FOR NICKEL

Item	Elasticity Assumption	Cost (U.S. $ millions) Assuming Selected Percentage Gaps of:		
		.5 percent	1.0 percent	2.0 percent
Consumer transfer to producers	−1.0	165.2	304.1	518.3
	−2.0	82.6	152.1	259.1
U.S. consumer transfer to foreign producers	−1.0	33.04	60.82	103.7
	−2.0	16.52	30.42	51.8
World loss in welfare	−1.0	4.62	17.17	62.89
	−2.0	2.31	8.58	31.45
U.S. welfare costs	−1.0	1.06	3.95	14.46
	−2.0	.53	1.97	7.23
Total U.S. cost	−1.0	5.68	21.15	77.35
	−2.0	2.84	10.55	38.77

Table 9
U.S. FIRMS' SHARE OF DEEP-SEA MINING REVENUES FROM FOUR MINERALS

Mineral	1985 Output [a]	Prices (1971 average)	Revenue
Manganese (thousands of tons)	750	40.00 per ton [b]	30,000,000
Copper (thousands of tons)	90	.52 per pound	93,600,000
Cobalt (thousands of pounds)	39,750	2.20 per pound	87,450,000
Nickel (millions of pounds)	210	1.33 per pound [c]	297,300,000

[a] Fifty percent of 1985 output. [b] Average price 1970 through 1972. [c] Year-end price.

Because these are funds transferred from consumers to producers, the actual net costs would be distributed quite unevenly among countries. Countries that produce more than they consume would gain at the expense of countries that consume more than is domestically produced. For the United States, which imports considerable quantities of nickel, the transfer would be quite large.

In 1985, the United States will account for approximately 23 percent of world nickel consumption. Imports of nickel in 1985 would, at 1973 prices, be in the area of 217 thousand tons, and this import demand represents approximately 20 percent of world demand for nickel. If we assume that these proportions would not change as a result of higher prices, the transfer from the United States to the rest of the world would be considerable and would range from $16.5 to $103.7 million per year (Table 8).

Let us now look at world welfare costs—the deadweight loss attributable to the general misallocation of resources. Estimates of these are given in Table 8. These costs range from $2.3 to $62.9 million. These are not especially large, but they are deadweight costs for only one mineral and for one year, and they are likely to grow over time. The U.S. share of this welfare loss ranges from $.5 million to $14.5 million. The U.S. share is based, it should be noted, on the U.S. share of total consumption. Table 8 shows the *total* cost to the United States in 1985 under various gaps and elasticities, and these range from $2.8 to $77 million *per year* at 1985 levels of consumption.

A restrictive regime could easily cause a gap between desired consumption and production of 2 percent or more. If seabed production reduces this gap by 2 percent, the United States will *save* nearly $78 million in 1985, and such savings will become greater each year after that.

We have limited our cost estimates to only one mineral. The potential savings from not having a restrictive regulatory regime could be far greater with respect to each of the other minerals. A pound of cobalt, for example, is far more expensive than a pound of nickel today, and seabed production would potentially supply all of U.S. needs and exceed the anticipated world demand. Similarly, the manganese needs of the U.S. could be largely accommodated by seabed production in 1985. In addition, rough but very conservative calculations on copper reveal potential U.S. savings ranging from $17 to $65 million for various elasticities, and the amount of the shortfall that seabed production could close. If savings of the same order of magnitude could be achieved for each of the other minerals contained in nodules, a nonrestrictive regime might be worth nearly $310 million per year to the United States at 1985 consumption rates, and considerably more in later years.

In summary, a restrictive regime would be costly to the United States, to all other consumers, and to world producers and consumers alike as a result of deadweight losses. Accordingly, acceptance of a restrictive seabed regulatory authority in the law of the sea negotiations would be economically undesirable, not only for the United States but for the world.

U.S. Interests and Revenue Sharing on the Deep Seabed. Unfortunately, it is not only the choice of regime which could harm U.S. interests. There is also the question of revenue sharing. The United Nations has adopted the concept that the oceans are the "common heritage of mankind," and unfortunately this concept has been interpreted by many to mean that producing nations or firms should share their revenues with less-developed countries.[17]

To get an approximate idea of the magnitudes that may be involved in acceptance of the revenue-sharing notion, some rough calculations on the revenues derived by the U.S. firms from deep-sea exploitation are provided in Table 9. This shows 50 percent of deep-sea minerals produced by U.S. firms in 1985, the average prices which prevailed for each of these minerals during 1971, and the total real value of production, assuming real prices are the same in 1985 as in 1971.

The three-firm industry portrayed, with all three firms being American, shows aggregate revenues conservatively estimated at $508 million in 1985. The full six-firm industry would have aggregate revenues of roughly $1 billion in 1985, and if 1971 prices prevailed in 2000, aggregate revenues would be in the $2 to $3 billion range (rather than $5 billion) as a consequence of the excess of supply over demand for some minerals and the resulting downward pressure on prices.

The more commonly mentioned revenue-sharing percentages range from 10 to 50 percent of total revenues obtained from deep-sea production. Abstracting from the question of whether a deep-sea mining industry could exist with a royalty of 50 percent, application of these percentages would mean that between $50 and $250 million would be turned over by the United States to the international community in 1985, and more in future years. These are considerable sums, and, if anything, the value of deep-seabed production is understated because of the use of 1971 prices and conservative estimates of mineral recovery. Accordingly, the revenue-sharing issue may be one that the law of the sea negotiators should treat thoughtfully, lest they give away substantially more by treaty than should be given away to attain concessions in other areas.

The method of levying taxes is another aspect of the revenue-sharing question which deserves consideration. Quite clearly, the level of taxation is important, but the mechanism for levying taxes could also have a considerable effect on the efficient allocation of resources between deep-sea and land-based mining. Of utmost importance is the fact that royalty taxation is among the more pernicious forms of taxation devised by man. The percentage royalty, because it artificially increases the marginal cost of production, leads to premature shutdown of mining operations. In contrast, a lump-sum tax, say $50,000 per year per mine, has no marginal production effect.

Summary. In this section, we have examined the growth of world and U.S. demand for the mineral resources obtainable from manganese nodules. We have also

---

[17] Derived from United Nations, *Yearbook of International Trade Statistics, 1969,* and United Kingdom Geological Sciences, *Statistical Summary of the Mineral Industry, 1964-1969.*

seen how the economically efficient exploitation of these minerals can, to a relatively great degree, help to satisfy increasing world and U.S. demand for these minerals. Given this situation, it was argued that the choice of a deep-sea mining regulatory regime by the law of the sea negotiations was crucial, because the type of regime selected would largely determine the pace of exploitation and consequently the rate at which the world enjoys the benefits of these resources. In particular, the selection of a free-access/free-timing claims registry system was supported, since this would interfere least with the efficient exploitation of the deep sea's mineral resources. Finally, it was pointed out that U.S. interests are sensitive to the concept of revenue sharing and that, if set as a percentage of value of production, the rate should be set low; preferably it should be a low lump-sum tax.

The Coastal Economic Zone and the Delimitation of the Continental Margin

The continental margin, which is a natural undersea prolongation of the continental land mass, encompasses three areas: (1) the continental shelf, which extends horizontally from the shore a variable distance averaging 100 miles and is ordinarily no deeper than about 200 meters; (2) the continental slope, which gradually slopes to the rise at a depth of approximately 2500 meters; and (3) the continental rise, which is the generally steeper transitional area between the slope and the ocean floor, the foot of which has an approximate depth of 4000 meters.

Under the 1958 Geneva Convention on the Continental Shelf, coastal states have exclusive control over natural resources on the continental shelf up to the 200-meter depth and beyond to "where the depth of the superadjacent waters admit to the exploitation of the mineral resources." Thus, the 1958 convention extends the coastal states' jurisdiction over the natural resources of the ocean bed to at least 200 meters, but does not extend coastal state jurisdiction beyond the territorial sea for fishing, research, or navigational purposes. Because the "exploitability" and "adjacency" concepts are vague, there has been considerable controversy about the outer limit of coastal state jurisdiction. One of the expressed purposes of the law of the sea convention is the settling of this controversy by negotiating the boundary between the coastal state economic area (CSEA) and the deep seabed which, according to some proposals, would be controlled by the deep seabed authority.

A large majority of coastal states now favors extension of broad coastal jurisdiction over living and mineral resources beyond the proposed twelve-mile territorial sea and beyond the continental shelf, to at least two hundred miles from the shore, or from some other baseline such as the territorial sea. The economic resources of the margin include marine life, minerals, and petroleum resources. Minerals of value include sand and gravel, oyster shells, placer minerals, phosphate, and

56

manganese nodules. Gold, platinum, tin, and chromite deposits are located off the coasts of Alaska, Oregon, and California; manganese nodules of relatively little economic value are located on the Blake Plateau off the Atlantic Coast.

By far the most valuable minerals on the continental margin are oil, gas, and natural gas liquids.[18] Despite past production of more than five billion barrels of crude on the U.S. continental margin, little is known about the extent of petroleum resources located there with the exception of those found at depths of less than 400 to 500 feet off the Pacific and Gulf coasts. No hard estimates are available for the Atlantic Coast because exploratory wells have been prohibited. Pacific and Gulf coast explorations have been governed by leasing procedures presumably to prevent diminution of bids, whereas the Atlantic drilling has been prohibited for environmental reasons.

Numerous formulae have been advanced to delimit the boundary between coastal state jurisdiction and the international seabed jurisdiction. The five outer limits—12 miles, 200 miles, 200 meters, 2500 meters, and 4000 meters—presented in Table 10 represent a fair range of the formulae used in the delimitation discussions.

Assuming a 4000-meter depth as the seaward edge of the continental margin, the United States margin includes an area of 1.8 million square nautical miles, an estimated 395 billion barrels of oil, nearly 2000 trillion cubic feet of natural gas (341 billion barrels of crude equivalents), 60 feet of natural gas (341 billion barrels of crude equivalents), and 60 billion barrels of natural gas liquids (41 billion barrels of crude equivalent), which, assuming that $10 is the price per barrel of crude, has a total value of $7.8 trillion.[19]

---

[18] The projected value of offshore recovery of sand, gravel, shell, and so on, is estimated to total $180 million in 1985. See U.S. Senate, Commerce Committee, "The Economic Value of Ocean Resources to the United States."

[19] Unlike most of the estimates made in this study, the estimates of the value of petroleum resources on the U.S. continental margins are on the high side of the range. First, we have used a price of $10 per barrel which is slightly below the current c.i.f. import price of $11.50 per barrel; however, the $10 price is most likely above the real long-run equilibrium price. It is a simple task, however, to scale down the value estimates by whatever real price one believes to be appropriate.

The quantity estimates are more difficult to reconcile, because there is considerable disagreement among geologists as to the quantity of potential recoverable petroleum resources on the U.S. margin. Basically, we used official published U.S. Geological Survey data. After several discussions with survey geologists, we adjusted the quantities within the various components of the margin, but we retained the total quantity (395 billion for oil) for the entire margin to a 4,000-meter depth. However, we currently have reason to believe that these estimates are too optimistic. The U.S. Geological Survey is preparing another study which will revise their previous estimates downward, but we have not been able to determine by how much. Their new estimates should be released by May 1975, however. The National Petroleum Council has prepared estimates which suggest that there are undiscovered oil and natural gas liquids resources of 127 billion barrels on the outer continental shelf (0-200 meters) to which we must add the measured (35.3b), indicated (5.1b), inferred (18.0b), and measured natural gas liquids (6.5b), which totals 192 billion barrels. Their estimate of total oil resources (192 billion

The 200-meter isobath has legal precedence in the 1958 Geneva convention and has been loosely equated by many with the depth on the seaward edge of the continental shelf. Approximately 26 percent of the estimated potential recoverable petroleum resources on the U.S. continental shelf are believed to lie between the U.S. coastline and the 200-meter isobath. Because virtually all of the current exploration and drilling activity has occurred within the 200-meter isobath, the quantitative estimates within this region are more accurate than in the others. Although current technology does not permit operation much beyond 200 meters, Table 10 shows that nearly three-quarters of the U.S. continental margin's petroleum resources are estimated to lie beyond 200 meters. However, most of the petroleum resources beyond the 200-meter isobath lie within the landward side of the 2500-meter isobath.

Although all offshore petroleum production has occurred in depths of less than 200 meters, current technology, subject to a few refinements (especially in pipeline laying and maintenance), permits extensive exploratory drilling and production up to the 400-meter isobath. It is anticipated that mobile drilling and underwater wellheads will permit operation up to the 1500-meter depth before the end of this decade. Further advances in semi-independent subsea units are expected to permit operation up to 2000 or 2500 meters and beyond by the end of the next decade.[20]

If the outer limit of the coastal economic zone were to be established at 2500 meters rather than at twelve miles or 200 meters, the United States could obtain large quantities of additional petroleum resources. At 2500 meters, the United States would obtain $6.8 trillion in petroleum resources (85 percent of the total value of the margin), whereas it would acquire $2 trillion (26 percent) a 200 meters, but only $0.5 trillion (6 percent) at a twelve-mile outer limit (territorial sea). Beyond 2500 meters (2500 to 4000 meters), the United States would add $1 trillion (15 percent) to its exclusively controlled petroleum resources although it should be noted that most of this increment is located within the Arctic Zone where the operating and environmental costs will delay development for two decades or more. At the present time (February 1975), the most commonly

---

barrels) on the outer continental shelf is greater than our estimate of oil and natural gas liquid of 117 billion barrels.

A noted geologist, L. G. Weeks, has estimated world offshore petroleum resources to total 2,272 billion barrels. Prorating this amount by the area of the U.S. continental margin (827,00 square nautical miles) to total world area on the continental margin to a 3,000-meter dept (13,771,300 square nautical miles) we obtain a U.S. prorata share of 136 billion barrels. On problem with this estimate is that we do not know what measure Weeks used to define offshor areas. If he used a broad definition of 4,000 meters, the estimate of 136 billion barrels woul probably have to be considered a conservative one.

[20] A UN study has estimated that North America may have nearly 16 percent of the estimate recoverable reserves on the world's continental shelf. This is more than any other part of th world except, of course, the Middle East. See UN A/AC. 138/87, June 1973.

Table 10

QUANTITIES AND VALUES OF POTENTIAL PETROLEUM RESOURCES RECOVERABLE FROM THE U.S. CONTINENTAL MARGINS[a]

Intervals	Oil (billions of barrels)	Gas (billions of barrels of crude equivalent)	Natural Gas Liquids (billions of barrels of crude equivalent)	Value of Oil	Value of Gas	Value of Natural Gas Liquids	Total Value	Percentage of Total (within interval)
					($ billions)			
0–4,000 meters[b] (foot of rise)	395	341	41	$3,950	$3,410	$410	$7,770	100
0–200 meters[b]	100	88	17	1,000	880	170	2,050	25
0–2,500 meters[b]	340	301	35	3,400	3,010	350	6,760	85
0–12 miles[b]	25	21	3.5	250	210	35	495	6
12 miles—200 meters	75	67	13.8	750	670	138	1,558	20
200 meters—4,000 miles	295	253	24	2,950	2,530	240	5,720	74
0–4,000 meters within 200 miles[c]	340	296	36	3,400	2,960	360	6,720	86
0–4,000 meters outside 200 miles	55	45	5.5	550	450	55	1,055	14

[a] Geological quantities based upon a revised internal government paper prepared by John P. Albers of the U.S. Geological Survey. These estimates are currently being revised by the Geological Survey. (See footnote 19, p. 57.)

[b] 200 nautical miles or, of less than 200 nautical miles, theoretical division of seabed based on U.S. State Department map (Washington, D. C.: U.S. Government Printing Office, 1971).

[c] Areas exclude Hawaii and insular possessions, based on work of S. Freqon, U.S. Geological Survey (1973). Petroleum volumes based on calculations of S. Schweinfurth, U.S. Geological Survey (1969).

Table 11

ESTIMATED COSTS OF REVENUE SHARING FOR ALTERNATIVE DELIMITATIONS OF THE U.S. CONTINENTAL MARGIN

Intervals	Annual Revenue Sharing, 2 Percent of Value of Production, 50 Percent Depletion over 25 Years ($ billions per year)	Annual Revenue Sharing, 5 Percent of Value of Production, 50 Percent Depletion over 25 Years ($ billions per year)
0–4,000 meters	$3.11	$7.77
0–200 meters	.82	2.05
200 meters–250 meters	1.88	4.71
2,500 meters–4,000 meters	.40	1.01
12 miles–200 meters	.62	1.56
12 miles–4,000 meters	2.91	7.28
200 meters–200 miles	1.87	4.67
200 meters–4,000 meters	2.28	5.72
12 miles–200 miles	2.49	6.23
4,000 meters beyond 200 miles	.42	1.06

discussed policy options on the width of the continental margin are either 200 miles, or 200 miles or the edge of the margin, whichever is farther seaward.[21]

Alternative delimitation methods of the coastal seabed economic area (CSEA) and the related values are presented in Table 11. From the data given, it is obvious that substantial resources would be added to U.S. jurisdiction if the United States were able to obtain agreement on 200 miles or the edge of the margin (4000 meters), whichever is farther seaward; or, subject to some beneficial trade-off, 200 miles or 2500 meters.

An issue closely associated with the delimitation of the CSEA is the concept of revenue sharing as proposed in President Nixon's "common heritage of mankind" announcement in May 1970. Revenue sharing on the continental margin is strongly endorsed by those countries with narrow margins, those less technologically advanced, and a few developing coastal countries which (incorrectly)

[21] The former ambassador of Malta, Arvid Pardo, who is widely credited with initiating the law of the sea conferences in his November 1967 speech before the United Nations, has argued that the width of the CSEA is irrelevant unless there is an agreement on the baselines from which the CSEA is to be measured. Otherwise, according to Pardo, countries could, as Bangladesh has done recently, declare that their countries' baselines begin at an isobath which is located a considerable distance off their shores. Arvid Pardo, "Comments on Caracas and Predictions for the Future," *Perspectives on Ocean Policy: Conflict and Order in Ocean Relations* (Johns Hopkins University, 1974); and Ambassador Pardo's comments printed in this volume, pp. 161-66.

believe they would reap few benefits from the extension of coastal state control over the margins. There are many mechanisms of revenue sharing, the most widely discussed of which is a fixed royalty payment based upon the value of production at the wellhead or mine site. Table 11 presents the estimated annual, and the nondiscounted accumulated, revenues which the United States would have to pay to the international community for production on its margins if the royalty rates were set at 2 percent and 5 percent of the value of production. These estimates must be interpreted with extreme caution because they are based upon the rather shaky geologic estimates and stock values presented in Table 10. Furthermore, they are derived from the assumption that the rate of depletion of petroleum resources located on the margin will be on average a constant 2 percent per annum over a twenty-five-year period, or that 50 percent of petroleum resources will be depleted over twenty-five years.

Annual revenue sharing for petroleum production on the entire U.S. margin is estimated to cost more than $3 billion per year at a 2 percent royalty, and nearly $8 billion per year at a 5 percent royalty. If the landward base line of the CSEA is the twelve-mile territorial sea, and the seaward limit is 200 miles, estimated shared revenues will be $2.5-$6.2 billion per year. Thus, even at relatively low royalty rates, the United States would incur substantial payment obligations if revenue sharing were adopted.[22]

Another way of interpreting the data in Table 11 is to assume that a royalty rate of 2.5 percent is levied on taxed resources produced within the deep seabed and that no royalty is levied within the CSEA. If the seaward limit of the CSEA were 2000 meters rather than 200 meters, the United States could save between $2 and $6 billion per year in revenue sharing. The data, although based on crude estimates, strongly suggest that the United States would gain access to considerable quantities of petroleum resources and would save billions of dollars in revenue sharing if the CSEA were extended to the edge of the margin and if revenue sharing were excluded from the CSEA.

Although there would be significant benefits to the United States of extending coastal state control to the edge of the margin and not sharing revenues obtained from production on the margin, it may be necessary to forgo these in order to secure benefits of greater value. One consideration often raised is whether the benefits obtained by a wide U.S. coastal economic zone will be greater than the additional costs which will be imposed on those U.S. firms producing on the margins of other countries. An important part of the answer to this question lies in the type of investment guarantees that are negotiated for the CSEA and the continued adher-

---

[22] In Senate Commerce Committee, "The Economic Value of Ocean Resources to the United States" (p. 13), it is estimated that cumulative production on the CSEA from 1974 through the year 2000 would amount to $400 billion (1973 prices). Assuming constant depletion rates over this period, estimated shared revenues would be approximately $300 million per year at 2 percent and $750 million at a 5 percent royalty.

ence to the treaty's provisions by coastal states. The wider the CSEA, the greater will be the revenues paid to the coastal states by U.S. oil companies and consumers, and the smaller will be the revenues transferred to the international seabed authority. Oil companies will have more alternatives for negotiating production rights if coastal states, rather than the seabed authority, have control over the margins. In addition, the United States would gain exclusive control over, and certain access to, considerable resources on its own wide margin. Given these factors, it appears that one could conclude that it would be in the economic interests of the United States to negotiate the extension of the CSEA from twelve miles to the edge of the margin (4000 meters).

When considering CSEA trade-offs on other issues, the rational strategy for the United States is to be certain that it gains at least as much as the potential value of petroleum and other resources located on the margin. The United States might be able to obtain support for its positions on other issues by falling back to a 2500-meter seaward delimitation of the margin, a move which should not prove excessively costly, although other nations can also effectively recognize this fact; any further inland movement of the outer delimitation line, however, would be very costly and should be traded away only in return for highly valued and tangible benefits on other issues.

Freedom of Transit through Straits

The traditional three-mile limit of territorial seas—ocean areas over which adjacent countries may exercise complete resource and navigational control—was derived from the limited ability of coastal states to protect their exclusive jurisdiction. Initially this was defined by the three-mile range of land-based cannons. Despite advances in weapons technology, the three-mile limit concept, originally advanced by Grotius in *Mare Liberum,* obtained until the Truman Proclamation of 1945 asserted U.S. jurisdiction and control over those natural resources located on the accessible subsoil and seabed of the U.S. continental shelf. In 1953, Congress "ratified" this proclamation by passing the Outer Continental Shelf Lands Act establishing rules and procedures for the leasing of property on the U.S. continental margin for purposes of mineral extraction. Although neither the act nor the proclamation established territorial claims, they appear to have served as catalysts to the claims of other nations over resources and territorial seas. Prior to 1945, virtually all countries of the world recognized the three-mile limit to the territorial sea, whereas in 1975 only 29 of the 149 coastal states recognized this limit. Currently, fifty-four countries claim a twelve-mile territorial sea, and at least eight claim a territorial sea of 200 miles.[23]

---

[23] For a more lengthy discussion of the traditional development of territorial seas, see K. Clarkson, "International Law, U.S. Seabeds Policy and Ocean Resource Development," *Journal of Law and Economics,* vol. 17, no. 1 (April 1974), pp. 117-42.

If the width of the territorial sea is extended from three to twelve miles in the law of the sea negotiations, as is widely anticipated, most navigable straits will fall within the confines of territorial waters, because most straits are less than twenty-four miles in width. Under the current three-mile territorial sea regime, most of the significant straits contain high seas corridors in which vessels passing through straits are not subject to any legal controls by straits states. Extension of the territorial sea to twelve miles, as proposed by many countries, would eliminate the high seas corridors of approximately thirty important straits.

Almost as important as the width of the territorial sea is the degree of control exercised by straits states within the territorial sea. The doctrine of "innocent passage," which originated in customary international law and is codified in the 1958 Convention of the Territorial Sea, permits ships to navigate through the territorial sea if their passage is not "prejudicial to the peace, good order or security of the coastal state." It also prohibits charges "levied upon foreign ships by reason of their passage through the territorial sea," though it would seem that this convention would not prohibit fees to ease traffic congestion or to pay for safety of navigation aids provided they were nondiscriminatory among nations.

The doctrine of innocent passage raises a number of problems. First, submarines must navigate on the surface and show their flags; second, overflight of the territorial sea by commercial and military aircraft requires prior consent of the straits states; [24] and third, the doctrine is subject to varying interpretations, hence may lead to abuse by controlling states. For example, states may, as Malaysia has done, construe innocent passage to mean that they can protest movement by oil tankers on the theory that such passage is not "innocent" because of the possibility of pollution. In addition, states may either prohibit or require prior notification of movement by military vessels on the grounds that such passage is not "innocent."

The United States has traditionally pressed for narrow territorial seas and for the right of "free transit" through straits, permitting ships and aircraft to travel from one part of the high seas to another unmolested and without prior notification.

The 1958 Convention on the Territorial Sea also failed to define the methods for measuring the inner boundaries of the territorial sea around archipelagos. As a result, some archipelagic states, such as the Philippines and Indonesia, have claimed that the inner boundary should be determined by drawing a straight line connecting the outermost islands in the archipelago. If these claims are finally accepted internationally, they will result in a broader territorial sea and increased coastal state control over the oceans in or around the archipelagos.

---

[24] The (Chicago) Convention on International Civil Aviation and the International Air Services Transit Agreement provide international navigation transit rights over the national territory of contracting states for civil aircraft. These rights, however, are not extended to state aircraft, including military, customs, and police services.

Although U.S. decision makers may not explicitly recognize or confront the implicit trade-offs between the straits and archipelago position of the United States and its position on the deep seabed or on other issues, such trade-offs are implicit in the negotiating and bargaining process in the law of the sea negotiations. If the United States could obtain a lasting and enforceable agreement on a highly valued issue by sacrificing on issues of less value, such a trade-off would be rational. Before such trade-offs are made, however, it is essential that reliable and realistic studies be made on all of the issues. Although some economic data have been obtained on other issues, there have been virtually no systematic studies of the straits/archipelago issues. Considerable emphasis has been placed on the possibility that straits countries and archipelagos could arbitrarily prohibit transit of U.S. vessels for environmental, political, or economic reasons. Politically motivated actions could be aimed at the United States directly or indirectly through one or more of its allies. If the law of the sea negotiations fail, such actions obviously are possible, though it is not clear how probable they would be, nor how a law of the sea treaty might effectively reduce this probability. Further, if such actions do occur, it is not clear that they would inflict very serious damage on the United States.

Many straits states are major U.S. trading partners and would be unlikely to charge high tolls or prohibit passage of vessels carrying cargo between them and the United States. Because of adverse political and commercial repercussions, they might also be reluctant to engage in actions that would seriously jeopardize U.S. trade with other countries. Second, straits countries must consider the possibility that the United States and its allies would employ alternative routes and modes of transportation or that they would obtain their goods and services from countries which are located on different trade routes. It should be noted that there are heavily used straits which do not now have high seas corridors, for example, Skaggerak, and which are not the sites of undue harassment.

Despite the pressures on straits countries to minimize harassment on international shipping, incidents might occur. If we assume that some incidents would occur, we need to know the probability of occurrence and the costs such episodes would impose, in order to judge rationally the potential problems.

When analyzing the costs of straits closure or expanded territorial seas, one must consider both military and commercial navigation. Unfortunately no quantitative studies have been made available on military navigation; only a few preliminary quantitative studies have been made of the costs to commercial navigation.

One of the more impressive of the qualitative studies on military and commercial navigational interests has been conducted by Robert Osgood.[25] Of all the straits which might potentially be closed by extension of the territorial sea, Osgood

---

[25] Robert E. Osgood, "U.S. Security Interests and Ocean Law," *Ocean Development and International Law,* Spring 1974, pp. 1-36.

cogently argued that only three of military importance might actually be closed to U.S. naval forces; of the ten straits of economic significance, he concluded that only five might seriously be threatened by closure. While the underlying logic of the arguments provides a qualitative understanding, robust decisions concerning trade-offs are still not possible until some estimate of the probable magnitude of costs is made.

Along these lines, it is necessary to proceed on a case-by-case basis. That is, we need to examine the costs of closure for each particular strait, combine their estimates, and then compare the total of such costs to those of negotiating concessions which might be made in order to achieve agreement on the free transit issue. A complete case-by-case approach is beyond the realm of this paper. However, using two alternative methods, we do explore the magnitude of the costs to the United States resulting from closure of two economically important straits.

If the Straits of Dover, through which 22 percent of waterborne U.S. imports and 27 percent of U.S. waterborne exports pass, were to be closed, the incremental transit costs of using diversionary water routes would amount to approximately $35 to $45 million per year.[26] Assuming that 25 percent of all U.S. waterborne trade travels through the Straits of Dover, the cost of closure of all straits would be less than $140 to $180 million per year. This assumption of proportionality is rather heroic, but it must be pointed out that the effects of closing the very costly straits will be at least partially offset by the closure of straits having low-cost alternatives.

A recent study by David B. Johnson compared the costs of transporting oil from the Persian Gulf under the present three-mile territorial sea regime and under a hypothetical 200-mile territorial sea regime. The shortest route from the Persian Gulf to the United States is via the Red Sea and the Suez Canal, a distance of 8,546 miles. When the recently reopened Suez Canal is dredged to its former depth, draft limitations would still prohibit its use by loaded 250,000 deadweight ton (d.w.t.) tankers, though they might be able to transit the canal on the return ballasted journey.

At the present time, when U.S.-bound tankers leave the Persian Gulf they may proceed either in a westerly direction to the Gulf or Atlantic coasts of the United States or in an easterly direction to the U.S. Pacific Coast. The Treasury study posed the following question: what would happen to the costs of transporting a barrel of oil to the East and West coasts of the United States if a territorial sea of 200 miles were established along each coast and archipelago, excepting, of course, the Persian Gulf states? [27] Table 12 presents data on comparative costs of the alternative routes.

---

[26] This is based on estimates of the cost of avoiding the strait plus the reduction in U.S. exports that would occur as a result of the higher transportation costs.

[27] At its narrowest point, the Straits of Hormuz, which connect the Persian Gulf with the Indian Ocean, would fall within the twelve-mile territorial waters of Oman or Iran. If the Persian Gulf

Although the round-trip Suez Canal route is impossible at present, the canal could be deepened to accommodate 200,000 d.w.t. tankers; in that case oil transport costs would be $1.00 per barrel. If 2.5 millions of barrels per day (mmb/d) were shipped to the U.S. East Coast through the Suez Canal, the oil transportation bill for one year would be $913 million. The present route for transporting oil from the Persian Gulf to the East Coast of the United States is around the Cape of Good Hope and costs approximately $1.20 per barrel or $1.10 billion annually. If a 200-mile territorial sea were established, it is assumed that U.S.-bound tankers would travel at least 200 miles off the coasts of Mozambique and South Africa. This would add ten cents per barrel to transportation costs, or less than two-tenths of a cent per gallon of gasoline. Total annual costs of shipping 2.5 mmb/d to the East Coast of the United States is $1.19 billion, which means that the incremental costs imposed by a 200-mile territorial sea on transporting oil from the Persian Gulf would be less than $100 million annually. Despite many comments that an extended territorial sea would "jeopardize" the transportation of crude to the U.S. market, the additional costs of a 200-mile territorial sea are considerably less ($91 million) than the differential costs imposed by the closure and limitations of the Suez Canal necessitating transit around the Cape of Good Hope ($182 million).

While Alaskan North Slope oil and Indonesian oil will probably supply the East Coast of the United States, some proportion of oil from the Persian Gulf may be sent to the West Coast. A considerable increase in distance to the West Coast would be made necessary by the hypothetical closure of the Malacca-Singapore straits and of the 200-mile band around non-U.S.-controlled islands. The current route from the Persian Gulf to San Francisco, utilizing the Malacca-Singapore straits, costs $1.14 per barrel. If U.S.-bound tankers had to avoid the territorial sea of other countries, the per-barrel transportation costs would be $1.47; less than one-half of one cent would be added to the price of a gallon of gasoline.

Assuming that 2.0 mmb/d of Persian Gulf oil will be sent to the U.S. Atlantic Coast and .5 mmb/d will be sent to the U.S. Pacific Coast each year, the annual cost differential between the currently viable routes and the routes dictated by a 200-mile regime is $137 million. Over a twenty-five-year period, a hypothetical 200-mile regime would result in additional nondiscounted oil transportation costs of between $2.3 billion (import to U.S. East Coast only) and $3.4 billion (import to East and West coasts) in 1973 dollars (nondiscounted).

states act as a unified cartel, they can levy only one monopoly price; they can exert their monopoly power on oil or on transit, but not on both. Control of the straits does not increase the potential monopoly power of the cartel, although it may increase relative bargaining power of the strait states within the cartel. Hence, if the cartel is not charging the profit-maximizing price, the strait states, if so inclined, do have additional leverage within the cartel which, subject to the independent transportation alternatives of the other oil-producing states, could have the effect of increasing oil prices.

Table 12

ROUND-TRIP TANKER TRANSPORTATION COSTS UTILIZING
ALTERNATIVE ROUTES FROM THE PERSIAN GULF

	To Philadelphia			To San Francisco		Differential Costs between Normal Routes & 200-Mile Regime Routes
	Suez Canal	Cape of Good Hope	200-mile regime	Malacca-Singapore Strait	200-mile regime	
Per barrel costs (dollars)	1.00	1.20	1.30	1.13	1.48	—
Total annual costs ($ millions)						
Assuming 2.5 mmb/d to Atlantic Coast	913	1,095	1,186	—	—	91
Assuming 2.0 mmb/d to Atlantic and .5 mmb/d to Pacific Coast	730	876	949	206	270	137
Nondiscounted costs, 1976–2000 ($ millions)						
Assuming 2.5 mmb/d to Atlantic Coast	22,825	27,375	29,650	—	—	2,275
Assuming 2.0 mmb/d to Atlantic and .5 mmb/d to Pacific	18,250	21,900	23,725	5,510	6,750	3,425

Note: It is assumed that all trips are made in 250,000 d.w.t. tankers at 1973 time-charter hire rates and that bunker fuel is priced at $70 per ton. Light loading for the winter weather zone located 200 miles off Cape of Good Hope is included in cost estimate for 200-mile regime as well as a small time differential for an adverse current.

These two studies are far from definitive. They should lead to the conclusion that free transit through straits and archipelagos is valuable, but they suggest that the costs of limited access to straits and expanded territorial seas may not be dreadfully high. The right of free transit for the military and commercial navigation of the United States and its allies is valuable, but this right, like that of free access to the seabed's resources, is not beyond economic quantification and analysis. Additional studies need to be made of other trade routes, alternative supplies of raw materials, and possible effects on our allies. In particular, defense is such a vital goal that there should be serious attempts to *quantify* the value of free transit for specific routes, considering the costs of alternative routes, modes of delivery, and different methods of accomplishing strategic and tactical missions of the United States and its allies.

International Pollution Standards

A country can suffer significant ocean pollution caused by vessels of other countries. This is one of the reasons why the law of the sea conference seeks to achieve international agreement on pollution standards on the high seas and in coastal state economic areas. This is a laudable goal, for pollution potentially causes externalities harmful to innocent parties. However, there are a number of other international organizations, such as the International Maritime Consultative Organization (IMCO), which are currently working on this legitimate concern. Insofar as this problem is already under consideration, its inclusion in the already crowded list of law of the sea negotiation topics may not be optimal.

The major argument for international pollution standards is that they are necessary to prevent individual countries from establishing significantly divergent standards in their own economic areas. Such fears, however, may not be legitimate on economic grounds.

The danger in a regime of varying standards is that any given country might establish higher standards than other countries, resulting in increased shipping costs for those using their sea lanes. For example, countries might agree upon a 200-mile coastal state economic area with coastal state pollution control rights with *minimum* international standards. Subsequently, a country contiguous to an important trade route could arbitrarily impose stringent vessel design criteria. Such an action might necessitate the refitting or replacement of ships using this route, or force noncomplying vessels to travel outside the area. However, since all of the vessels owned by or trading with the country imposing the restrictions would have to conform to the new specifications, the adoption of such criteria would probably result in considerably higher costs of navigation for this country relative to others.

Thus, there would be powerful economic incentives for not imposing standards higher than the international standards. In fact, it seems likely that standards higher than the international average would be imposed only by rich nations that are very worried about pollution, only modestly dependent upon trade, and feel they can bear the extra costs and international competitive disadvantage. These nations might well be best negotiated with on a bilateral basis, with a carefully tailored quid pro quo.

Another possibility is that no international standards whatsoever be established. In the early days of the railroads, gauges were not standard, and myriad conflicting rules developed in different countries. In the case of the railroad, however, this situation arose because no one had foreseen its eventual consequences. If such costs are foreseen, there will be general, government-enforced agreement to avoid them. In fact, in the United States a standard gauge was generally adopted by the railroad companies, with no government intervention. Therefore, the railroad example is really an argument for the lack of necessity for formal international agreement on harmonization.

At the present time, there is no consensus among the law of the sea negotiators as to what the fundamental basis of international pollution standards should be, and there is less agreement on specific proposals regarding explicit criteria. However, the setting of international standards will involve costs, the magnitude of which must be considered. Some understanding of the size of these costs might be achieved by a quick examination of the probable costs to the United States of adoption on a multilateral basis of a particular set of very popular oil tanker design criteria.

In the fall of 1973, the International Maritime Consultative Organization met to consider the adoption of a regulation requiring barges and oil tankers of a given size to be segregated-ballast tankers.[28] The original U.S. position was that all tankers of 70,000 deadweight tons or larger (contracted for after January 1976)

---

[28] Vessels transporting oil generally carry cargo on only one leg of each round trip voyage. When not carrying cargo, these ships must be provided with weight (ballast) in order to achieve seaworthiness and proper propeller immersion, and to facilitate landing in port. Crude oil tankers are ballasted with sea water. At one time, tankers loaded ballast directly into the cargo tanks which became intermixed with the remaining oil. To protect the area around the loading port, the oily ballast was discharged at sea and replaced with clean ballast, which was discharged at the port. Today, nearly 80 percent of the tankers use an alternative technique called load-on-top (LOT) which reduces, but does not eliminate, the amount of oil discharged into the sea. A third alternative involves the use of tankers which are constructed with separate tanks for cargo and ballast. This system, known as segregated ballasting, virtually eliminates operational oil spills. However, there is some danger that the skin of the ballast tanks could be ruptured. An additional layer of steel sheet makes "double-skin" ballasted tankers more likely to withstand external shocks to the vessel. For additional information, see Joseph D. Porricelli, Virgil F. Keith, and Richard L. Storch, "Tankers and the Ecology," *Transactions of the Society of Naval Architects and Marine Engineers*, vol. 79 (1971), pp. 174-77; and *Safer Tankers and Cleaner Seas* (New York, N.Y.: Exxon, 1972), pp. 12-14.

be double-skinned segregated-ballast tankers. The actual outcome of the conference was that tankers of 150,000 deadweight or more (contracted for after January 1978) were to be single-skinned segregated-ballast tankers, a requirement significantly less stringent than the original U.S. proposal.

Although questions may be raised concerning the wisdom of selecting the criteria, the immediate interest here is the cost of imposing these design standards.[29] For the world as a whole, the annual costs of transporting oil in 1980 using single-skin segregated-ballast tankers would be an additional $54 million to $125 million, depending upon the minimum size selected for imposing this standard. If double-skin segregated-ballast tankers were used, the additional oil transport costs would be $153 million to $358 million, depending upon the minimum size for the requirement. For the United States, corresponding estimates are an additional $10 million to $26 million annually for single-skin and $28 million to $75 million for double-skin segregated-ballast tankers.

The magnitude of these costs is substantial, and the use of segregated ballast for oil tankers represents only one of many conceivable facets of a possible general international agreement on pollution control. Accordingly, it is incumbent upon policy makers to understand fully and specify quite carefully the possible gains from such standards prior to granting concessions in order to achieve international agreement in this regard.

The explicit benefit derived by the United States from adoption of segregated-ballast design criteria is the prevention of economic losses due to vessel source oil pollution (such as damage to fisheries, recreational losses, and so on).

With respect to the single-skin segregated-ballast requirement, the benefits may well be negative; due to the deeper drafts of the ships, increased accidental oil spillage will probably more than fully offset the reduction in operational oil spillage. For the double-skinned segregated ballast, the annual reduction in pollution damage would be a maximum of $7 million. Accordingly, an incremental investment of $10 million to $75 million in obtaining segregated-ballast tankers does not appear to be prudent: costs exceed benefits by a wide margin.

The above illustration serves to underscore the fact that the imposition of international pollution standards by the law of the sea conference could result in substantial costs to the United States and to the world. Moreover, the benefits from such standards appear to be considerably less than the costs. Accordingly, additional serious thought is necessary prior to supporting such international standards and, more important, making substantive concessions in order to achieve agreement on international standards.

---

[29] For the complete treatment of this general issue of segregated ballast as well as full discussion of the cost computations, see P. A. Cummins, D. E. Logue, R. D. Tollison, and T. D. Willett, "Oil Tanker Pollution Control: Design Criteria vs. Effective Liability Assessment," *Journal of Maritime Law and Commerce,* forthcoming.

Fisheries

The issue of coastal state control of fisheries located on the adjacent continental margin has probably generated more political interest within the United States than any other issue. Yet the basic fisheries problems and issues are unknown to most U.S. citizens. Because of the complexity of the fishery issue, it cannot be discussed thoroughly in this essay. Only a summary discussion of the fisheries issue and some indicative data will be presented.

Current law of the sea negotiations on fisheries have been generated by two practical considerations. The first is a very practical problem arising from the fact that some coastal countries have unilaterally extended their areas of exclusive control. Under current international law, it is generally recognized that coastal states shall only exercise exclusive control over living marine resources within twelve miles of the coastal baseline. Some nations, notably Peru, Ecuador, and Mexico, have unilaterally extended their exclusive fisheries zones as far out as 200 miles. Consequently, one of the major purposes of the law of the sea negotiations is to settle disputes over the extent of exclusive zones and to obtain common agreement on the extent of coastal state jurisdiction.

The other impetus to negotiations is the so-called common-pool, or open-access problem, which arises from the fact that fishery resources are not owned by individuals. The mobility of fish and the difficulty of identifying and tracking them makes property rights in fisheries too costly to assign and to enforce.[30]

Property rights in fish, unlike those in most other resources, can be exclusively acquired only by producing (harvesting) the fish (the right of capture); it is not possible to establish property rights to fish swimming in the ocean. This lack of individual property rights causes each fisherman to ignore the fact that the costs of future harvests of a species depend upon the future stock of that species. Fish harvested today reduce tomorrow's stock and the size of tomorrow's stock affects tomorrow's harvesting costs. If each fisherman could be assigned a specific school of fish, he could manage the stock of that school so that he and society would obtain the maximum economic benefits over time, including the time at which he might want to sell this stock to someone else. Because such exclusive property

---

[30] Two classic economic articles on fisheries are Howard Scott Gordon, "The Economic Theory of a Common-Property Resource: The Fishery," *Journal of Political Economy,* vol. 62 (April 1954), pp. 124-42, and Anthony Scott, "The Fishery: The Objectives of Sole Ownership," *Journal of Political Economy,* vol. 63 (April 1955), pp. 116-24. A few examples of other articles are Ralph Turvey, "Optimization and Suboptimization in Fishery Regulation," *American Economic Review,* vol. 54 (March 1964), pp. 64-76; Vernon L. Smith, "The Economics of Production from Natural Resources," *American Economic Review,* vol. 58, no. 3 (June 1968), pp. 409-31; and Colin W. Clark, "Profit Maximization and the Extinction of Animal Species," *Journal of Political Economy,* vol. 81, no. 4 (September-October 1973), pp. 950-61; and R. J. Sweeney, R. D. Tollison, and T. D. Willett, "Market Failure, the Common-Pool Problem, and Ocean Resource Exploitation," *Journal of Law and Economics,* vol. 13, no. 1 (Spring 1974), pp. 174-93.

rights cannot be assigned, each individual fisherman knows that if he abstains from "overfishing," his rivals will not, and that his individual abstention will have no noticeable effect on the stock of fish; hence, there is no incentive for any individual fisherman to conserve.[31]

This common-pool free-access characteristic of fishing has caused the over-fishing of many species and the virtual elimination of others, at a time of increasing world demand for protein. Thus, the second problem focusing concern on fishery resources in the law of the sea negotiations is really the need to develop workable resource management plans. The most widely discussed operative criterion to be employed in these management plans is a concept called maximum sustainable yield (MSY).

In very simple terms, the MSY concept means that the annual yield or fish harvest should be constant and should be the difference between the positive input of reproduction and the output caused by natural mortality. This constant should be maximized over time through the correct control of the stock of fish by regional or international fishery management commissions.

In Figure 1, the stock of a particular species of fish is charted on the horizontal axis and the annual yield or harvest is graphed on the vertical axis. Given any size stock of the species, the sustainable yield curve (SYC) shows the amount of fish which may be caught without causing an increase or decline in the stock. The maximum sustainable yield occurs at stock S_1, which will sustain an annual harvest of C_1. Thus, the goal of fishery management, if the sustainable yield curve can be discerned, is to achieve a stock of S_1 and to limit the annual harvest to C_1. Economists dispute the value of the maximum sustainable yield concept in fishery management, because it leads to the economically "wrong" stock of fish and often to wasteful restrictions that harm both fishermen and society.[32] The determination of the MSY quantity for each species, the size of the corresponding stock, the distribution of yield, and the suboptimality properties of the MSY concept when economic considerations are introduced, produces a multitude of problems too lengthy and complicated to explore here. However, the MSY concept unfortunately retains its popularity among law of the sea negotiators, and is currently being used by international and regional fishing commissions such as the Inter-American Tropical Tuna Commission.

There are at least four major fishery options which the United States could adopt in the law of the sea negotiations. The first is a continuation of the existing international framework giving coastal states control over (1) all fishery resources within the twelve-mile contiguous fisheries zone, which may be incorporated into a twelve-mile territorial sea, and (2) those sedentary resources, such as crabs,

---

[31] For a further analysis, see Richard J. Sweeney, "The Controversy over the Traditional Theory of Fisheries," OASIA Discussion Paper 75-1 (1975) and "Second-Best in Fishery Regulation," OASIA Discussion Paper 74-10 (1975), U.S. Department of the Treasury.

[32] Ibid.

Figure 1
FISHERY DEPLETION

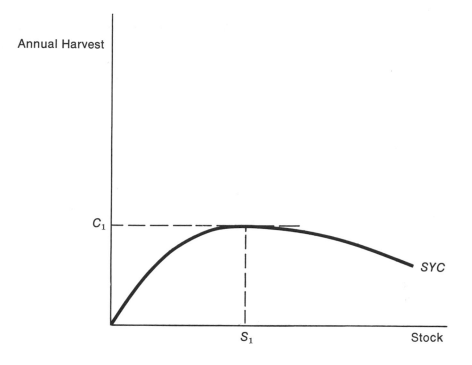

over which the 1958 Convention on the Continental Shelf authorizes coastal states to exercise exclusive jurisdiction. Nonsedentary fishery resources beyond twelve miles would have to be managed through international or regional management organizations in which the United States would participate through treaties and executive agreements.[33]

A second option is the so-called species approach, introduced by the United States in 1972, which grants the coastal state preferential rights to all its coastal living resources beyond the territorial seas to the limits of their migratory range. Coastal states in which anadromous species (of primary importance, salmon) were spawned would have the authority to regulate the stocks and would have preferential rights to the species throughout their migratory range on the high seas. Coastal states might establish management quotas and conservation measures subject to international standards; compulsory dispute settlement procedures and their management standards would be based on the criterion of maximum sustainable yield, possibly as qualified by "relevant" economic and environmental factors,

---

[33] At the present time the United States is a party to eight conventions establishing international management commissions and twelve bilateral agreements dealing with specific fishery management questions.

though such considerations are not made operational in the proposals. The coastal state might reserve for its flag vessels that portion of the annual allowable catch of coastal and anadromous species which it could harvest. The remaining portion would be left for harvesting by other states that would be permitted access under reasonable and nondiscriminatory conditions set by the coastal state, though with due consideration for "historical" fishing rights, with the coastal state having virtual discretion on this decision.

A third approach is a specified but nonexclusive coastal fishery resource zone, perhaps incorporated into the coastal state economic area (CSEA). Two hundred miles is the width most generally suggested for this zone. Coastal state authority over the fishery resources in this zone would be subject to international standards and compulsory dispute settlement, but its jurisdiction would extend only to the seaward edge of the zone. Occasionally coupled with this approach is the establishment of an international management regime for highly migratory species (for example, tuna and whales). This international organization would determine the maximum sustainable yields and the allocation of quotas.

The fourth and last alternative is an exclusive fishery zone within which the coastal state has complete control over the management and allocation of all fishery resources. The coastal state could decide on the quantity of the harvest it would assign to its flag vessels and the quantity it would allocate to other countries. It could also specify the conditions and price under which such access would be granted. This approach, too, could be coupled with an international management regime that would control the harvest of highly migratory species outside of the coastal states' fishery zones.

Table 13 is useful in evaluating which of the above options is most beneficial to U.S. interests. In 1973, slightly more than three-fifths of the total value of U.S. commercial landings were caught within twelve miles of shore. An additional 21 percent were caught *within 200 miles of U.S. shores (and beyond, presumably)*, whereas only 17 percent were caught in international waters off foreign shores. Because these data do not include sportfishing, they tend to underestimate the value of fish caught within twelve miles of shore. These data, coupled with the knowledge that other nations (especially the U.S.S.R. and Japan) catch considerable quantities of fish (especially salmon) within 200 miles of the U.S. shore, suggest that it would be in U.S. interests to opt for an exclusive fishery zone of 200 miles (excepting whales and tuna), plus an international mechanism for controlling all migratory fish, including those found within the 200-mile coastal zone. Although coastal fish may not migrate much beyond the 200-mile zone, they do migrate considerable distances along the shore and thus cross international borders. For the United States, bilateral agreements with Canada and Mexico would be necessary to manage the stocks of fish that regularly cross the coastal zone boundaries. Because only two other countries are involved and because the

74

Table 13

VALUE OF COMMERCIAL LANDINGS OF FISH AND SHELLFISH
BY U.S. FISHING CRAFT, 1973

($ thousands)

Species	0–3 Miles	3–12 Miles	12–200 Miles	International Waters off Foreign Shores	Total Value
Shrimp	$ 59,364	$ 54,037	$ 87,203	$ 40,703	$241,307
Salmon	108,339	12,515	4,099	160	125,113
Tuna	474	1,502	15,512	114,085	131,573
Crabs	36,620	40,869	10,596	1	88,086
Menhaden	65,946	7,321	9	—	73,276
Others	170,082	14,242	84,972	12,098	311,445
	$440,825	$160,486	$202,391	$167,098	$970,800
Percentage of total	45%	17%	21%	17%	100%

Source: U.S. Congress, Senate, Committee on Commerce, *The Economic Value of Ocean Resources to the United States,* 93d Cong., 2d sess. (December 1974).

species are relatively few in number, a regional agreement should be inexpensive to enact and to enforce, especially compared to any sort of multilateral convention or regulatory scheme.

Although the exclusive-zone approach, on balance, may be in the best interests of the United States, certain negative features should not be overlooked. First, certain nations, including the United States, have a comparative advantage in distant-water fishing off the shores of other countries. If the exclusive 200-mile zone is adopted, less efficient fishermen will be substituted for more efficient ones and there will be a global decrease in world fish production and an inefficient use of labor and capital. Second, most coastal countries do not enjoy long coastlines like those of the United States and its neighbors; hence, in many areas such as the west coast of Africa or the Mediterranean Sea, numerous countries would have to agree on the collective management of the species; consequently the bargaining and transaction cost would be appreciably higher. Third, in the more tropical climates there are hundreds of species of fish, making any kind of species management very cumbersome. It can be argued, however, that the transaction costs of species management are high, whether such management is done by the coastal state, a regional body, or an international regime. We have no definitive suggestions to make on this complicated issue except to note that in certain regions, possibly North America, the externalities and transaction costs are likely to be relatively low; if so, a national or regional management plan is preferable to an all-encompassing, universal treaty.

Conclusion

In our attempt to cover a substantial amount of factual material within a short space, we have been prevented from incorporating other data and discussing noneconomic objectives. Economic efficiency, viewed in its more traditional and narrow way, is not the only goal which the United States should pursue in the law of the sea negotiations; however, as a result of the papers presented at this Treasury/AEI conference and the numerous articles cited in the papers, it is obvious that the consistent analytical framework of economics has been applied to the law of the sea and a considerable proportion of the relevant data has been provided. Apart from a few admirable but isolated articles, where is the analytical framework of the political objectives? Where are the data? Where is the analysis of the trade-offs? We do not underestimate the importance of the political objectives, nor the harsh reality of the political environment; in fact, we have tried to incorporate part of the latter into our analysis. Neither, however, do we appreciate the rejection of economic analysis on the simplistic basis that it ignores long-term political objectives—Q.E.D. We simply want to urge that all objectives be analyzed and evaluated in a consistent and effective manner. It is in the best interest of the United States to develop, *de minimus,* more analytical sophistication, empirical investigation, and negotiating astuteness than was manifested in the infamous Russian wheat deal of 1973.

Although we have emphasized the economic interests of the United States, we are very much aware that policies that will lower revenue transfers by the United States and other Western countries will be criticized because they supposedly vitiate all substance of the "common heritage of mankind." We believe that our negotiators and those of other countries are erroneously interpreting the "common heritage of mankind" when they focus solely on the production side of the market. Certainly some revenue sharing from production may be justified, but we fear that excessive reliance on this interpretation may more realistically reflect the common heritage of politicians—which is not identical to that of mankind—because centralized control of production and the distribution of revenues provides more political power than the diffusion of benefits directly to the world's consumers. A negotiated treaty investing individual countries with coastal economic areas or deep-sea property rights which could be freely traded or leased, a treaty protecting the private or public investments of other countries, prohibiting the cartelization of the ocean's resources and the navigational routes on the ocean, and encouraging the exercise of the comparative advantages of individuals and countries, would result in greater economic well-being for citizens throughout the world and thereby more effectively cultivate the "common heritage of mankind."

INSTITUTIONAL MECHANISMS FOR DEALING WITH INTERNATIONAL EXTERNALITIES: A PUBLIC CHOICE PERSPECTIVE

Robert D. Tollison and Thomas D. Willett

Our paper is probably the most theoretical paper prepared for this conference. Since our background is primarily in economics, our major objective is to illustrate how economics can be useful in the study of the law of the sea negotiations.[1] Our purpose is not so much to talk about law of the sea specifically as it is to illustrate how concepts from the economics of public finance and public choice can be useful in analyzing the types of problems that have emerged in the law of the sea negotiations (certainly one of the most complex international negotiations ever to take place). We do, however, apply our approach to several specific issues in these negotiations, including ocean resource exploitation, ocean pollution, and the concept of the oceans as the common heritage of mankind. The general theme of our remarks will be that, given the difficulties of reaching international agreement, it would seem wise to concentrate efforts at international agreement on those areas in which agreements can make the greatest contribution. To do this, of course, it would be necessary to determine the relative difficulty of achieving agreement in the various areas. We specifically address ourselves to three broad questions concerning the negotiations.

In the first section we look at the relevant trade-offs involved in designing policies and institutions to internalize international externalities. For our purposes here, we define an externality as the uncompensated side effects (positive or negative) of an activity on parties not directly involved in the transaction. An example of a prominent externality in the law of the sea negotiations is ocean pollution, where shippers and consumers of products dependent upon ocean shipping for transportation pose a potential externality to the quality of the marine environment. We stress in this section that the mere existence of an international externality does not lead to the conclusion that it should be internalized at the highest level of government possible. Thus, it is particularly important to recognize that merely showing that the market is failing to perform perfectly or that there

---

[1] We emphasize, however, that ours is a public choice perspective. In this paper this means the application of economic analysis to decipher what the substantive political and economic aspects of various issues are. Methodologically, then, we are situated between economics and political science and will hopefully have some things to say that will be useful to policy makers and scholars in both areas. For a more extensive discussion of the theory of public choice, see J. M. Buchanan and R. D. Tollison, eds., *Theory of Public Choice* (Ann Arbor: University of Michigan Press, 1972).

is some scope for gain from coordination of national policies is not sufficient to establish a clear case for international action. The need for caution in taking market or national government failure as a prima facie case for international intervention is reinforced by the recognition, derived essentially from contributions to the theory of public choice, that "perfect intervention" by governments or international organizations is as rare as the "perfect competition" of economists' models in real economic systems. Likewise, even where some degree of externality is imposed upon the whole community of nations, if the significant portion of the externality is concentrated on a smaller number of countries, then in an imperfect world, it may be more desirable for attempts at international action to be concentrated on this smaller number of countries. The issues here correspond closely to those of desirable patterns of fiscal federalism within a nation-state. Our general conclusion in this section is that not every externality needs an international body to deal with it. Since governments are not perfect intervenors, one must look at the relevant trade-offs in externality control in each case.

This approach is applied within the context of specific issues in the current international negotiations on the law of the sea. Specifically, we examine first the potential externalities from the exploitation of ocean resources, and conclude that there is no economic rationale for the international regulation of deep-ocean economic activity, except for the specific case of fish that reside primarily in international waters. Second, we examine oil pollution control, including the externalities that can arise from the harmonization of pollution standards. Our basic conclusion in this discussion is that the costs of not having internationally agreed upon pollution standards have been generally overstated relative to the benefits.

In the second section of the paper we discuss the concept of the oceans as the common heritage of mankind. It has appeared to many observers that acceptance of this concept requires the creation of an international regulatory authority to control access to ocean resources and to tax and control the operations of firms developing ocean resources. In this section we analyze the common heritage concept and derive from public finance and public choice principles an operational formulation of it consistent with liberal economic principles.

In the third section we extend the discussion of the law of the sea negotiations to consider questions bearing on the process of the negotiations as such. We argue that the prospective gains from international action must be weighed against the costs of securing international agreement and the potential diversion of scarce collective decision-making resources from other more important areas. We specifically examine the effect that the number and complexity of issues can have on negotiations. In particular we stress the importance of not having too many issues in the same negotiating forum and relate this point to the slow rate of progress in the law of the sea negotiations. We also stress the importance of agenda setting in determining collective outcomes.

Our main conclusions in this section are twofold. First, we argue that there is a strong theoretical case for weighted voting in international organizations and agreements, although such voting systems are often hard to implement in practice. Second, we conclude that there is a strong case for including more than one issue in a set of negotiations so as to allow greater scope for compromises which are technically efficient. As the number of issues increases, however, the difficulty of discovering and implementing technically efficient solutions may also increase. Thus, where information costs exist, it is possible to go too far in increasing the number of issues dealt with in a particular forum. It seems possible that in the current comprehensive law of the sea negotiations, the number of issues may have been pushed past the point of optimum trade-off.

Fiscal Federalism and the Control of International Externalities

A methodological error often made in discussions of public policy is to assume that market failure automatically implies government intervention. But this unexamined alternative, too, produces externalities and is clearly not a perfect remedy for private market failures. In the context of the law of the sea negotiations, this fallacy frequently leads to the assumption that market failures should be internalized at the highest possible level of international agreement (the United Nations). Although economists should make this mistake less readily than others, the economics profession is somewhat to blame for engendering the general idea that the simple application of Pigovian taxes and subsidies is a cure-all for market failure. In recent years, however, such writers as Buchanan, Coase, and McKean have pointed up some of the problems with the simple Pigovian logic.[2] At the international level it can, in particular, obscure many of the advantages of bilateral and regional agreements to control externalities, and in a broad sense it simply ignores the costs of lost diversity where the amount of externality control desired varies widely among individual nations. In this section we first review briefly the basic trade-offs mentioned in the economic theory of fiscal federalism for determining the optimal level at which to regulate market failures, and then explore the problems in applying this approach by looking at the technical aspects of selected law of the sea issues.

---

[2] See, for example, J. M. Buchanan, "Politics, Policy, and the Pigovian Margins," *Economica,* n.s. 29 (February 1962), pp. 17-28; Ronald Coase, "The Problem of Social Cost," *Journal of Law and Economics,* vol. 3 (1960), pp. 1-44; and R. N. McKean and J. R. Minasian, "On Achieving Pareto Optimality: Regardless of Cost," *Western Economic Journal,* vol. 5 (December 1966), pp. 14-23. Pigou, however, has some modern defenders. See, for example, W. J. Baumol, "On Taxation and the Control of Externalities," *American Economic Review,* vol. 62 (June 1972), pp. 307-22.

The economic theory of fiscal federalism stresses the determination of the optimal size of polities and is based on the principle of perfect correspondence. Perfect correspondence occurs when the jurisdiction that provides the public good or regulates the public bad includes the entire set of homogeneous individuals who consume the good or bad, and only these individuals.[3] This, however, is clearly a limiting case. In a more realistic case of international externality, benefits or costs taper off spatially from some point of origin and are not spread equally among the members of a given polity.[4] This type of benefit or cost incidence makes it important to look at the technical aspects of particular externality problems in determining the relevant level of government to regulate the externality. Rigid application of perfect correspondence in this setting could lead to the determination of the consumption levels of most public goods at an extremely centralized level with a subsequent loss in the advantages of decentralized provision of these goods.

In practice the application of the correspondence principle suggests that one should equate the marginal costs and benefits from expanding the number of individuals in the relevant jurisdiction. Many trade-offs are possible in arriving at the optimal jurisdiction size. Among those treated in the literature are diversity in individual demands (that is, the decentralization theorem),[5] costs of collective decision making,[6] consumer mobility,[7] governmental interdependence,[8] and, in an explicitly normative model, the equality of total utility over the issue set among the members of a polity (that is, the equal-stake requirement).[9] The decentralization theorem emphasizes the optimality of local public-goods supply where there is a geographic diversity of individual demands for the good and there are no cost

---

[3] For definition see Wallace E. Oates, *Fiscal Federalism* (New York: Harcourt Brace Jovanovich, Inc., 1972), pp. 33-35. Also, see the discussion in Richard A. Musgrave, *Fiscal Systems* (New Haven: Yale University Press, 1969), pp. 292-320.

[4] See Musgrave, *Fiscal Systems,* p. 296, for a clear discussion of the problem posed to the theory of fiscal federalism by tapering benefits and costs.

[5] See Gordon Tullock, "Social Cost and Government Action," *American Economic Review,* vol. 59 (May 1969), pp. 189-97; and Yoram Barzel, "Two Propositions on the Optimum Level of Producing Public Goods," *Public Choice,* vol. 6 (Spring 1969), pp. 31-37.

[6] See Gordon Tullock, "Federalism: Problems of Scale," *Public Choice,* vol. 6 (Spring 1969), pp. 19-29.

[7] See Charles M. Tiebout, "A Pure Theory of Local Expenditures," *Journal of Political Economy,* vol. 64 (October 1956), pp. 416-24, and "An Economic Theory of Fiscal Decentralization," *Public Finances: Needs, Sources, and Utilization,* ed. James M. Buchanan (Princeton, N.J.: Princeton University Press, 1961), pp. 79-96; James M. Buchanan and Richard Wagner, "An Efficiency Basis for Federal Fiscal Equalization," in *The Analysis of Public Output,* ed. Julius Margolis (New York: Columbia University Press, 1970), pp. 139-58; and James M. Buchanan and Charles J. Goetz, "Efficiency Limits of Fiscal Mobility: An Assessment of the Tiebout Model," *Public Economics,* vol. 1 (April 1972), pp. 25-44.

[8] See Gordon Tullock, "Federalism: Problems of Scale." Also, see Mark V. Pauly, "Optimality, 'Public' Goods, and Local Governments: A General Theoretical Analysis," *Journal of Political Economy,* vol. 78, no. 3 (May/June 1970), pp. 572-85, and the references cited there.

[9] See Dennis C. Mueller, "Fiscal Federalism in a Constitutional Democracy," *Public Policy,* vol. 19 (Fall 1971), pp. 567-94.

advantages to centralized provision of the public good. In effect this argument suggests that the incentives for decentralization are likely to be greatest where the diversity in local demand is considerable. The trade-off involving the costs of collective decision making is especially important in the law of the sea negotiations, and we shall have more to say about it later in the paper. In short, there are administrative and voting costs to having multiple decision-making entities. Consumer or voter mobility causes special problems. In some respects mobility increases the gains from decentralized decision making, because consumer-voters may locate as a function of their preferences for mixes of private and public goods. On the other hand, where such factors as congestion costs become important, mobility can be a mixed blessing to consumer-voters already living in a given polity. Governmental interdependence stresses the problems covered by externalities that occur across jurisdictional boundaries. This trade-off suggests decision making on a more centralized scale than purely local supply. Finally, the equal-stake requirement emphasizes the requirement that voting rights should be tailored to individual stakes in a collective decision. We shall also have more to say about this potential trade-off later in the paper.

A broad trade-off that we particularly wish to emphasize at the international level is that between diversity in individual (national) demands for the control of international externalities, and centralized procedures to internalize international social costs and benefits. If we take the economist's view of optimality as tailoring economic outcomes to fit individual preferences as closely as possible, then decentralized provision of public goods will typically be more efficient unless centralized provision has some inherent cost-saving advantages.

There has been a tendency in the literature to assume that efficiency in externality control requires the same tax-price for all communities.[10] This does not necessarily follow, and as stressed by the decentralization theorem, where people have different tastes, fiscal mechanisms should be tailored to reflect this diversity.[11] Much of this discussion centers on the question of factor mobility, stressing that where factors are immobile different tax-prices will be optimal. Even in the case of factor mobility, different tax-prices will still be optimal where the costs of mobility are properly accounted for. Mobility does, however, cause some special problems. Competition among local communities can lead to undercutting of tax prices to control local externalities to secure local industry. This is more likely to be a problem where the local competition takes the form of bidding for tax havens (such as the location of head offices or the registry of a ship) than in

---

[10] See, for example, J. Stein, "The 1971 Report of the President's Council of Economic Advisers: Micro-Economic Aspects of Public Policy," *American Economic Review,* vol. 61, no. 6 (September 1971), pp. 531-37.

[11] For a suggestive treatment of a specific example, see R. C. Amacher, R. D. Tollison, and T. D. Willett, "The Economics of Fatal Mistakes: Fiscal Mechanisms for Preserving Endangered Predators," *Public Policy,* vol. 20 (Summer 1972), pp. 411-41.

the case of industrial pollution. In domestic economies, as Sherman and Willett stress, there can be a problem (though usually overrated) of lowering pollution standards to bid for industry when there are local employment benefits.[12] This is probably more of a problem within regions, however, than among countries. Within regions substantial employment effects may develop from factor mobility because of resultant changes in aggregate demand. Among countries, however, where exchange rates can change, there may be sectoral impacts of industrial relocation, but there would be no problem of deficient effective demand causing additional long-run unemployment. We discuss this issue in more detail later in this section.

Of course, in practice the choice between diversity and centralized control of externalities is not so simple. For example, in the derivation of correspondence the spatial patterns of benefits and costs from the provision of the public good (or bad) are assumed to be contained in the jurisdiction that provides the good. As stressed above, a more realistic case is one in which benefits or costs taper off spatially with increasing distance from a point of origin.[13] This type of benefit or cost incidence can lead to interjurisdictional externalities, because jurisdictional lines, derived from considering the trade-offs noted above, will typically not coincide with the area of benefit or cost incidence. In this case it is important to find mechanisms that allow optimal control of externalities while maintaining as much diversity in individual demands as possible. In other words, most practical applications of the correspondence principle would lead to consideration of the trade-offs among the various costs and benefits of greater conformity. The main point here is that it is inconceivable that we would want to internalize every spillover of costs or benefits among nations at the international level. In any approach to international externalities emphasizing diversity, schemes of optimal control will emphasize the importance of choosing the optimal level of decision making on the issue.

It is especially important to note that while this complication of tapering benefit or cost incidence can be solved by applying a varying benefit tax (as stressed by Musgrave), it is difficult to conceive of a solution in terms of a workable voting system. Capricious outcomes can result where individuals with small interests in a spillover problem are given a full vote in the determination of the outcome. This sort of structure of voting rights can lead to intensity problems, where voting may not maximize social welfare. That is, partial taxation and equally weighted voting rights for tapering externalities can lead to capricious results.

Intensity problems have been much discussed in the literature on voting theory.[14] The typical statement of the problem depicts the victory of a lethargic

---

[12] See R. Sherman and T. Willett, "Regional Development, Externalities and Tax-Subsidy Combinations," *National Tax Journal,* June 1969, pp. 102-23.

[13] See Musgrave, *Fiscal Systems.*

[14] For a discussion emphasizing that no solution exists for intensity problems, see R. Dahl, *A Preface to Democratic Theory* (Chicago: University of Chicago Press, 1956).

majority over an intense minority, to the detriment of either one's sense of equity or efficiency. One of the simplest of all democratic processes illustrates one type of intensity problem: a local referendum to increase the property tax by a stated amount and use the funds to build a new school. This situation can easily lend itself to an intensity problem. For example, a majority of the voters may not have children and may be slightly opposed to the measure because of the (let us say) small tax increase that accompanies it. The parents of school-age children may be intensely in favor of the tax-school package, however, because of the poor condition of the existing school. Thus, the parents would lose to a relatively indifferent majority in the defeat of the school issue. Conversely, one could envisage a situation in which the parents are in the majority, the proposed tax increase is substantial, the present school is in good condition, and the nonparents are "tyrannized" by the passage of the tax-school referendum. In either case the lesson is clear—for one-man-one-vote majority rule on separate issues to have normative authority, each voter must have an equal expected welfare gain or loss from the outcome of any given issue. We have addressed this type of problem in a separate paper stressing that weighted voting where voting rights are tailored to individual stakes in spillovers is the appropriate voting analog to the varying benefit tax.[15] While we do not wish to go into the theoretical justification for this voting analog here, we do wish to emphasize the general desirability of tailoring voting processes to reflect voters' stakes in issues. In the case of the law of sea, the application of this type of voting model would stress weighted voting rights where issues are decided at the highest level; it would also argue for more decentralized decision making on externality issues that affect smaller subsets of United Nations members.

To conclude this brief discussion we wish to emphasize that it is crucial to analyze specific externality problems with respect to the basic trade-offs involved in deciding at what level they should be handled. Basic questions that must be addressed would be: (1) the nature of the externality—does it exist, is it worth the cost of doing something about it, and over what domain does it occur; and

---

[15] See our "A Voting Mechanism for Fiscal Federalism where Spillovers Taper Off Spatially," unpublished manuscript, Cornell University, 1973. For further discussion and theoretical justifications of the type of voting sytem presented in the text, see Mueller's "Fiscal Federalism" and the following papers by Dennis C. Mueller, Robert D. Tollison, and Thomas D. Willett: "A Normative Theory of Representative Democracy," in *Democratic Representation and Apportionment: Quantitative Methods, Measures, and Criteria,* Annals of the New York Academy of Science, vol. 219 (9 November 1973), pp. 5-19; "Representative Democracy via Random Selection," *Public Choice,* vol. 12 (Spring 1972), pp. 57-68; "On Equalizing the Distribution of Political Income," *Journal of Political Economy,* vol. 82 (March 1974), pp. 414-22; "The Utilitarian Contract: A Generalization of Rawls' Theory of Justice," *Theory and Decision,* vol. 4, no. 3, pp. 345-69; "Solving the Intensity Problem in Representative Democracy," in *The Economic Approach to Social Policy,* R. C. Amacher, R. D. Tollison and T. D. Willett, eds. (Ithaca: Cornell University Press, forthcoming). Also, see Dennis C. Mueller, "Constitutional Democracy and Social Welfare," *Quarterly Journal of Economics,* vol. 87 (February 1972), pp. 60-80.

(2) the efficiency of organizations designed to deal with the spillover. It is possible that some of the externalities at issue in the law of the sea negotiations, when subjected to this sort of technical analysis, would appear to be best handled by bilateral or regional agreements at a far more decentralized level of decision making than a conference of United Nations members, each with a full vote on all issues. In the remainder of this section we examine the technical aspects and trade-offs of several law of the sea externality issues.

Regulation of Ocean Resource Exploitation [16]

Three resources that have received much interest in the law of the sea negotiations are fish, oil, and manganese nodules. The feeling is widespread that serious inefficiency is likely to result if these resources are not subjected to international regulation. In part, this feeling arises from the well-known difficulties fish and oil encounter because of the common-pool problem. This is a particularly timely question, since two major issues in law of the sea negotiations are an International Seabed Resource Authority (ISRA) to regulate the deep seabed (manganese nodules will be the major resource here in the near term) and international commissions to regulate fish species that are highly migratory (such as tuna) or spend their lives partly in fresh water and partly far at sea (that is, anadromous species such as salmon).

In the case of certain resources that have common-pool properties, competitive private market activity may lead to inefficient resource usage. These common-pool features of resource exploitation may create divergences between private and social costs and benefits, that is, externalities, and in the face of resulting "market failure," some form of collective agreement among producers or government action may be called for in order to achieve a fully efficient outcome.[17]

---

[16] The discussion considered under this heading is based on a larger study by R. J. Sweeney, R. D. Tollison, and T. D. Willett, "Market Failure, the Common-Pool Problem, and Ocean Resource Exploitation," *Journal of Law and Economics,* vol. 17, no. 1 (April 1974), pp. 179-92.

[17] It should also be noted at the outset that the characteristic of nonreproducibility of resources is not analogous to the common-pool problem and does not give rise to a divergence between private and social costs. Indeed, one of the two major subsets of the general common-pool problem is the effect of the stock of resources on their rate of reproduction. Arguments that unregulated market activity will lead to too rapid a depletion of nonrenewable resources are based on a belief that the market system generally has not led to correct investment and production decisions because private decision makers have failed to use socially appropriate discount rates. There is not a unanimity of views within the economic profession as to whether or not there is substance to this argument. Divergent views on this subject have been expressed in the literature on growth as an objective of government policy and in the partially related literature on the appropriate discount rate to be used in government decision making. It must be recognized that the contrary point of view requires government policies to influence rates of investment and exploitation to achieve economic efficiency and does not imply that ocean resources be singled out for special treatment. In other words, whatever general tax incentives or other measures are deemed desirable should be applied to firms operating in the ocean as well as within domestic economies. There is no economic case for applying special measures to ocean resource exploitation on these grounds.

The fundamental cause of any common-pool problem is the difficulty of identifying, keeping track of, and asserting property rights over some part of the resource in question. As a consequence, each person with access to the resource has an incentive to exploit currently as much as he profitably can, thus neglecting the effects of his actions on resource availability in the future, since he cannot hope to reap the future benefits that would result if he were to forgo some current profit. This neglect of the future leads to excessive rates of exploitation of fish and oil under competitive conditions. The fisherman who lets a fish go has no very great chance of catching it (and its offspring) later when it is larger (and has bred). Some other fisherman gets the benefit of this provision for the future, so the first fisherman has no incentive to let the fish go. The oil producer in a given pool who moderates his current flow risks allowing other producers to pump oil he could have had, and since each producer in the pool understands this, all pump too rapidly.

Fish and oil each add particular new elements to the general common-pool problem, since the future stock of fish depends on current harvesting, and the *efficiency* of pumping oil, as well as the quantity derived from pumping, depend on others' acts. But, to repeat, the common-pool problem turns crucially on the difficulty of identifying, keeping track of, and assigning property rights over a resource, and this difficulty is perhaps why these resources are generally treated as common property, whose ownership is established by seizure because it is not feasible to establish property rights in advance.

The absence of property rights in nodules might suggest by analogy that nodules could be subject to the "common-pool" problem that arises in fisheries and oil production precisely because of lack of property rights. This, however, is not the case. Nodules are not like fish since they do not move around and since apparently the reproduction rate of nodules is *independent* of the total stock of nodules.[18] Nodules are not like oil in that they do not flow from one mining site to another, that is, the action of one dredge head does not interfere with that of another. Thus, the externalities inherent in the common-pool problems caused by fish and oil do not apply to nodules.

This basic economic analysis suggests that there is no rationale based on the economic theory of the common-pool problem for regulating ocean mining. In the case of oil it seems sensible to suggest that since the relevant externality extends only over a given oil pool, producers will have sufficient incentives to reach

---

[18] To be exactly accurate, it should be noted that there is some dispute among geologists about whether there is a stock-reproduction process among nodules. However, if it exists, this process has a very small effect on nodule production, and from an economic point of view, there would not have to be a single owner of nodules to internalize the small external effects of such a reproduction process. Indeed, probable mining-plot sizes are large enough so that dispersed ownership of nodule sites could internalize this effect. The appropriate analog in fishing would be that of many private owners of catfish farms, where the problem of the net reproduction rate of catfish is handled appropriately by market decisions.

collective agreements to internalize these spillovers. And since oil pools are localized, even where called for, government intervention should be on the national or local level, rather than on the international level.

Finally, in the case of fish there is a clear rationale for international regulation of some species. Highly migratory species, such as tuna, that swim through many national waters do call for international regulation as a first, best solution.[19] Species that live in the ocean but stay in particular national waters are not candidates for international regulation, but in terms of the domain of the relevant common-pool problem are candidates for some form of national fishery regulation.

As this abbreviated discussion of ocean resources suggests, it is helpful to analyze the substantive aspects of any proposed externality problem to be sure that it exists and that some form of regulation is called for. For one thing, such analysis points up clearly that the absence of such regulation will not lead to chaos in ocean mining. The definition and protection of property rights should be sufficient to ensure efficient and orderly production in ocean mining. The alleged case of externalities associated with nodule mining was shown not to be significant, and hence ocean mining should not be a candidate for regulation on these grounds. Recognition of the importance of discovering the domain of international spillovers can therefore be quite useful in framing sensible negotiating positions on such issues.

In closing this discussion we should note that two potential cases of market failure caused by problems of defining and enforcing property rights which might affect nodule production are pollution and claim-jumping among sites of production. In the former case, the problem of pollution, for which enforcement costs are not excessive, is probably most efficiently handled by the assignment of liability to ocean producers for the costs of any excessive environmental degradation which they may cause. We discuss this problem in the next section. Claim-jumping, on the other hand, is a problem of property rights. Investigation of the factors which are likely to promote or deter claim-jumping suggests, however, that the nodule mining industry is not likely to display the type of claim-jumping behavior that was prevalent in the Old West.[20]

Thus, while clear delineation of property rights through a mechanism such as the U.S. proposal for licensing would be desirable, the absence of such a regime would not be likely to generate serious economic inefficiencies, at least until the number of mining operations begins to approach the number of prime mine sights, a development that is unlikely to occur during this century.

---

[19] It should be noted that the analysis only shows that government action *could* improve the competitive market performance. A badly regulated fisheries system could, of course, perform less well than an imperfect, unregulated market. The conclusion that some form of government regulation, either national or international, may help matters in commercial fishing is discussed extensively in the literature on the fishery.

[20] See Sweeney, Tollison, and Willett, "Market Failure, the Common-Pool Problem, and Ocean Resource Exploitation."

In summary, while fears have often been expressed that economic chaos would result from the failure of a comprehensive law of the sea treaty, economic analysis suggests that this would not be the case. In the case of mineral resources there is no economic case for international regulation, and while an international claims registry to establish property rights (by auction in the case of competing claims, as the United States has proposed) would be desirable, failure to establish such a mechanism would not be likely to lead to severely adverse economic effects. Economic analysis does suggest that there is a case for international agreements to preserve stocks of fish that reside in international waters.

Any number of analysts have asserted that if a comprehensive law of the sea treaty is not developed, the world will be plunged into chaos.[21] The presumption clearly is that if a broad multilateral agreement over the jurisdictional issues being considered in the law of the sea treaty cannot be achieved, there will be no incentive for nations to make bilateral arrangements among themselves or to work within the limits of existing international law, seeking opinions from the World Court whenever issues arise that are unprecedented in extant international law. Without in any way denigrating the desirability of reaching a good law of the sea treaty, we must point out that it is very disappointing, as a matter of analysis, to see how frequently chaos, or perhaps war, among nations over resource privileges is depicted as the only alternative to a multilateral law of the sea treaty. Such a view overlooks the fact that there is a wide array of alternative approaches to the preservation of economic and political order. In many instances, the conflicts and inefficiencies caused by the absence of an international regime may be minimal or nonexistent. In cases where there is the greatest need for international agreements, bilateral or regional arrangements may frequently form the basis for satisfactory outcomes, and in some instances may lead to more desirable results than would be achieved from broader multilateral agreement.

Given the various important aspects of arrangements for international fiscal federalism, there is no easy shorthand way for determining the appropriate institutional structure for internalizing international externalities, nor for ascertaining the costs of the absence of an international agreement. While economic, political, and public choice theory and the results of many studies of particular policies and organizations provide us with powerful aids in approaching these issues, particularly in suggesting pitfalls to avoid, these must be painstakingly applied to particular types of externalities and institutional alternatives on a case-by-case basis.

Many of those who predict "chaos without a comprehensive treaty" also tend to envision chaos unless all ocean activity is tightly regulated and heavily taxed, or indeed performed directly by an international organization. This view

---

[21] For example, see Patrick A. Mulloy, "Political Storm Signals over the Sea," *Natural History,* vol. 82, no. 6 (December 1973), pp. 87-90; Gregory De Sousa, "Ocean Management and World Order," *Columbia Journal of World Business,* Summer 1974, pp. 123-28; and a three-part series, "Chaos at Sea," in *Saturday Review World,* vol. 1, nos. 14-16 (November and December 1973).

is most often applied to living and nonliving resources, namely fisheries and minerals; but it is also applied to "resources of use" of the oceans, principally scientific research and freedom of navigation for ships. The argument is that without close international supervision and taxation of all of these resources, the benefits of exploiting them may accrue disproportionately to a single country, thus violating the "oceans as common heritage of all mankind" concept, which we discuss separately below.

Unfortunately, such tight controls or quite onerous tax burdens, if accepted, may only serve to heighten international tensions by inducing conflict; hence, they may be more likely to result in chaos than would the absence of any treaty. Of more immediate concern, however, is the fact that if rigid international control over many of the resources in question were introduced, it might be such a great deterrent to private ocean activity that no one would benefit except a few land-based producers of minerals whose gains would be exceeded by the losses of the rest of the world due to high prices.

Harmonization of Externality Control: The Case of Ocean Shipping

Another consideration of some importance in the law of the sea negotiations is that the measures used to control externalities may themselves generate other types of externalities. A good example of this is the case of shipping. Our impression is that the case for harmonization of shipping standards has been greatly over-stated, but let us discuss the specific reasons why we feel this way.

Among the many issues involved in the law of the sea convention is the problem of establishing minimum international ocean pollution standards. The rationale supporting the view that there should be a single international standard is that standards which vary widely from the coastal areas of one state to another would cause large increases in the shipping costs of international trade since ships might have to travel substantially longer distances to avoid having to comply with the particularly stringent rules of a single coastal state bordering a trade route. Furthermore, ships from more pollution-tolerant states might gain an "unfair" competitive advantage over ships from states less tolerant of pollution.

The position that, without uniform international standards, chaotic shipping conditions would result is dubious. The proponents of single standards argue that without a single standard, in particular a vessel-design and construction standard, countries are likely to impose bizarre standards, and that there would be no effective means by which coastal states neighboring those with very lax standards would be able to control pollution coming from adjacent waters. The first argument is weakened by the recognition that countries which behave in their rational self-interest will not increase their own shipping costs substantially by imposing highly specialized pollution-reducing vessel construction standards. To

88

the extent that its standards are at wide variance with those of the rest of the world, a country's costs will increase more than proportionally. The second argument would be false if an effective liability system were established under which polluters would be made to bear the full cost of environmental repair.

By requiring owners and operators to build ships with highly effective pollution abatement capability, nations could achieve significant reductions in oil damage, but the cost of implementing this technology could exceed its benefits to society. Moreover, to the extent that different countries would prefer to make different trade-offs between pollution control and the availability of other goods and services, cost relative to the social benefit could be greater for one country than for another. The same result as that attained by dictating a particular technology could conceivably be achieved through a system imposing liability for damages on the party responsible for pollution. The latter approach would have the advantage of avoiding undesirable hindrances to innovation and perhaps introduction of more cost-effective pollution-abatement equipment and procedures. It would also leave the choice of technology to those who could be expected to be most familiar with relative costs. The use of liability assignment, of course, hinges on reasonable information costs. Where such costs are reasonable, liability assignment may be an effective way to ease the requirement of harmonization. In effect it lessens the problem of inconsistency in achieving pollution objectives.[22]

It is useful at this point to recall the earlier discussion of coordination of pollution control measures and local tax-prices on pollution. Where there is high factor mobility, efforts of countries to impose high levels of costly pollution control on local firms may be frustrated by the movement of firms to other countries willing to accept lower levels of pollution control. Here a basic trade-off is involved. The most efficient application of antipollution techniques would require a uniform pollution policy across the entire area of high factor mobility. However, such a

---

[22] For an extensive theoretical and empirical treatment of the issue of standard versus liability assignment to control oil tanker pollution, see P. Cummins, D. Logue, R. Tollison, and T. Willett, "Oil Tanker Pollution Control: Design Criteria vs. Effective Liability Assignment," *Journal of Maritime Law and Commerce* (forthcoming). The reader interested in the costs and benefits of a particular set of design criteria (segregated-ballast construction) proposed for oil tankers by the United States should also consult this paper. It demonstrates in a rather dramatic fashion the dangers and costs of failing to consider appropriate alternatives to stringent rules when confronting environmental issues generally. In particular, the costs of segregated ballasting are estimated on an annual basis. These are then compared to an alternative but more conventional technique for reducing the operational discharge of tankers bringing oil to the United States. The results indicate that segregated ballasting will be somewhere in the range of 1.75 to 4.5 times more expensive, and strongly suggest that the notion of imposing such costly design criteria should be reexamined. In addition, estimates of the benefits of reducing total oil discharges to the standards implied by segregated ballasting are examined. As it turns out, the annual incremental cost of segregated-ballast construction relative to the imputed annual net dollar value of benefits (that is, benefit in excess of these achievable by the alternative method of controlling discharge) yields a ratio of approximately twenty to one. Although the scientific data upon which the benefit estimates are based are not as complete as would be desired, the magnitude of the ratio itself is cause for concern over the wisdom of adopting segregated ballasting to achieve these standards.

policy constrains all parties to accept the same level of pollution control while many communities might prefer different levels of pollution control. For instance, lower-income countries would probably want to give up fewer economic goods and services in exchange for cleaner air and water than would higher-income communities, that is, they would want to buy less pollution control. If factor mobility were perfect, there would be no choice for the larger community but to have a completely unified pollution policy. However, in realistic situations where mobility may be reasonably high but not infinite, there is a trade-off between the effectiveness of the application of pollution policy and the allowance for diversity in choice by the different communities.

A similar situation occurs with respect to macroeconomic policy in the international community. Under fixed exchange rates, the higher the level of interdependence between national economies, the more difficult will it be for a country to follow macroeconomic policies sharply different from those of its trading partners. For a given difference in the rates of inflation in two countries, for instance, the size of the resulting balance-of-payments disequilibrium will be greater, the higher level of interdependence between them.

There is no unique answer to this general question, what is the most desirable trade-off of greater coordination to increase the effectiveness of policies chosen, versus greater sovereignty or autonomy in the choice of policies to pursue? The best combination will vary from case to case depending upon the costs of following independent policies and the strength of different subgroups' desire to choose the policies to be followed.

With respect to the international community and the degree of divergence in the desired policies, it is clear that desires for independent national policies are sufficiently strong that full centralization of economic policy making would not be optimal, but on the other hand the spillovers between many countries are sufficiently great that some degree of policy coordination would be desirable.

We do have a powerful method available to countries, but not to regions within a country, which can help to reduce this dilemma or trade-off between independence and the efficiency of policy implementation. This is the use of exchange rate adjustments to offset the effects of differing sets of underlying economic or policy influences in different countries. Differing desired choices of rates of inflation, employment, and growth between two countries can be rendered consistent with each other by adjusting the countries' relative exchange rates in line with the resulting difference in balance-of-payments trends. In other words, by appropriately adjusting exchange rates, the spillovers from trading partners' macroeconomic policies can be reduced, and the scope for efficiently following independent policies can be increased. This is true even in the case of environmental policies discussed above. If a region of a country, or a country without the option of adjusting its exchange rate or border taxes, decided to raise its

90

pollution control requirements much higher than those of its trading partners, then even without factor mobility the private costs of its industries would be raised and their competitiveness would decline, resulting in a trade deficit and deflationary pressures. However, where exchange rate or border tax adjustments are possible, this tendency for overall competitiveness to decline could be offset by a depreciation of the exchange rate or increase in general import taxes and export subsidies, thus averting the domestic deflationary pressures which would otherwise result. While specific industry impacts and possible reallocation costs would remain, ability to vary effective exchange rates means that a country need not bear the general macroeconomic costs of depressed economic activity as a result of adopting higher pollution control standards in the same way that such higher costs could cause a generally depressed region within a nation. Thus, the need for coordination of antipollution measures among countries is less than it is among regions within a nation in terms of side effects on the level of economic activity.[23]

In general, then, it is our impression that the need for the harmonization of shipping standards has been greatly overstated. Indeed, international transportation would be a low priority candidate for harmonization as opposed, say, to tax policies. The prospective efficiency gains from harmonization of shipping standards are low, and the benefits of lost diversity may be substantial. The moral of the story: do not overrate the costs of nonuniformity in analyzing international externalities.

"The Common Heritage of Mankind": Alternative Interpretations

Some may fully accept our arguments thus far but go on to raise the objection that, since the oceans have been declared the "common heritage of mankind," does this not in itself make these resources different and hence call for their detailed regulation for the benefit of all? We turn now to this question, and as will become apparent, we conclude that operationalizing the common heritage concept does not have to imply strong regulatory measures over ocean economic activity. Initially, however, a brief review of the origin of the common heritage concept may be helpful.

In 1967, the Maltese ambassador to the United Nations, Arvid Pardo, urged his fellow UN delegates to promote a sincere interest in, and affirmation action by their home countries for, developing a new approach to oceans policy. He argued, in essence, that existing international law was inadequate to deal with the problems that could arise from the diverse forces—technology, population, and nationalism—that were combining to bring chaos to the oceans and conflict among nations. He asserted the need for a comprehensive law of the sea treaty covering virtually every aspect of the oceans' use and of international jurisdiction over their resources.

---

[23] For a discussion of the latter case, see Sherman and Willett, "Regional Development, Externalities, and Tax-Subsidy Combinations."

In his now famous speech of 1 November 1967 before the United Nations, Pardo suggested that "the seabed and the ocean floor are a common heritage of mankind and should be used and exploited for peaceful purposes and for the exclusive benefit of mankind as a whole." [24] Moreover, he expounded five main principles for the proposed treaty:

> . . . the seabed and the ocean floor underlying the sea beyond the limits of national jurisdiction as defined in the treaty are not subject to national appropriation in any manner whatsoever.
>
> . . . the seabed and ocean floor beyond the limits of national jurisdiction shall be reserved exclusively for peaceful purposes.
>
> . . . scientific research with regard to the deep sea and ocean floor, not directly connected with defense, shall be freely permissible and its results available to all.
>
> . . . the resources of the seabed and ocean floor beyond the limits of national jurisdiction shall be exploited primarily in the interests of mankind, with particular regard to the needs of poor countries.
>
> . . . the exploration and exploitation of the seabed and ocean floor beyond the limits of national jurisdiction shall be conducted in a manner consistent with the principle and purposes of the United Nations Charter and in a manner not causing unnecessary obstruction of the high seas or serious impairment of the marine environment. [25]

Since the notion that the deep seas form part of the common heritage of all mankind has already been widely accepted (and we accept it), ocean resources should be developed for the common benefit of all, though the sharing ratios in these benefits are an open question. However, it has appeared to many that acceptance of this principle would of necessity require the creation of an international regulatory authority to control access to ocean resources, and to tax and control the operations of firms developing ocean resources. Indeed some have even argued that the common heritage concept implies that development of ocean resources by private firms and individuals should be prohibited and that only an international authority should be allowed to operate beyond the limits of national boundaries. In this section we attempt to analyze the meaning of the common heritage of mankind from the standpoint of economic and public finance theory and suggest an operational formulation of this concept that is consistent with liberal economic principles.

A far more appealing way to make operational the concept of the oceans as the common heritage of all mankind is to approach the problem from an economic perspective, fashioning fiscal mechanisms to accomplish this task. In particular, emphasis should be placed on distinguishing the kinds of free access

---

[24] Excerpted from *Woods Hole Notes,* February 1974, in U.S. Congress, Senate, Subcommittee on Minerals, Materials, and Fuels of the Committee on Interior and Insular Affairs, *Mineral Resources of the Deep Seabed,* p. 1324.

[25] Ibid., pp. 1324, 1325.

that cause no damage to others, and the issues of access to ocean resources generally. In the former case, a good example of which is scientific research, we quite agree that free access is the appropriate policy. Of course, where conflicts of basic freedoms occur, some resolution of rights will have to be made. A good, though improbable, example here would be the case of a scientific ship taking up residence in a heavily travelled channel. In this case we would have to look at the basic trade-off involved in deciding on freedom of scientific research versus freedom of transit.[26] In general, however, free access for scientific research and similar activities should present few problems.

In the case of the freedom of access to ocean resources, extreme confusion has arisen, particularly over natural resources, from the identification of those who physically exploit a resource with those who obtain the benefits from exploitation. This involves the fallacy that physical ownership conveys all the benefits from exploitation to the producer, which is simply not true. The exploitation of real ocean resources, such as manganese nodules, hydrocarbon deposits, and fisheries, will generate three major types of economic benefit. First, consumers throughout the world will benefit from the greater availability and lower prices of the resources obtained. Second, exploiters may find this a more attractive opportunity than others available, generating higher profits and wages than would otherwise be the case. Third, this new activity may represent a marginal addition to the world's tax base.

In the particular case of the exploiters of the resources to which access is free, as the United States proposes, producers should earn a competitive, or normal, rate of return on their invested capital. Perhaps the concern with the ownership of the means of physical production per se derives from some emotional attachment to the land; or perhaps a better analogy would be concern over the great profits that have been made in the discovery of lodes of certain minerals (such as gold) in the past. In that case, of course, producers were not making a normal rate of return; they were earning rents. If ocean mining could be considered analagous to gathering suddenly discovered sunken treasures, then the economic implication would be that producers were making excess returns. The U.S. proposals for free access *and* auctioning of competing claims to ocean resources serve to resolve this type of problem. The common heritage concept suggests that revenues from competitive bids for a claim, which under free access should reflect the rental value of the property, should go into the pool of funds for revenue sharing. In practice these revenues would be negligible for the foreseeable future because property rights to claims will not be scarce. Conceptually, however, competitive bidding for access to property rights in ocean claims sets

<hr>

[26] See K. Clarkson, "International Law, U.S. Seabeds Policy and Ocean Resource Development," *Journal of Law and Economics*, vol. 17, no. 1 (April 1974), pp. 117-42, for a discussion of some of the trade-offs involved.

the appropriate scarcity values for access to these resources, and revenues for such bidding should go into revenue sharing.

In general, then, we accept the concept of the oceans as the common heritage of mankind, but we would formulate a different set of requirements to make the concept operational in an economic sense. These are threefold:

(1) Potential consumers of ocean resources should not be discriminated against in the purchase of ocean resources. The existence of a competitive market will bring about this result.

(2) Potential exploiters should not be discriminated against in seeking access to ocean resources. This may be achieved by an international authority whose power to impede access to ocean resources is nondiscretionary and minimal.

(3) Not only should the citizens of the countries of origin of the expoiting firms benefit from the expansion tax base represented by the ocean resource industry, but all should benefit, via the sharing of the revenues raised from taxation of ocean resource exploitation and from competitive bids for property rights to ocean resources. Access to ocean resources should not be restricted so as to monopolistically raise revenues at the expense of distorting the efficient allocation of resources.

Whereas our preceding analysis has suggested that implementation of the concept of the common heritage of mankind dictates that the full amount of revenues from competitive bidding should be shared internationally, the result of full sharing does not carry over to the taxation of ocean resource exploitation. The expansion of world "taxable capacity" [27] represented by the exploitation of ocean resources will represent only a small fraction of the taxable capacity of ocean industries. A large portion will represent a diversion of taxable capacity from domestic economies. We suggest that, consistent with the common heritage concept, only the increment to world taxable capacity should belong to the international community. Thus the appropriate treatment of the tax revenues derived from ocean resource exploitation beyond the limits of national jurisdiction is that of revenue sharing. We shall argue below that in these circumstances it is the smaller fraction of tax revenues which should accrue to the international community. First, however, let us briefly discuss some questions concerning the form and extent of taxation of ocean resource exploitation.

In general the standard taxation criteria of efficiency and equity would suggest that there is nothing special about mineral production that merits taxation.[28]

---

[27] Taxable capacity is a standard public finance measure of the revenue produced by the tax system. The greater the per capita or group incomes, the greater, presumably, the taxable capacity or the ability to generate revenue.

[28] See D. Logue, R. Sweeney, and T. Willett, "Optimal Leasing Policy and the Development of Outer Continental Shelf Hydrocarbon Resources," *Land Economics* (forthcoming) for a general discussion of the principles of taxation as applied to offshore resources.

However, given that land-based mineral production is taxed, there may be a second-best case for taxation of ocean resource production. In this case, if levels of taxation of ocean resource production do not exceed those on comparable land-based resource production, namely minerals, then this taxation may not represent a serious hindrance to the exploitation of the resources of the sea. Within this constraint, the theory of taxation would suggest that a direct tax that does not affect production, such as a profits tax, would be preferable to an indirect tax, such as a royalty tax. But, whereas the direct tax has economic advantages, it would be complex to administer, while the royalty tax, relatively easy to administer, is economically less desirable. In practice the choice between the two types of taxation would depend on the relative weight placed on production distribution due to royalty taxation, and the administrative costs of profit taxation.

Part of the case for revenue sharing derives from the expansion of the world tax base involved in the exploitation of ocean resources, whatever approach to actual taxation is adopted. It is important to recognize, however, that the full amount of new tax base represented by ocean industry is not a net addition to the world's tax base. In part the expansion of revenues from ocean industry will come at the expense of the domestic tax bases of countries whose firms undertake ocean activity (this labor and capital would otherwise presumably have been employed at home, albeit in less advantageous pursuits), and also in the tax bases of countries whose firms face less advantageous markets because of competition from ocean-based production.[29] Because the differential economic advantage of ocean resource development is likely to be relatively small at the margin, the percentage share that should be allocated to the international community likewise should be low, perhaps on the order of 10 to 25 percent.

There are also, of course, a host of important considerations concerning the dissemination and the use of the revenue accruing to the international community. First, one might argue that there is a case for the regulation of the production of ocean wealth on the grounds that without tight regulation an existing inequity in the distribution of income among countries will be perpetrated. Accepting, for the sake of argument, that the latter inequity exists, we want to stress that a regulatory solution does not follow from this argument. In the first place, it is unclear how the benefits of an open-access regime would be distributed. This would depend to a large extent on the incidence of per capita consumption of ocean resources across countries.[30] Also, the traditional theorem stressing that it is more efficient to redistribute income through transfers of purchasing power than through price controls on particular goods holds in the case of the redistribution of wealth produced from oceans. This really repeats our earlier point, that the extent

[29] This is actually an example of an externality imposed by adjustments to taxation. For a discussion of such externalities, see J. M. Buchanan, "Externality in Tax Response," *Southern Economic Journal,* vol. 33 (July 1966), pp. 35-42.
[30] For some evidence on this point, see the paper in this volume by D. Johnson and D. Logue.

of revenue sharing is conceptually distinct from the issue of open access to ocean resources.

Second, it has been pointed out that in the usual case of international taxation, the host country collects a tax on full production where international corporations operate within alternative national boundaries. The full value of local production is taxed and allowed as a credit against taxes in the country where the corporation legally resides. In the case of the expansion of taxable capacity from the development of ocean resources, however, the measure of the expansion of taxable capacity is the net expansion of capacity after the relevant resource reallocations from land-based to ocean-based activities has taken place. As we pointed out, the desired revenue-sharing weights would be placed on this margin. In the usual case of international taxation, taxing the full value of domestic production derives from both legal and economic considerations, and basically reflects the fact that we do not have an international tax base against which to apply a standard set of tax rates. The present system does have an economic rationale to the extent that the payment of the tax by foreign investors reflects a charge for their consumption of local social overhead capital. In the oceans, however, there is the creation of an international tax base, and here we need to be careful to assess the desirable tax rates against the correct economic measure of increased taxable capacity. Also, there would be no consumption of social overhead capital in the oceans against which to levy a charge.

A third point that might be raised addresses the issue of whether competitive access to ocean resources would reflect competitive bids for ocean production sites. This is an important question that would have to be answered by examining the structure of the relevant mineral industries related to ocean mining. It is our impression that the available evidence indicates that this would not be a problem, and that in fact ocean production of minerals would be a major threat (via entry of new production) to existing and potential land-based mineral cartels.[31] A complete study of the structure of these industries, however, needs to be done.

Our general considerations, then, are quite compatible with the basic form of revenue sharing proposed by the United States in this treaty negotiation (an internationally set tax on ocean production, the proceeds of which are divided between an exploiting firm's government and the international community), but they do suggest a lower percentage distribution to the international community than the range mentioned in the 1970 U.S. draft treaty. They suggest that it is quite possible to accept the concept that the ocean beyond the limits of national production is the common heritage of mankind, without this leading to the necessity for extensive resource control on the part of an international authority. Furthermore, the implementation of this approach need not even hinge upon the

---

[31] See R. C. Amacher and R. J. Sweeney, "International Commodity Cartels and the Threat of New Entry: Some Implications of Ocean Minerals Resources," *Kyklos* (forthcoming).

existence of a treaty, but could be undertaken unilaterally by any country which had the wherewithal to exploit ocean resources.

Toward a Theory of Optimal Negotiations [32]

The law of the sea negotiations are among the most complex negotiations ever to take place. There has been much comment on the lack of apparent progress in the negotiations thus far, and the sheer number of issues involved is frequently mentioned as one reason for this. In the first part of this paper we discussed why theoretically it is not wise to attempt to internalize every international spillover at the highest level possible. In this section we will sketch some tentative elements of a theory of optimal negotiations, which emphasizes the possible costs of considering every issue related to law of the sea in one centralized forum. We hope that this analysis will be helpful in discussion of the advantages and disadvantages of a unified law of the sea treaty on all issues, versus less comprehensive agreements on specific areas.

In the simplest model of economic exchange, trade between individuals typically merges because they place different marginal values (given by the slopes of their respective indifference curves) on the goods they are trading. The analytical apparatus often used by economists to depict trade is called the Edgeworth box, and trade takes place in this setting until the contract curve is reached.[33] The understanding of the economic theory of exchange is really quite simple when thought of in terms of movements to mutually beneficial positions within an Edgeworth box. Analytically, this is depicted as points along the contract curve where the contract curve is defined as the points of tangency between individuals' indifference curves. At these points of tangency the individuals place the same marginal value on the combination of goods being traded, and hence trade ceases. Trade within an Edgeworth box to reach the contract curve may be characterized as positive sum in the sense that both parties are benefited by exchange. Trade that moves individuals along the contract curve may be thought of as zero sum in the sense that what one party gives up the other loses. This is a situation of pure conflict. A final category of trades could be characterized as negative sum in the sense that an individual would not voluntarily engage in such trade, because the expected value of trade would be less than the original endowment which he could retain by not trading (playing the game). Normally, these latter types of trade are not quantitatively important since most trade that we observe is voluntary. A well-known axiom of politics, at least domestic politics, however, is that

[32] The discussion in this section is taken from our forthcoming book on *International Economic Interdependence: A Public Choice Perspective,* to be published by Heath Lexington.

[33] See A. A. Alchian and W. R. Allen, *University Economics: Elements of Inquiry* (Belmont, Calif.: Wadsworth, 1972), pp. 47-49, for a clear discussion of exchange theory in terms of an Edgeworth box diagram.

one cannot refuse to play. Moreover, as we shall see, the possibility of negative-sum trade has to be considered in international negotiating processes. We can now turn specifically to the issues involved in optimal negotiations.

An important question in the context of international relations is, at what level of aggregation should decisions among nations be made or discussed? That is, how many issues should be included in a decision-making package and at what level of the respective governments should trade in matters of international policy take place? While we cannot give precise answers to these questions, we can elaborate some general principles by employing some concepts from the foregoing discussion. It will be useful to remember that the objective of trade is presumably to reach the contract curve (an agreement satisfactory to both parties), and the following discussion will be largely couched in such terms.

When negotiations take place on a single issue, and side payments are not possible, the agreement reached by two parties may be off the technically efficient contract curve. In order to divide the benefits from the agreement in a mutually satisfactory manner, it may be necessary to accept compromise outcomes which are off the contract curve, that is, which leave open the possibility of changes that would raise the utility of both parties if direct side payments were possible.[34]

Where the contract curve is clear and well understood by all parties, the aggregation of issues is quite helpful to the process of reaching international agreement. This follows since attempts to reach agreement by focusing on one issue at a time are likely to be frustrated by the limited ability of participants to make direct side payments in international negotiations in order to reach the contract curve.[35] Aggregating issues and dealing with them at the highest level allows greater scope for indirect trades to come closer to the contract curve. In this way, vote trading in legislatures may contribute to more efficient outcomes.[36] A multiplicity of issues creates more possibilities for indirect trades leading to productive agreements.

However, there may also be problems in aggregating issues. Frequently there is a fundamental disagreement about the nature of the contract curve. In other words, there is no agreement on what is best with respect to a particular policy. A good example of this situation would be the issue of fixed versus flexible exchange rates in the international monetary system. In such a case, it may be best not to aggregate underlying issues or decisions; aggregation of issues would in general intensify government-to-government conflict.

---

[34] A point which we do not discuss in detail here but which we feel is quite important in the context of the theory of optimal negotiations is the importance of agenda setting. For a very interesting discussion of this aspect of voting theory, see C. R. Plott and M. E. Levine, "On Using the Agenda to Influence Group Decisions: Theory, Experiments, and an Application," California Institute of Technology Working Paper No. 66, November 1974.

[35] See Albert Breton, "Public Goods and the Stability of Federalism," *Kyklos,* vol. 23, no. 4 (1970), pp. 882-901, for a related discussion of this point.

[36] See Mueller, Tollison, and Willett, "A Normative Theory of Representative Democracy."

A similar case could occur where there is some degree of consensus among experts about the nature of the contract curve, but where the issues involved are so complex that the higher-level decision makers who are making the trade-offs will not be able to understand them. Hence, complexity of issues will sometimes restrict the degree to which they should be aggregated for discussion or decision.

In some of these cases it is better, then, not to aggregate or defer issues or decisions and to allow discussion to be handled at a lower level in the government-to-government process. The nature of the work at this lower level would be the presumably technical task of clarifying the nature of the contract curve.

What we have stressed so far in this section is the importance of more issues, not more actors. A point that has an important bearing on the highly centralized manner in which the law of the sea negotiations have taken place concerns the effect of increasing the number of actors in dramatically increasing decision costs. In this setting, where the number of actors is increased against a given number of issues, it is more difficult to reach optimal collective agreements.[37] For one thing, the transactions costs of keeping track of more details on issues is increased immensely. That is, it becomes incredibly difficult for the actors to be informed on the relevant trade-offs among all issues and all actors, and to consummate trade-offs among various coalitions.

Indeed, an optimal outcome is not even assured by the provision of an enforceable mechanism for international collective decision making. Where voting power differs substantially from the distribution of potential costs and benefits derived, collective outcomes may be both inequitable and inefficient.

Attempts to skew the costs and benefits of outcomes by the majority of countries may result in the underprovision of the public good in question. Essentially, the provision of the international public good is a mixed-motive game, with the scope for potential benefits to all from the provision of the public good yielding cooperative elements, the positive-sum aspect of the game, while the desire to minimize one's share of the cost of providing the public good leads to competitive zero- or negative-sum elements. To attempt to secure too great a share of the benefits is to run the risk of failing to provide the good at all, or in sufficient quantities. The prospect for underprovision in such circumstances is increased by the fact that it is usually far easier for nation states to withdraw from international agreements than it is for citizens to withdraw from the effective jurisdiction of national political decisions.

Even in organizations with weighted voting there is considerable difficulty in designing the appropriate basis for weighting. This is compounded both by the changing positions of countries over time and the possibility of enormous variation of "interests" with respect to different issues. In formal organizations, as voting

---

[37] An interesting question in its own right involves the determination of the optimal number of issues relative to actors.

procedures are generally instituted, it is difficult if not impossible to vary voting weights to correspond appropriately to the realities of various situations. In practice, some scope for varying effective voting weights is provided by vote trading on various issues. The workability of such systems, however, is itself dependent upon there being some reasonably stable pattern of interests over a reasonable period of time. The discrete nature and importance of the issues which face the international community tends to necessitate ad hoc responses outside of overly formal international institutional arrangements. Thus, even if more efficient voting mechanisms were instituted within our formal international arrangements, we would still need flexibility for the ad hoc development of new forums and institutions as major new situations arise. Although some inefficiency is undoubtedly generated by multiplying ad hoc and formal international forums and institutions, it is likely that any fully optimal pattern would display considerable untidiness, and would change over time.

Finally, in some cases not enough is known about an issue to define a reasonable policy, and the contract curve might be characterized as fuzzy. A particular example of this type of problem in the law of the sea negotiations is the procedure of referring technical issues on which agreement cannot be reached to the World Court. This seems to be a poor way to reduce decision costs on complicated issues. In general, what criteria would one follow in referring technical issues to be decided after general agreement on principles is reached? First, it would seem optimal to delegate decisions on specific technical details where the potential benefits of reaching general agreement on principles is high. Where technical details relate to the substance of the agreement, however, as is frequently the case, it would not be sensible to leave them to be decided until after general agreement is reached. For instance, agreement in principle that there should be free access to ocean resources could easily be undermined if considerable discretionary power were in fact given to an international authority to regulate licensed firms.

Conclusion

Reaching international agreements is difficult, and the law of the sea negotiations are an excellent example of the difficulties involved. Our main point is that negotiators should concentrate on areas where agreements can render the largest contribution. Collective decision-making resources are scarce and must be allocated to achieve the greatest benefits from international negotiations. Thus, negotiators must take care to understand the technical trade-offs involved in the relevant issues. Market failure per se is not a sufficient basis for justifying international agreements to control externalities. Costs must be weighed against benefits in particular cases, recognizing that perfect intervention by governments or

100

international organizations is not possible. Likewise, in deciding which level of government will control externalities, we must consider the dimensions of the externalities. In some cases in the law of the sea negotiations this will mean emphasizing bilateral or regional agreements to handle international spillovers. Finally, we have sketched a tentative theory of optimal negotiations that emphasizes the difficulties of trying to decide upon all issues in a given area of negotiations in a single forum, and the theoretical advantages (and practical difficulties) of applying weighted voting in international negotiations.

COMMENTARY

Seyom Brown

I am going to comment mainly on Dean Osgood's paper and make just a few elliptical remarks about the other papers.

I agree basically with Osgood's tactical conclusions. First, our work at Brookings tends to support the conclusion that unimpeded passage through straits is important for the United States, but not essential to its strategic nuclear capability—though this work is still preliminary. Also, I agree with his conclusion that antisubmarine warfare devices would not be threatened in such a way as to really constitute a security threat to the United States. Of course, we work with unclassified material, so our judgment is based upon a good deal of speculation and conjecture as to what is happening in this field. But I think this is a sound conclusion, too.

I also agree with his conclusion that strategic overflight opportunities for the United States may be threatened by a restrictive straits regime, but that this is a larger issue than the straits regime, per se. If the United States has to deal with the obstruction of strategic overflight, it is not going to be substantially affected in the way it deals with that by the existence or the nonexistence of a particular treaty. The interference with strategic overflight usually comes during a rather intense crisis, and that has to be dealt with in another way.

His paper is sound, I think, in indicating that serious diplomatic and tactical problems are more likely to emerge as a result of the hampering of naval mobility in smaller conflicts and local wars, than in strategic war.

However, I begin to differ with him when he concludes that agreements on straits passage do not really require such a universal treaty, but can probably be adequately handled by maintaining favorable political relations with the states involved. The problem with this approach is that restrictions which may be imposed unilaterally by any particular straits state, or coastal state—say, restrictions on navigation with the ostensible objective of interfering with or impeding only a particular kind of activity in some waters, directed only at a particular country—may well spill over and affect other ocean uses and other actors.

The interdependence of uses within the congested areas is one of the reasons why some of us feel that leaving the maritime order, leaving changes in patterns and rules, and indeed the implementation of rules, to ad hoc, mainly bilateral interactions between states is not a sensible way of managing these relationships. Indeed, over the long term, it is probably the least efficient and least effective way.

States should be accountable to the larger community of ocean users in order to promote the efficient and effective use of the oceans, as well as to control conflict. One is largely giving up what would be a desirable ocean order by going to a bilateral, or a very limited multilateral, mode of working out differences.

Now, I think that Osgood comes out where he does because of his structuring of the alternatives. The alternatives that he would like, he considers to be unfeasible. Probably the best one would be a treaty that allowed for unimpeded passage, but realistic political analysis indicates that we are not going to get that kind of treaty. Another alternative would be a treaty that conceded just about everything to the strait states and to the coastal states, that accepted a maritime order based upon absolute coastal state sovereignty in important international waterways. Perhaps you could get that, but he would not want that. The third alternative is the one that would seem to produce the best outcomes, given the impossibility of the first and the undesirability of the second—namely, no treaty to speak of, but ad hoc, modus-vivendi types of interactions.

I think that this eliminates, however, a fourth alternative which would be more desirable and should not be considered infeasible. I think it is too early to interpret what is going on as portending the collapse of the negotiations. In the middle of any big and complicated international negotiation, countries are still posturing, asserting their maximum demands, and the incentives for agreement have not yet really come to the fore.

There could be a treaty—and I think that this indeed is the U.S. government's objective—with international accountability provisions and processes built into it. This treaty would stipulate the minimum rights of the maritime states and the minimum rights of coastal and strait states, and it would leave a lot of gray areas to be worked out through consultative and, perhaps, adjudicatory processes. These would constitute a buffer in bilateral conflict situations that in many cases could escalate to a level at which third parties would be inhibited from doing what they need to do in some of the most congested areas of the ocean.

That treaty should be the objective, and as long as it is still possible to foresee such an outcome, it appears to me that it's worth exploring all of the intricacies and continuing with the very difficult negotiating process, which may take a few years yet, in the international forum, despite the preference the economists have expressed in their papers for limited-actor negotiating forums.

Let me just say a few words about the ideas that came across to me in the economists' papers. I am not an economist and therefore will not deal intrinsically with the economic arguments they presented. It appears to me that the economists we heard today are structuring their analysis too neatly, assuming that efficiency criteria are the main ones, and the heaviest ones, for evaluating the economic worth of particular regimes. To be sure, some assertions were made about distributional objectives and about the benefits that could be diffused throughout the world to consumers if there were aggregate increases in resources. I am not challenging the proposition that aggregate increases in resources would result from the particular regimes they have advocated; but the assumption that a diffusion of benefits throughout the world would result remained at the level of assertion; there was no real analysis of how that diffusion or distribution of benefits would take place. It appears to me that assessment of the failure of the existing open-access, free-use regime and the evaluation of substitutes, whether they are national authorities or international authorities, has to be based partly on norms other than efficiency. There should be a broader and more explicit normative framework to such an analysis or evaluation than I found in the economic papers. I had to infer what the broader normative framework was.

In the normative framework to which, it appears to me, the United States must be committed internationally—not simply for reasons of altruism, but for very profound political reasons—the distribution of income and rent, and the ecological health of the sea itself are more important than ever before. The analysis must be very sensitive to the great uncertainties about what can really harm the sea and what effects may be irreversible. This observation, incidentally, makes one want to take the public-choice paper considerably further than it went in theory. One wants to take further empirically what appears to me to be their very sound suggestion on the way to handle externalities. The notion that one should not, simply as a result of the discovery of externalities, set up a centralized, universal decision system, or regulatory system, I think is very sound.

The question of how wide the circle of directly affected actors is, is an empirical question which does not—when you examine some of the issues that we are looking at—lead one to the conclusion that there can be a narrow circle of actors in some important realms. Tollison and Willett granted this point with respect to fisheries. I would suggest that with respect to a lot of the environmental problems, the circle of actors whose preferences really have to be taken into account is quite wide, and the costs inflicted upon them, which also have to be taken into account, are great.

This is, of course, an empirical question, but it may mean that the economists' promise of a path away from multiple-actor as well as multiple-issue negotiating forums and regulatory institutions is not really a path away from that at all. There may be regional institutions that could fulfill this function, but they may be very, very complicated and involve all kinds of actors of various sizes. Thus they may create almost as many problems—and sometimes even more problems—than would a simple broadening of the membership base of a regulatory institution. Again, these are empirical questions which, under closer examination, may indicate that the economic theory does not really lead to any better solution than other types of analysis do.

In addition to the norm of ecological health of the sea, the sense of legitimacy of any regime should be taken into account. The common heritage of mankind, to be sure, is the "common heritage of politicians." But what is the alternative to dealing with the common heritage of politicians? Politicians are brokers for what they, rightly or wrongly, perceive to be the interests of various groups of people. I wonder whether what is being suggested is a return to a kind of international economic system without these brokers?

The politicians, who represent nationalist sensitivities, have to be taken into account, as does the notion that what is done in the sea has to be done with reference to the concept that the sea belongs to all.

Joseph Nye

Our subject this morning is U.S. interests and methods of choosing among them. I would like to focus on the efforts made in the papers to apply economic rationality—the normative aspects of the liberal economic model—and to show where it succeeds and where it fails. I regard the Tollison and Willett paper as having been more successful, and the Johnson and Logue paper as somewhat less successful, in making that application.

Political scientists often use the abused term "national interest." Sometimes, it refers to the residual product of a fight among constituencies. Whatever the vector is at the end of the fight it is called the "national interest." It does not seem to me that we have to let it go at that. There are at least two normative principles that we can use to distinguish which interests should prevail over others. It seems to me that long-run interests should prevail over short-run interests, given an appropriate social discount rate, and that those interests that are more widely shared among the American people should prevail over those which are only partially shared. This means that issues such as security and aggregate economic interests tend to be at the core of the national interest.

Now security, as Robert Osgood points out in his paper, has a military component and an economic component. He wrote primarily on the military aspects. Economic security, on the other hand, is a matter of relative vulnerability. Oil cartels, potential mineral cartels, or embargoes are clearly important factors for assessing economic security in the oceans. To increase economic security, control over seabed resources is quite important, but control need not mean monopolization of the revenues that accrue from those resources. In other words, one can be opposed to the kind of International Seabed Resources Authority that some less-developed countries propose but also be in favor of broad revenue sharing. Such

106

revenue sharing might go beyond revenues derived from nodules, which are really not expected to provide much revenue, to include shelf hydrocarbons.

It seems to me that Tollison and Willett, using the liberal economic model, have the right perspective and that Johnson and Logue have the wrong one when they worry about the cost of $2 to $6 billion in potential revenue sharing. Such revenue sharing, which amounts to some 0.2 percent of our gross national product, might be a very economical investment from a long-term national-security point of view. Now, what does revenue sharing have to do with national security? The last paragraph of Osgood's paper provides a good answer. Osgood points out the sensitivities of less-developed countries and the importance of using carrots as well as sticks in trying to develop the law and international order that we want. The long-run U.S. interest in the oceans, it seems to me, is in preserving some form of international order. I think the United States also has a long-run interest in development, in establishing a rising floor under global poverty. Even if only for its symbolic value, we have a long-run interest in preserving the concept of the common heritage of mankind in the oceans issue.

If the last paragraph of Osgood's paper is correct, 0.2 percent of the gross national product is quite an inexpensive security investment. It seems to me that the Johnson and Logue view is rather short-sighted. Someone arguing for their position might reply that if the United States wants to achieve these long-run objectives, it can always give aid. However, that would eliminate the symbolic effects I have already mentioned, as well as the benefits of having this revenue transfer from the world's commons occur outside our domestic political process. Intergovernmental aid involves a myriad of extraneous political problems. To take a recent example, it is not a good thing to have the International Development Association (IDA) replenishment tied to extraneous questions such as the ability of American citizens to purchase gold. Now, Johnson and Logue might reply, "That is politically irresponsible. It is a giveaway of our resources." However, the point is that the resources are not yet ours. This is part of what the law of the sea conference is about—the establishment of these property rights.

Thus, I believe that it is in the long-run national security interests of the United States to favor significant revenue sharing, such as 10 percent of oil beyond 200 meters, from all countries having per capita incomes of more than $2,000. These funds could go to the World Bank for loans to the least-developed countries. That leaves the middle group of less-developed countries unaffected, but the richer countries would forgo some revenues in favor of the least developed countries. This could contribute considerably to the sense of legitimacy that is necessary to maintain a new oceanic order.

Why this emphasis on revenue sharing? I would like to demonstrate its importance by stepping back from the question of revenue sharing and talking about the problems of conference diplomacy—where we are in the politics of rule making in the international system. There is currently a trend in the United Nations system toward larger and more unwieldy conferences, and these conferences lead to a tremendous incongruence of power resources inside and outside the conference diplomacy arena. As Willett and Tollison point out, that discrepancy grows when the number of countries in the conference, and the number of issues on the agenda, increase. The law of the sea conference in which we are now engaged is merely a worst case in a trend that has been going on since the first United Nations Conference on Trade and Development session in 1964.

What sort of response should we make to this? First, we can distinguish between what large conferences can do and what they cannot do. There are four basic functions that international conferences and institutions can carry out: (1) provision of information; (2) norm formation—establishment of certain basic norms; (3) regulation, and (4) operation. These functions form a crude ascending scale of difficulty. Conferences with broad scope and number are often quite useful for the first two functions, where one wants to diffuse information and reach a broad agreement on norms. They are extremely bad for functions three and four, where one wants detailed negotiation and efficient operation.

I conclude from this that the U.S. position on the law of the sea should start by distinguishing the instruments which are useful in achieving our various objectives. As Gary Knight's paper for this afternoon makes clear, we want to achieve our objectives through a variety of procedures. From the law of the sea negotiations, we want to establish certain norms, whether through a framework treaty or a general resolution—for example, a restriction on the continuing extension of national jurisdictions, a "no national lakes" resolution. We want to reinforce such basic norms as the "common heritage."

At the same time, we would turn to a second instrument, regional and bilateral agreements, to achieve a number of our other objectives. For example, a great many of our problems connected with fisheries and pollution affect only Mexico and Canada and can be handled most easily in quiet negotiations of the type which has often characterized our relations with our neighbors.

A third point, which Knight's paper also raises, is the use of military force. The use of force is dangerous, but the defensive use of force plays an important role. Both the economic papers say there is little risk of claim-jumping in deep-sea nodule mining, because the self-interests of miners will prevent it. But this is a good example of the failure to take into account symbolic political values. Although there may be no rational economic interest in claim-jumping, for symbolic political purposes, a country might decide to send out a gunboat to harass those whom it considers to be stealing from the common heritage of mankind. In this kind of situation, the presence of American military ships at an early stage in the game might be very important in preserving international law. Indeed, it might have been better in the tuna disputes in the 1950s for the United States to have used a defensive show of naval force rather than to have come out with the Fishermen's Protective Act.

A fourth type of instrument, again referred to in Knight's afternoon paper, is domestic legislation. We want legislation which, if imitated, will lead to the formation of good international law. If we look at the traditional way in which law was formed in the days of British hegemony, we can see that the discrete use of force at the margin helped to create the rules of the sea, but good behavior at home was also essential. The British, in fact, were quite good about policing their own domestic constituencies and obeying the laws which they imposed upon others.

The last of the five instruments that we can use for achieving our long-term objective of establishing a peaceful and just oceans order is revenue sharing, which might be called the carrot that makes it less necessary to use the stick. Significant revenue sharing would show that we are serious about an international order for the oceans that emphasizes the common interest rather than merely our selfish interest.

Having said this about objectives and instruments, let me add one final and brief word about tactics. Tollison and Willett are correct in their skepticism about a seabed authority that restricts production, but I think the tactics we have used to explain our basis for skepticism to other countries have often been somewhat inept. We should not try to explain our position in terms of the abstract benefits of the market, because this argument is viewed by other countries as self-serving American ideology. After all, the free market benefits the player who starts out with a large pile of chips. Whether or not it is true that the Americans are extolling the market solution out of self-interest, the U.S. position certainly appears to be self-serving.

Let me describe a situation I witnessed to illustrate what I mean. A Treasury representative, in a speech similar to these two economic papers, argued that the free market would provide for the interests of all. A representative from a copper-producing, less-developed country rose and branded this as U.S. ideology designed to cover up our narrow self-interest. This representative then argued that the solidarity of the less-developed countries on the seabed question showed that their common interests lay in a restrictive seabed resource authority. There is obviously a fallacy in that less-developed country's position, but I must say that the U.S. representative fell right into the hands of his critic. He replied with ideology, the ideology that urges us to think of ourselves as "consumer citizens of the world."

What we should have done, and what we should do in the conference, is reply with fact. We should carry out studies of potential losses of consumer surplus by non-metal-producing less-developed countries. Suppose we found that for a given country there was a $50 million loss in consumer surplus forgone, and then pointed out that this is the equivalent of two IDA loans. Then we could ask that country whether it still wanted to maintain an ideological coalition at that level of cost. I think we would get a response somewhat different from the one we get when we argue in terms of abstract market ideology.

So, if we go back to Johnson and Logue, who argue that they are engaged in an analysis of empirical evidence, from the perspective of the United States, I conclude that what we need is not a narrowly defined U.S. perspective, but a broader perspective developed through research on costs and benefits other countries may anticipate as well as those the United States may expect. If economic rationality is to be introduced into the law of the sea negotiations, I would be the first to applaud it, but the manner of introduction matters very much.

Roland McKean

It was my understanding that I was to comment on the Tollison-Willett paper, so I am afraid that most of my comments will pertain to it. I might say at the outset, however, in defense of the Johnson-Logue paper, that I assumed they were deliberately looking at U.S. economic interests and that they would not necessarily oppose revenue sharing to a greater extent, or assigning initial property rights in a different way, in order to promote greater equality or wealth-distribution or other objectives.

I agree with most of the points made by Tollison and Willett and with the positions they take. Their analysis strikes me as being generally correct and important, and I like their skepticism about the "perfect intervention" theory of government. I will try, nonetheless, to be the devil's advocate and emphasize some of the qualifications that they recognize but do not stress much, and elaborate a bit on some of their arguments.

Regarding this matter of property rights in ocean resources, they correctly give considerable attention to the advantages of simply defining and enforcing property rights to the manganese nodules. These are not, inherently, common-pool resources, and yet, like the gravel around the Black Sea, or like a communal forest, the resources would be used uneconomically if they were treated like a commons.

Tollison and Willett concede that enforcement of property rights may not be a simple matter, but they suggest that claim-jumping, either by rival producers or by nations, is not likely to be a major problem. I do not feel confident of that. Claim-jumping by rival producers, if we ignore the government support of one side or the other, can probably be discouraged at relatively low cost; it is not too difficult to detect invasions and defend a mine, either under the land or under the sea.

110

But I am not so sure that the threat of take-over by a nation is small. After all, nationalization of foreign enterprise on land—somewhat easier, of course, because the assets are usually within the nationalizing country's boundaries—has not been uncommon. If this threat of take-over is significant, it would presumably deter mutual exchange or deter development. And it raises the question, how could property rights to ocean resources be more effectively enforced? Bilateral agreements and reliance on the present state of international law may be the best one can do, but it is not a fully satisfactory way of promoting development and exchange. For instance, property rights within the United States would be less certain, I think, if each of the fifty states were an independent, sovereign unit making bilateral agreements.

Among nations, some of the bargainers can, as the authors mentioned, make one nation "an offer that he cannot refuse," or perhaps more pertinent, make a second or a third offer that cannot be refused. Consequently, it seems to me that a bilateral agreement, like Sam Goldwyn's oral promise, will often not be worth the paper it is written on. In addition, such agreements can inflict spillover costs and right infringements on other firms or nations that have little bargaining power.

I think we have to face the fact that the international sphere is much like anarchy, in which enforcement costs are relatively high and private. Property-exchange systems may not work as well as we would like. Indeed, these writings on ocean resources remind me of the literature on the economics of anarchy by indicating the voluntary agreements that would arise automatically and those that would not.

In the absence of world government, what can one expect of a world court, of an international claims registry, or of a comprehensive international agreement? One can expect that some rights will be enforced through mutual threat of retaliation by either cost imposition or benefit withholding, the means described in any analysis of anarchy. The final arbiter is perhaps the balance of terror and all the relevant strategic considerations. Each nation may restrain itself somewhat for fear of setting in motion a chain of repercussions that would in the end be very costly to itself. Unless the stakes become very high, these informal mechanisms may serve adequately, as the authors apparently feel they will, to enforce property rights. If Demsetz was correct, American Indian tribes apparently adhered, for a while anyway, to an agreement that assigned property rights to the trapping of beaver—without establishing a world Indian government. However, if the ocean resources, say the petroleum deposits, become sufficiently valuable, I would predict some claim-jumping. Still, that prediction might apply to land as well as ocean resources.

In any event, while I may be less optimistic about claim-jumping than Willett and Tollison, I admit that a comprehensive international agreement might do little to alleviate my concern. Perhaps I should add, too, that I am not advocating world government, because it would bring its own species of costs. In effect, I am regretting the lack of an ideal world.

The second topic I would like to touch on is the liability for damages that Tollison and Willett suggest as a way of coping with pollution. Here I have no quarrel with them, but I would like to elaborate on a point that they mentioned. Assigning liability for damages done by ocean polluters, which again is a property rights matter, is probably the preferred way of coping with this problem, if detection, damage estimation, and policing costs are low. If these costs are sufficiently high, however, it may be economical to turn to indirect or "meat-axe" techniques, or to a combination of measures. One customary example is that assigning liability to motorists who discard litter as they drive along the highway would handle that type of pollution very well if the costs of detecting litterers, determining damages in individual instances, and enforcing the judgments were not too large. Given the probable magnitude of such costs, however, it may make sense to retreat to "meat-axe" fines or penalties, or simply to have government take charge of cleaning up the litter.

Few people *retreat* to "meat-axe" policies, however; instead they advocate harsh remedial policies as a first choice. My favorite example is the suggestion that we reduce economic growth in order to check pollution—a very clumsy, indirect kind of mechanism, a bit like diminishing the municipal water supply in order to reduce prostitution.

In the face of the disadvantages of various solutions, one should, of course, weigh the pros and cons of the alternative policies; and the mixture that is preferred, as the authors note, is preferred partly on the basis of the policing and intervention costs associated with it.

Some people favor, as a corollary to the "perfect intervention theory" of government, the "perfect regulation theory" of regulatory agencies. I share the skepticism about this theory and wish to underline some of the reasons. What such agencies actually do depends largely on the costs and rewards to officials and personnel of taking various actions. As is well known, regulatory agencies often seem to be captured by the groups they are supposed to regulate, by some group that has a relatively large stake per group-member in the outcome of regulatory decisions. I am not sure who might capture an international regulatory body, but I have no confidence that such a body would ultimately have incentives to pursue economic efficiency or any other objective to which most people would agree some weight should be attached.

Given all the talk about common heritage, I would like to elaborate a bit about an issue touched upon briefly by Tollison and Willett—conservation of resources for posterity. These authors correctly point out that if one believes that we should set aside more nonrenewable resources than the market will automatically preserve for posterity, this belief should affect attitudes toward all resources, not just ocean resources.

If there is to be conservation of exhaustible resources, we might prefer to use worldwide taxes rather than other forms of worldwide regulation to achieve this goal. But personally, I seriously doubt that many persons are willing to make significant sacrifices for the sake of distant posterity. I fancy that I am one of those who feel sorry for posterity, and I would like to drop in for a day or two a hundred years from now, but I really do not think I would want to trade places with distant posterity. I look upon the future as being perhaps a nice place to visit, but I would not want to live there.

Nonetheless, even if I am sorry for future generations, and sentimentally drawn toward the idea of preserving mankind for a few more years than it would exist otherwise, I am very doubtful about what we really would be willing to sacrifice. (In my own case, I sometimes tell Gordon Tullock that I am worried about conservation not because I think posterity is so deserving but rather because I think the people today are so undeserving.)

Helping future populations looks to me like the public good to end all public goods, posing the free-rider problem to end all the free-rider problems. Posterity would appear to be almost infinitely large, at least if we succeed in keeping mankind going. The benefits—the conditions of the future—look the same regardless of a living individual's sacrifice. If we solved the first free-rider problem by compelling all existing people to contribute, the conservation of barrels of petroleum would still be a drop in the bucket when spread out over an infinitely large posterity. Thus a further free-rider problem appears. Even if all those alive today made their sacrifice, the public good that was produced—making things easier for the average man of the future—would still look insignificant. And today's sacrificers would have no assurance that tomorrow's free-riders, say the population of 2100 A.D., would not live it up and deprive the people of 2200 A.D., after all.

In any event, most of us are not willing to sacrifice much, even for our neighbors. Nobody is concerned much about the noise that his barking dog inflicts on his immediate neighbors, even though he knows the latter personally. To help unidentified automobile drivers in our own community, we are not even willing to use our turn signals. For total strangers living in our own culture, most of us seem to have little concern, and we display even less concern for strangers living in other lands. So it is really hard for me to believe that many persons are genuinely willing to sacrifice very many bottles of beer for the unborn, invisible, total strangers who may live a thousand years from now. I have a strong feeling that, no matter what my personal sympathies toward future generations are, leaving more resources for posterity is one of the more hotly debated nonissues around.

Ross D. Eckert

I am pleased to be able to serve as a substitute commentator on the Johnson-Logue paper in the place of Deputy Assistant Secretary Shields and Ambassador Stevenson, although I certainly cannot say that I speak for them or their agencies.

On the whole, I disagree with Professor Nye's comments on the Johnson-Logue paper. I think it is a good paper, and I think that the dichotomy between the small and the large that Nye describes is inapplicable here, because Johnson and Logue attempt to quantify some of the rather obvious costs of United States policy toward the law of the sea. Now, their numbers are not perfect; few numbers are. The accuracy of numbers will improve over time, however, and if they are at least ballpark figures, they suggest that the costs of present U.S. policy are rather large.

Let me focus on the aspect of the policy that I understand best, which is the one pertaining to the mining of manganese nodules. What is the situation? Here we have a nascent industry, perhaps to be stillborn, perhaps to be aborted, that would satisfy a significant portion of U.S. demand for raw materials. It would benefit not only the United States, but all consuming nations by providing minerals, steel, and other metals at lower prices than are possible now. That reduction in price may not be clearly perceived by us or by others, but it will be there nonetheless.

An unfettered exploitation of offshore resources would undercut cartels in minerals and possibly in hydrocarbons. Evidently ocean mining will not degrade the environment very much, and certainly will degrade it little compared to alternative land-based sources of production. So, on the whole, the ocean mining industry represents a marvelous opportunity. The intervention to regulate it, I think, is really the only factor that might foul up what will otherwise be a large benefit to mankind.

I want to take, however, one exception to their paper. I would call your attention to the discussion of regulatory regimes and the extent to which they might improve or worsen resource allocation. Johnson and Logue distinguish between, first, what they call a free-access, free-timing type of claims registry, and second, a powerful international seabed regulatory authority, that term derived from the 1970 U.S. draft treaty. They conclude that the first type of regulatory authority "would do nothing more than establish property rights and would, from the point of view of efficient exploitation of deep-sea minerals, be virtually costless. The second type could severely hinder resource availability and in so doing cause prices to be substantially higher than they otherwise would be [and] reduce the security of supply. . . ."

I am not sure that this distinction is well drawn. I have doubts of my own as to whether a claims registry would significantly enhance resource allocation;

in some areas it would clearly misallocate resources. To the extent that registration of claims in some detail became a qualification for exploitation, it would force exploiters to reveal proprietary information about the extent of these claims, and by forcing that information to become public before they would otherwise elect to release it, would result in a nonoptimal rate of investment in the search for valuable deposits and therefore a nonoptimal rate of exploitation. Even if this claims registry could be created and could limit claims, I do not see how it would have any enforcement power unless it were converted into the second type of regulatory authority.

It also seems to me that even a registry would politicize the decision of who is going to mine where. This would otherwise be decided independently by individual firms, through consortia or by a few bilateral agreements among nations that either have the technology or seek to purchase it. These would not necessarily be rich countries.

My second concern with the dichotomy they discuss is that *de minimis* regulation (the registry proposal) cannot always be confined to that level over time. What Johnson and Logue have drawn is a dichotomy between a regulatory regime that appears to do very little and one that appears to do a lot. Even if we could all agree, or if the participants in the law of the sea conference could agree to draft a treaty that would create this *de minimis* regime, I do not see how we could bind it constitutionally to that character forever. A regime of the first type would probably have strong incentives to become eventually a regime of the second type, a result that Johnson and Logue would find objectionable.

So it seems to me that once you start down the path of regulation, even if you create a weak, feckless regime, you are likely to wind up with something quite different.

I also want to say that I think the possibility of minerals cartels as raised in this paper is a bit overdrawn, as we know from a dozen years of observing the situation in the Middle East. The difference between an attempted cartel and a successful cartel is very sharp. And even when political interests, as a result of war and other things, have prompted that cartel to be as successful as possible, it still can have some weaknesses. The development of minerals cartels would only be promoted by creating a strong international regime that could act as a joint clearing house for apportioning quotas among various countries.

To close, I want to echo a remark made by Professor McKean, and again take issue with Professor Nye, on one point. Obviously Professor Nye is correct in noting that there can be noneconomic reasons for jumping manganese nodule claims. A nation may well perceive that its vital interests are at stake in jumping someone else's claim. But, I wonder how a treaty would constitute a serious obstacle to an action of that kind.

DISCUSSION

EDITOR'S NOTE: Arvid Pardo criticized the papers for their assumption that the negotiations would limit national jurisdiction to 200 nautical miles. He argued that there have been no proposals suggesting precise criteria for drawing straight baselines, and without precise criteria states will continue to expand their jurisdiction. Pardo therefore advocated some type of international mechanism to deal with all uses of ocean space beyond national jurisdiction. He argued that if this is not done, a division of the oceans will be inevitable.

Clinton Whitehurst asked Robert Osgood if anything were preventing the United States from codifying its interests in the law of the sea, and if those interests were identical to those of the Soviet Union.

Francis Christie argued in response to the Tollison-Willett and Johnson-Logue papers that lower mineral prices that result from ocean mining may not significantly reduce the price of end products for the consuming nations. Second, he wondered how consumers might be protected from cartels formed by seabed mineral producers. Responding to the Johnson and Logue paper, Christie speculated that one may not want regional arrangements with regard to fisheries, but rather, benign neglect. William Cline argued that what Tollison and Willett cite as the common heritage of mankind would accrue in proportion to the pre-existing world income distribution. Thus in a sense the assumption that the current distribution is the appropriate distribution for new wealth would be a value judgment.

Myres McDougal argued that for the most part the papers and the discussion undercut existing law and showed no understanding of the process by which international law is made. The present law is customary law based on retaliation and reciprocity. This customary law is an important base of power, and it should not be overlooked or undercut in the present negotiations. Lewis Alexander expanded on this point with respect to straits. He argued that there are now certain rules regarding straits and that these should be a starting point in the negotiations.

117

Richard Sweeney remarked that government regulation intended to make deep-sea mining "optimal" will not work and will only succeed in generating a little bureaucracy. Sweeney answered Christie's question by arguing that the deep-sea miners chance of forming a cartel would be improved greatly by a strong ISRA. He concluded by agreeing with Christie's modified position that fishery regulation may not be a good idea, given the very poor performance of past regulatory agencies in this area.

ROBERT OSGOOD: My paper suffers from at least two limitations that tend to give a distorted view of the total realm of considerations involved in thinking about what sort of ocean regime we can reasonably work toward and what means we can use to work toward it. One limitation is that I am talking about the implications of various regimes for security interests, with security defined fairly narrowly lest it become a rubric for every vital interest under the sun. Second, I concentrate on a negative point, which is that some of the positions that we have heretofore taken, as with respect to our interpretation of unimpeded passage, are not essential; however important they may be, they are not, by any stretch of my imagination, essential for security reasons. The kinds of security threats that may arise in the straits and with respect to the extension of jurisdictional claims of the United States, when security interest is involved, are probably not going to be dealt with effectively by the law of the sea treaty, but will depend upon other factors. The primary factor is our political relations with the few states that really can affect us seriously in this respect.

My major point, given these two limitations, is that we should not expect law to do too much—not that we should dismiss law, and particularly not customary law. We are now in a stage of international ocean politics in which customary law is developing. It is important not only to consider the modi vivendi and the bilateral and informal relationships, but also, as Seyom Brown says, to try to develop some kinds of multilateral laws and regulations. I would emphasize that in doing so we have to draw a balance between the interests of the coastal states, the straits states, the maritime states, and other users, and that there is a danger in insisting upon too much being codified into law or upon the law being too heavily weighted toward our interests—the danger that we might end up getting much less than we could with a more modest approach to the development of customary law.

This relates to the other question that was asked. If the Soviet Union and the United States agree on their interests as expressed in a law of the sea regime, is it still the case that we are in danger of too rigid a codification of our interests in law, given the political context? The answer in my mind is surely yes, because

118

what I am eager to avoid is a polarization of interests on a north-south, rich-poor, coastal-maritime-state basis.

In order to mitigate that danger, it seems that we have to emphasize the complexity of the structure of interests that must be considered in approaching legal or other kinds of accommodations with coastal states, so that all of the less-developed countries, all the coastal states, and so on do not think of their interests as monolithic and as necessarily opposed to the interests of some other category of states. That is my general attitude. As for the specific consequences of the kind of regime I think is feasible, over time, what kinds of general principles are worth getting agreement upon, and what gray areas, as Seyom Brown calls them, need to be worked out—I just have not had the occasion to explain my solution to these problems.

PROFESSOR LOGUE: Both Professor Nye and Mr. Brown characterized our study as too neat an analysis, because, I think, we did not stress the trade-offs nor factor political considerations into it. To expect this was to misunderstand our approach, insofar as we were principally concerned with the U.S. position and the economic issues involved. To try to lump all these issues into one document, political and economic as well, is something that has yet to be accomplished satisfactorily. We hope that we have provided a starting point, at least, in focusing upon the actual figures involved in the economic issues, that is, the cost. We never intended this to serve as a negotiating document, but rather as an input into the strategy formulation.

The second point I want to raise concerns the notion of distributional objectives. Seyom Brown talked about the notion of the diffusion of benefits and the methods by which they would be diffused, and Professor Nye raised the issue of consumer surplus and asked how much of that would be transferred as a result of lower prices.

Some of our further work, which is not included in the preliminary draft but does appear in the final version, suggests, for example, that the consumer surplus of nickel lost, or potential consumer surplus of nickel lost, as a result of a very rigid regulatory regime for the world as a whole may amount to something on the order of $570 million per year by 1985. With respect to all four commodities found in the manganese nodules, the loss of consumer surplus might be on the order of $3 or $4 billion a year for the world as a whole.

Of that, the loss to the United States is only about $70 or $80 million with respect to nickel, and maybe $300 to $350 million with respect to all four commodities. The diffusion of benefits of a nonrestrictive regime, therefore, is quite broad and certainly accrues not only to the United States. Moreover, most of the land-based production of the commodities in question is concentrated in a very few less-developed countries and, therefore, the large majority of less-developed countries will derive some benefits from lower prices.

With respect to the notion of revenue sharing and the notion of brokers (politicians being brokers for the polity), and with respect to Nye's comments distinguishing between the short run and the long run, I am somewhat baffled, because these notions seem to be inconsistent. The history of policy making in this country and in others suggests that politicians tend to have very short-sighted views. Indeed, there was an excellent editorial in the *Wall Street Journal* recently by Irving Kristol, who very nicely analyzed the current energy debate raging between Congress and the White House, suggesting that politicians' objective functions generally are not those which might best serve the long-run interests of the world.

Returning to the notion of revenue sharing as only 0.2 percent of gross national product, I strongly emphasize that this misses the point. Indeed, we are discussing $3 billion and we should talk about it in those terms. The real question is, could we as a nation use that $3 billion more efficiently, or, to put it another way, could we buy an equivalent amount of defense for less than $3 billion by using another approach?

PROFESSOR TOLLISON: I would like to make three points. One is that we basically agree with Mr. Brown's contention that one does have to look at the specific cases and one does have to look at the empirical trade-offs in discussing given issues. In fact, one issue that Professor McKean noted specifically was that enforcement and detection costs in the issue of standards must be weighed when assigning liability for control of oil tanker pollution. We actually have looked at this case empirically, and on net the cost differential still cuts very strongly in favor of liability assignment. We agree with Mr. Brown that one does have to do the specific analysis of each case to reach a judgment.

Also I would respond to Brown's comments that we did not mean to leave the impression that bilateral or regional groupings were by any means superior forums in which to negotiate; we intended to say that in a negotiation so complex and with so many cross-cutting memberships, it would seem reasonable to expect there to be a wide variety of forums in which negotiations might take place, including highly centralized ones and highly decentralized ones.

A third point is that it is not apparent to me why Ambassador Pardo thinks that our assumptions are wrong, but perhaps that will come out in his discussion this afternoon, or perhaps we can clarify it at lunch. I did not understand the argument.

PART
TWO

ALTERNATIVES TO A COMPREHENSIVE TREATY

THE THIRD UN CONFERENCE ON THE LAW OF THE SEA: CARACAS REVIEW

Ann L. Hollick

The Caracas meeting of the Third UN Conference on the Law of the Sea is simply one act in a drama that began some years ago and will continue for some time. Caracas, in this sense, must be viewed in terms of its antecedents as well as its contribution to the development of an international legal regime for the oceans.

The First and Second UN Conferences on the Law of the Sea met in 1958 and 1960 respectively. The conventions produced at those conferences have not held up well in the face of rapid technological and scientific change. In 1970, only a decade after the second UN conference, the General Assembly of the United Nations voted to convene a third conference on the law of the sea to deal with a range of ocean issues. At present writing the Third UN Conference on the Law of the Sea has met for twelve weeks—two in New York in December 1973 and ten in Caracas from 20 June through 29 August 1974. The next round—eight weeks this time—is to begin on 17 March 1975 in Geneva, and subsequent sessions are contemplated for Vienna and/or Caracas.

The official goal of this lengthy series of discussions is to prepare a single treaty that will be both "comprehensive" and "widely accepted." Defining success in such terms virtually ensures that the third law of the sea conference will "fail" to carry out its official goal. With twenty-five agenda items (embracing sixty-three separate categories of major issues) and 137 delegations to the conference, a detailed treaty could not be widely accepted and a widely accepted treaty could not be comprehensive.[1] The task of the Caracas and other sessions, at least as officially defined, may be impossible. That is not to say that no treaty will emerge from the third conference. Indeed, the interest of the negotiators in achieving some tangible results from the drawn-out negotiations almost rules out the possibility that nothing will emerge. The treaty, however, will probably be either a widely accepted partial treaty or a comprehensive treaty accepted by a simple majority. The question posed by this outcome is whether the substance of the agreement will be desirable—from the U.S. or from the global perspective.

---

[1] If a comprehensive treaty were drawn up, a situation might develop in which nations approved it with reservations concerning those portions deemed unacceptable. If nations adhered in this manner, the net effect would be a treaty partially acceptable to a majority, rather than a universal or widely acceptable treaty.

Perspectives on Caracas

The Caracas session of the conference must be assessed from two points of departure—from the vantage point of the meetings that preceded it (those of the UN Seabed Committee [2] and of the procedural session in New York), and from the point of view of the structural problems built into the conference. Conclusions reached from the former perspective are far more optimistic than those drawn from the latter.

The Seabed Committee began in 1968 as an ad hoc committee of thirty-five members. It was converted into a permanent committee the following year, and in 1970 was designated as the preparatory committee for the law of the sea conference, with ninety-one members. Its most notable accomplishment in six years of meetings was the preparation of the agenda of twenty-five items, sixty-one subitems, and nineteen sub-subitems. The first session of the conference was held in New York from 3 to 15 December 1973 to deal with the organizational details of the election of conference officers and rules of procedure. With considerable difficulty, conference officers were elected by 11 December. During the remaining days, the delegates were unable to agree on the implementation of a "gentlemen's agreement" to seek consensus and the requisite majority for substantive decision making. The rules of procedure were therefore unresolved when the Caracas session opened.

Against this background, the fact that anything was accomplished at Caracas is all the more remarkable. Caracas, however, was notable for hard work, long hours, few polemics, and attention to detail. Negotiations on draft rules of procedure occupied the first week of the session, but at last agreement on a voting formula was reached and the rules of procedure were adopted. The agreed voting formula combines a "gentlemen's agreement" on efforts to reach consensus (in principle, that no voting on substantive matters will take place until all efforts to reach consensus or general agreement have been exhausted) with a requirement for substantive decisions of "a two-thirds majority of the representatives present and voting provided that majority shall include at least a majority of the states participating in that session of the Conference."

The conference created three main committees to deal with substantive issues, a general or steering committee, a drafting committee, and a credentials committee. The three main committees are holdovers from the subcommittees of the UN Seabed Committee, and agenda items are allocated unevenly among them. The First Committee is responsible for seabed mining beyond the limits of national jurisdiction. Of the three committees, only the First Committee had undertaken sufficient preparatory work to have elaborated the major alternatives on most

---

[2] Committee on the Peaceful Uses of the Seabed and the Ocean Floor beyond the Limits of National Jurisdiction.

issues concerning the legal regime for deep-seabed mining. The committee's work program at Caracas developed around three issues: (1) the economic implications of seabed mining; (2) the issue of who may exploit the area beyond the limits of national jurisdiction (Article 9); and (3) the rules and regulations governing exploitation (which evolved into a question of the conditions of exploitation).

The Second Committee was assigned fifteen agenda items dealing with a variety of law of the sea matters. These include the territorial sea, the economic or resource zone, the continental shelf, fishing, and navigation. The Second Committee devoted the Caracas session to the completion of what was essentially preparatory work. The committee began by holding general debate on each of the fifteen agenda items before it. Once the debate on each item was concluded, the chairman, Andres Aguilar (Venezuela), with the assistance of the Secretariat, prepared a working paper reflecting main trends in national policies on each item. The working papers were in the form of draft treaty articles. When a working paper was ready, the general debate was interrupted. The whole committee proceeded to review and revise the text, and each country had a chance to ensure that its views were incorporated. In this fashion, the working papers went through two revisions. The end product was a series of fifteen working papers presenting the major alternatives in treaty article form, to serve as the basis for future negotiations.

The Third Committee was entrusted with the preservation of the marine environment, scientific research, and the development and transfer of technology. The committee created two informal groups—one to deal with pollution, the other with scientific research. The pollution working group began with very general draft articles on preservation of the marine environment. Little progress was made on the formulation of a general obligation to preserve the marine environment due to developing-country insistence on a double standard on environmental questions. And with regard to vessel source pollution, the impasse continued over coastal state versus flag and port state enforcement. The scientific research group began with a few alternate drafts but reopened everything for discussion. It succeeded by the end of the session in drafting alternative formulations concerning the right to conduct research and the consent, participation, and obligations of coastal states.

Summing up the substantive work of the Caracas conference, it is clear that the three main committees worked diligently and by the end of the session had succeeded in sharpening different perspectives and preparing alternative treaty texts where they previously had been unavailable. Committees II and III in essence completed the preparatory work that should have been done before the conference, presumably laying the groundwork for future negotiations. In Committee I, however, where draft articles were available from the outset of the session, negotiation did not occur. This is a significant indication of the structural difficulties that face the third law of the sea conference and does not augur well for its outcome.

The two main structural difficulties facing the Caracas and future sessions of this conference are the size of the agenda and the number of negotiating parties. Whatever the capabilities of law of the sea negotiators, the task of negotiating durable international regimes for each of the ocean issues on the agenda in a single text is beyond the capacity of this political forum. Indeed the conference can be compared with an effort to combine in a single international decision-making process the issues before the Stockholm Conference on the Environment, the SALT negotiations, the UN Energy Conference, and the Rome Food Conference. The creation of optimum management regimes for matters as diverse as shipping, military transit, environment, living resources, petroleum, and hard minerals requires the isolation of each issue from the others and an approach to it on its own merits and in terms of its unique characteristics. The apparent goal of the third UN conference, however, is to trade these issues off in a political package rather than to develop management systems that will provide for the long-term use of ocean resources.

The second difficulty of the negotiating exercise—the number of participants—relates directly to the first. Presenting the nations of the world with a lengthy and heterogeneous list of negotiating issues creates numerous interest groups and subgroups on each topic. The groupings are based on level of economic development, geographical and resource situations, regional cohesion, and ideological differences. The broadest division is between the developed and the developing nations (the latter known as the Group of 77). This cleavage is most pronounced on the high-technology issues of deep-sea mining and scientific research. Other negotiating groups are based on geographical circumstances and the vagaries of oceanic resource distribution. These groups band together over the issue of extending coastal state jurisdiction. The land-locked and shelf-locked group of around forty nations has pursued the goal of either limiting the extension of offshore jurisdictions or, if extensions cannot be avoided, of gaining access to the resources of expanded coastal state jurisdiction of their neighboring coastal states. Nations that have continental margins extending beyond 200 miles want to ensure their jurisdiction over the anticipated petroleum resources of these areas, and another group of countries claims preferential rights to fisheries beyond their 200-mile zones.

Island and archipelago states pose a special set of problems. In extensions of jurisdiction, island states want to enjoy the same rights as continental states regardless of whether the islands or rocks from which these extensions are measured are inhabitable or even above water. Between the outermost points of archipelagic states, the intent is to draw straight baselines and claim archipelagic waters within—with 200-mile zones extending beyond that. However, coastal

126

states with islands belonging to other states off their shores oppose according them a full economic zone. A further complication rests in the developing countries' assertion that islands under foreign domination or control should not be allowed 200-mile resource zones.[3]

Other interest groups in the law of the sea conference are not unique to the oceans. The regional groupings of the United Nations are instruments for allocating chairmanships and decision-making rights in the conference. They also bring to the negotiations distinctive regional approaches. Soviet bloc attitudes toward ocean mining reflect their concern with protecting state enterprises and agencies and their traditional opposition to creating strong international organizations. African positions reflect a history of regional cooperation and close liaison between member states as well as the large proportion of African land-locked states. States bordering semienclosed seas such as the Caribbean and North Sea have fished each other's waters for decades and are attempting to develop new modes of allocating rights to dwindling resources. Member nations of the European Community have been preoccupied throughout the law of the sea conference with reaching agreed positions, but with only a modicum of success to date.

While the cohesion of states with shared interests may normally be a prerequisite to a successful international negotiation, it has proven counterproductive in the law of the sea discussions. The number and variety of issues yield too many groups with overlapping and cross-cutting memberships. This has created high transaction costs with efforts to coordinate policy within the groups absorbing so much time and energy that negotiation between contending groups rarely takes place. A prime example at Caracas was the work of the First Committee on deep-seabed mining. As the only committee to come to the conference with alternative treaty texts, the First Committee completed a third reading of the draft articles for a seabed-mining regime and then could not agree on the next issue to address. While the United States and other developed countries pressed for a discussion of and negotiations over rules and regulations to govern seabed mining, the Group of 77 opposed addressing this issue first. As a result of differences between producing and consuming countries, the Group of 77 was unwilling to risk internal division by considering detailed rules and regulations. Instead, the 77 preferred to focus on the broad issue of who may exploit the area (Article 9) on which they were in agreement among themselves, yet on which they were most sharply divided with the technologically advanced nations. This was just one of many instances in which the dynamic of intragroup negotiation detracted from and even precluded negotiations between the principal adversary groups at the conference.

---

[3] United Nations, Third Conference on the Law of the Sea, A/CONF.62/C.2/L.30, 30 July 1974.

There are a number of other impediments to the conclusion of a satisfactory law of the sea treaty. Some nations are interested in delaying the negotiations, either because their interests in the oceans are not yet clearly perceived or because they expect to realize gains in their position by delays. Working in the opposite direction in the developed countries are domestic pressures to resolve specific ocean regimes so that commercial and strategic users may go about their business without further uncertainties or delays. The opposing forces for delay and completion of the conference have complicated the process of reaching agreement. Until the final session is scheduled, no parties can be expected to make compromises. And until the major parties all agree that a treaty is necessary, the date of the final session cannot be set.

In 1973 U.S. officials told the Congress that 1975 was the final year when the conference must produce a treaty. Since then the administration has been careful to avoid specifying a probable treaty date, while still insisting that a treaty is necessary. Congress, however, is considering bills to immediately extend U.S. fisheries jurisdiction to 200 miles until a treaty is agreed upon, and to undertake seabed mining if there is no treaty by January 1976. In this situation it is useful to raise the question of what the U.S. interest is in this negotiating exercise. How will the United States be affected if there is or is not a law of the sea treaty?

The United States and the Third UN Conference on the Law of the Sea

From the U.S. perspective, it is difficult to foresee that any of the probable outcomes of the third conference will be seriously disadvantageous. In the unlikely event that no treaty results from the conference, the United States will nonetheless be able to protect its essential interests in the oceans. On the other hand, the majority sentiment that was evident at Caracas and that will probably be recognized in a statement to the UN General Assembly or a treaty is entirely in accord with U.S. territorial interests. That sentiment is for maximum extensions of coastal state jurisdiction—to twelve-mile territorial seas, to 200-mile resource zones, and to the living and nonliving resources adjacent to those zones. A partial treaty to this effect is being sought by the numerous island and coastal states at the conference. Whether or not the treaty contains detailed provisions for navigational and other international uses of the oceans, as the U.S. now insists is necessary, this country will benefit significantly from extensions of jurisdiction. Off its own lengthy coastline the United States enjoys substantial resources and would gain more territory (2.2 million square miles) than any other nation under a 200-mile economic or resource zone. The U.S. continental margin extends beyond 200 miles in some areas, as do its offshore fishery resources.

With regard to deep-sea mining, U.S. firms reputedly lead those of other nations in mining technology. Since a significant portion of the commercially attractive nodules could fall under the newly expanded national jurisdiction of

Pacific islands, enterprising firms may be invited by nodule-owning states to mine those resources, thereby evading whatever onerous restrictions might be incorporated in an international seabed authority. Indeed, if the provisions for a deep-seabed regime are too offensive to the developed nations in an era of resource scarcity, their governments may simply ignore the treaty and encourage their firms to go ahead with consortia arrangements providing for reciprocal recognition of the mining claims of others.

A primary U.S. concern, of course, is that coastal state expansion in the absence of a treaty will result in restrictions on navigation, whether of oil tankers or of military vessels. In the absence of treaty-guaranteed rights of transit through international straits, officials have argued, obstacles to navigation might be posed by coastal and straits nations. But when a number of developing nations are engaged in building their own merchant marines and others find themselves heavily dependent upon international commerce, it is difficult to foresee any international sentiment favoring restrictions on commercial mobility. However, the imposition of tolls to cover the costs of managing congested international straits is a possible development. It is true that coastal states strongly resent offshore naval activities of maritime nations, but it is equally unlikely that military transit will be prevented if the major naval powers remain united on this issue. No government would lightly risk the humiliation of having its challenge to straits transit resisted by the naval powers acting in concert. If, on the other hand, a straits state supported by a superpower closed a strait to transit by others, an international treaty guaranteeing free transit would scarcely provide an effective safeguard.

The projected outcome of a treaty (or statement) extending national jurisdiction but unable to effectively control and regulate deep-sea mining and navigation is doubly ironic. Since 1970 the United States has been foremost among those who have argued that a comprehensive and widely acceptable treaty is indispensable to this nation's interests in the oceans. Indeed the U.S. government has worked hard in moving its domestic interests to a more internationally acceptable position in the negotiations. The official premise of U.S. policy in this regard has been that an internationally agreed treaty is necessary to avoid conflicts in the oceans and to secure U.S. rights there. Yet it will be the United States, among other developed nations, that will benefit most if no treaty or only a minimal treaty emerges enshrining the expansionist tendencies at work in law of the sea negotiations.[4] The second irony becomes apparent when it is recalled

---

[4] Under a 200-mile zone, thirty-five countries will acquire 50 percent of the total ocean space to be enclosed. Among the thirty-five are ten "leading" countries that share among themselves 30 percent of the 200-mile zones. Lewis Alexander, "Geographical Factors and Patterns of Alignment," in *Perspectives on Ocean Policy: Conference on Conflict and Order in Ocean Relations,* Proceedings of the Airlie House Conference of the Ocean Policy Project, Johns Hopkins University, 21-24 October 1974 (Washington, D.C.: U.S. Government Printing Office, 1975), pp. 317-30.

that it was the developing countries, through the Group of 77, that pressed for recognition of 200-mile zones in a single comprehensive treaty as a means of countering the major maritime powers' interest in freedom of the seas. However, only a small number of developing nations will benefit—those with long coasts and abundant offshore resources. The big losers will be the landlocked and shelf-locked nations, countries with short coastlines, and countries with comparatively few resources off their coasts—most of them developing nations.

The Third Law of the Sea Conference and the Future

The foregoing observations raise in its most acute form the question of whether the treaty being sought at Caracas and elsewhere is desirable, in terms of international equity or efficient long-range management of ocean resources. It is contended here that no treaty may be better than the treaty that seems to be emerging from the present conference. As indicated earlier, significant pressures exist for some treaty outcome. The political nature of the forum and the diverse interests that are being accommodated in the negotiation determine that what does emerge will be the lowest common denominator—enormous extensions of national jurisdiction over ocean resources. With the exception of the landlocked and shelflocked, who will be either placated or ignored, every state should get something from this extension. Of course some will get more than others, the principal beneficiaries being certain developed countries, South America, and island states.

Proposals before the Caracas session indicate the shape of the treaty outcome. Twelve-mile territorial seas and 200-mile economic zones will be measured from new and extended straight baselines. In some cases proposed baselines measure up to 400 miles in length and in other cases they disregard land altogether and are based on water depths or geographical coordinates.[5] Additional claims are being made to continental margins and fishery resources which extend beyond the economic zone. Although more than twenty countries have margins reaching such distances, only a handful of states will benefit significantly and are active in pressing for coastal state jurisdiction over the resources of the continental shelf beyond the economic zone.[6] Other nations, such as those on the west coast of Latin America, that are not endowed with offshore mineral resources are seeking

---

[5] Arvid Pardo, "Comments on Caracas and Predictions for the Future," in ibid., pp. 383-405; UN, Third Conference on the Law of the Sea, A/CONF.62/C.2/L.30, 30 July 1974; A/CONF.62/C.2/L.49, 9 August 1974; A/CONF.62/C.2/L.70, 20 August 1974.

[6] Ignoring the effect of a 200-mile zone and measuring the continental shelf to a depth of 3,000 meters, the following nations combined control almost half of the continental margins of the world: Australia—1,445,400 sq. miles (10.83 percent of world margins); Canada—1,240,000 sq. miles (9.29 percent); Indonesia—1,229,800 sq. miles (9.21 percent); United States—862,600 sq. miles (6.46 percent); U.S.S.R.—735,900 sq. miles (5.51 percent); New Zealand—571,000 sq. miles (4.28 percent); Argentina—484,100 sq. miles (3.63 percent). U.S. Department of State, Geographer, International Boundary Study, Series A, Limits in the Seas, *Theoretical Area Allocations of Seabed to Coastal States*, no. 46, 12 August 1972.

130

compensation in the form of fisheries resources off their shores. Ecuador, Panama, and Peru therefore have claimed preferential rights to the living resources adjacent to their 200-mile zones.[7] Similarly, the United States, Canada, and the Soviet Union are seeking exclusive rights to salmon spawning in their rivers, regardless of their migratory range.

The area remaining beyond national jurisdiction will contain manganese nodules primarily, and of course nodules will also be found within newly expanded areas of jurisdiction. Given the limited resources that will fall to the international regime, the conference may decide that to achieve the compliance of the technologically advanced nations only minimal institutional machinery, combined with principles and codes of behavior for activities undertaken in the area, will be accepted.

The third major element of any treaty outcome relates to navigational rights within resource zones and through and over straits that will be covered by twelve-mile territorial seas. The United States, the Soviet Union, Japan, Great Britain, and other maritime nations have been united in their support of "unimpeded transit through international straits" and "no interference with non-resource uses of the economic zone." Indeed the United States and the Soviet Union have predicated their acceptance of an international treaty upon satisfaction of these navigation rights. Given this unyielding position, it is doubtful that the treaty will impose restrictions or controls on navigation through international straits regardless of the growing congestion and need for traffic regulation in these areas. It is likely, therefore, that states bordering on international straits will be nonsignatories. In the economic zone some legal formula will doubtless be devised that satisfies the coastal states' sentiment for sovereignty, while allowing an interpretation satisfactory to shipping and naval interests. The problems will arise in everyday usage as these different interpretations are applied. Coastal state application of international environmental regulations will probably also be couched in judicious language capable of alternate and conflicting interpretations.

The drawbacks of such an outcome, embodied in a treaty or other document, are apparent. The enclosure of major portions of the oceans will exacerbate existing international inequities and generate more conflicts than it resolves. The poorer landlocked and shelflocked nations will receive little if anything from the national extensions. And the shifting of boundaries itself will generate numerous disputes between neighboring countries. Where sharp regional hostilities exist, the resolution of these differences will be more like the Greek-Turkish conflict over islands than the adjudicated division of the North Sea.

Perhaps the most damaging criticism of the probable treaty is that it is a short-sighted response to the implications of a growing world population and a potential resource shortage. While national sovereignty may work for the man-

---

[7] UN, General Assembly, A/AC.138/SC.II/L.54, 10 August 1973.

agement of fixed mineral resources,[8] it cannot suffice to regulate marine pollution or certain stocks or ecological systems of fish. Indeed, given the past performance of nations in areas of exclusive jurisdiction, serious doubts must be raised about the capabilities of even the most developed countries to optimally manage the resources of large and arbitrarily drawn ocean zones.[9] Where the uses of an environment are multiple and interdependent, the management regime must be appropriate to the resource in question and will require cooperative international and national regulation.

The third law of the sea conference has generated no long-range schemes for the conservation and management of ocean resources. Nor has it given much attention to means of strengthening and improving existing international ocean institutions. By the time that the need for this has become critical and self-evident, the resultant treaty may have locked nations into positions they cannot yield. This prospect sharpens the question of whether no treaty would be better than the treaty that will probably be agreed in 1975 or 1976. At least a no-treaty result might allow future flexibility to devise necessary management institutions when the problems of congestion and ocean resource depletion become acute and schemes designed to optimize ocean resources become unavoidable. On the other hand, a no-treaty result could lead to the same extensions of jurisdiction by coastal states. Although not enshrined in an international convention, these extensions could eventually be accepted as customary international law. The result might, therefore, be the same in either case. Moreover, there is no assurance that if the present law of the sea negotiations were postponed for three to ten years, national governments would behave more wisely in developing an international regime for the effective management of ocean resources.

---

[8] When oil pools stretch across artificially drawn boundary lines, the result may be simultaneous and inefficient recovery of the resources.

[9] The record of international organizations, of course, has not been outstanding, but for different reasons. The inability to enforce decisions, rather than the parochial and interest-oriented nature of the decisions, has been at the root of most failures of international and regional bodies.

ALTERNATIVES TO A LAW OF THE SEA TREATY

H. Gary Knight

Since Ambassador Arvid Pardo first introduced the seabed question to the agenda of the United Nations General Assembly in 1967, the community of nations has devoted a substantial amount of time and effort to reaching a comprehensive and widely accepted agreement on a broad range of issues involving the use of the sea and the exploitation of ocean resources.[1] In 1970 the General Assembly called for convocation of the Third United Nations Conference on the Law of the Sea, and the first substantive session of that conference was held in Caracas, Venezuela, from 20 June to 29 August 1974. Although a substantial amount of preparatory work was accomplished at the Caracas session, there were no major breakthroughs in the negotiations and, in fact, no significant progress was made toward the drafting of agreed treaty articles on any of the twenty-five items, sixty-one sub-items, and nineteen sub-subitems on the conference agenda.[2] This result has led many observers, both within and outside government, to view pessimistically the prospects for achieving a comprehensive and widely accepted law of the sea treaty at the Geneva session of the conference to be held 17 March to 10 May 1975, or, indeed, at any subsequent session or sessions which might be held.[3]

Because important issues concerning the physical and economic security of the United States are involved in the law of the sea negotiations, it is important to assess the implications of failure to reach the desired accord, and to determine which alternative courses of action would best achieve U.S. policy objectives

---

[1] For background on the conference and the issues with which it is concerned, see H. G. Knight, "Issues before the Third United Nations Conference on the Law of the Sea," *Louisiana Law Review,* vol. 34 (Winter 1974), pp. 155-96; J. R. Stevenson and B. H. Oxman, "The Preparations for the Law of the Sea Conference," *American Journal of International Law,* vol. 68 (January 1974), pp. 1-32.

[2] The full conference agenda is reproduced in Knight, "Issues before the Third Conference," pp. 193-96.

[3] See H. G. Knight, "The Third United Nations Law of the Sea Conference: Caracas," *American Universities Field Staff Reports,* vol. 18, no. 1 (October 1974); T. Alexander, "Dead Ahead toward a Bounded Main," *Fortune Magazine,* vol. 90, no. 4 (October 1974), p. 129ff.; E. Miles, "An Interpretation of the Caracas Proceedings," Paper presented at the Ninth Annual Conference of the Law of the Sea Institute, Kingston, R.I., 1975; H. G. Knight, "Treaty and Non-Treaty Approaches to Order in the World Ocean" in *Perspectives on Ocean Policy: Conference on Conflict and Order in Ocean Relations,* Proceedings of the Airlie House Conference of the Ocean Policy Project, Johns Hopkins University, 21-24 October 1974 (Washington, D.C.: U.S. Government Printing Office, 1975), pp. 251-72.

in the event of such a failure.[4] Even if the conference should produce some sort of suboptimal agreement, an inquiry into alternatives has value in providing the U.S. negotiators (and, later, the U.S. Senate) with a basis for determining whether or not the nation's law of the sea interests would better be served by signing or ratifying such a treaty, or by seeking other alternatives. It is my purpose in this chapter to identify alternatives to a widely accepted and comprehensive law of the sea treaty and, in view of U.S. policy objectives, which will also be identified, to assess the value of each of these alternatives.

Preliminary Observations

Before identifying alternatives to a law of the sea treaty, three preliminary observations are in order.

1. The Effect of the Negotiations. The law of the sea negotiations and the conference, even though they may fail to produce the desired agreement, will have a profound effect on post-conference thinking and state actions. Throughout the discussions in the United Nations Seabed Committee and the conference, nations have determined their national interests and have expressed those interests by taking positions—either generally or in terms of specific draft treaty articles—on a wide variety of issues. The proposals made, and the reactions to them, have generated a dialogue which has greatly enlightened decision makers throughout the world about the nature of ocean space and its resources. Some nations have taken intransigent positions on issues which have significant domestic political implications and from which regression is not to be expected in the post-conference world. Still other nations have made clear their expectations about how others should behave in their use of ocean space and the exploitation of ocean resources. The consequences of deviation from those expectations have in some cases been made explicit. Thus, the failure of the conference will not mean time and effort have been totally wasted, but will provide the background from which future actions will emanate and, more important for the present, will give significant insights into the alternatives to a law of the sea treaty that will be viable in the future.

2. Forms of Nonagreement. As mentioned above, the desideratum of the diplomats negotiating law of the sea issues at present is an agreement that is both comprehensive (encompassing all of the major agenda items), and widely accepted (not

---

[4] For a general examination of United States policy toward the ocean and its resources, see A. L. Hollick, "Bureaucrats at Sea," in A. L. Hollick and R. E. Osgood, *New Era of Ocean Politics* (Baltimore, Md.: The Johns Hopkins University Press, 1974), pp. 75-131; H. G. Knight, "United States Oceans Policy: Perspective 1974," *Notre Dame Lawyer,* vol. 49 (December 1973), pp. 241-75.

unacceptable to any significant nation or group of nations). There are, of course, a variety of possible outcomes of the conference which fall short of these objectives. These will be briefly identified, because they have a bearing on the topic of alternatives to a law of the sea treaty. Among the possible "failure scenarios" are the following:

(1) *Total absence of agreement.* It is conceivable that the conference could terminate without producing any agreement on any agenda item. It is also conceivable that the conference could continue as a discussion forum, without reaching agreement, gradually taking second place in importance behind unilateral state action with respect to law of the sea issues.

(2) *Agreement on some but not all issues.* It is possible that the conference might reach agreement on some but not all agenda items. Obviously, those issues not reduced to written agreement would remain to be dealt with in some alternative format.

(3) *Unacceptable agreement.* The conference might produce agreement on some or all issues, but in such a form as to be unacceptable to one or more key nations or groups of nations. In that case, the minority would probably abstain from ratifying the agreement at all, or would ratify it subject to reservations which might gut the agreement of its essential meaning.

(4) *Inadequate agreement.* The conference might also produce an inadequate agreement on some or all issues, either an inarticulate statement of the lowest common denominator, or a vague agreement comparable to some of the provisions of the present Convention on the Territorial Sea and the Contiguous Zone and the Convention on the Continental Shelf.[5]

(5) *Resolution or declaration of principles.* Having failed to produce a treaty, the conference might decide to adopt a resolution or declaration of principles embodying a general consensus about the basic outlines of agreement on some or all of the agenda items.

(6) *Framework agreement.* Finally, the negotiators might agree on a treaty text elaborating the general outline of agreement on the major issues, leaving the vital details to subsequent negotiations or dispute-settlement mechanisms.

Regardless of which one or more of these options actually occurs—and some may occur with respect to some issues but not others—there will be a need for some alternative to the treaty method of developing law of the sea.

3. Ocean Policy Goals. In order to properly assess alternatives to a widely accepted and comprehensive law of the sea treaty, it is necessary to understand the objectives sought by the United States. There are two basic objectives, namely,

---

[5] Examples would include the innocent passage provisions of the Territorial Sea Convention [Article 14(4)], and the seaward extent and boundary delimitation provisions of the Continental Shelf Convention [Articles 1 and 6].

enhancement of world order, and protection of U.S. economic and security interests.

Enhancing world order means securing a stable and predictable regime governing ocean transit and the exploitation of ocean resources. Such a stable and predictable regime would bring about lower costs and reduce the potential for conflict. It also would allow for rational future planning for the oceans, since under stable conditions expectations about future conduct are generally fulfilled.

Of equal if not paramount importance is the protection of U.S. security and economic interests. Security interests include not only physical security from external attack but also protection of coastal and marine interests from impairment by, for example, pollution. Economic interests include primarily the acquisition of living and nonliving resources and of various forms of energy from adjacent waters. However, both security and economic interests extend beyond the coastal waters of the United States (and any economic zone over which it may have jurisdiction) to the protection of U.S. flag vessels (and other undertakings) wherever they may be on the world ocean, and to the preservation of the naval mobility necessary to the implementation of U.S. foreign policy, particularly with respect to nuclear deterrence. Thus it must be understood that protection of national economic and security interests has a global as well as a parochial component.

Alternatives to a Law of the Sea Treaty

It should be noted at the outset that the best method of achieving the policy goals stated above through alternatives to a law of the sea treaty will probably vary from policy area to policy area. An alternative that is deemed optimal with respect to securing supplies of seabed mineral resources, for example, may well be infeasible or too costly if applied to protection of distant-water fishing interests.

The basic practical alternatives to a law of the sea treaty for the United States would appear to be limited to the following:

(1) *Acquiescence in other nations' acts or agreements.* The United States could acquiesce in all unilateral, bilateral, and multilateral regimes established by other nations or groups of nations. It seems relatively certain that nations will proceed, following a conference failure, to protect their own perceived economic and security interests by taking whatever unilateral, bilateral, or multilateral actions they deem necessary. This may take the form of acts, proclamations, or written agreements. Although some of these unilateral actions are easily predictable, others are not so obvious. Among the types of jurisdictional claims that can be expected from certain nations in certain instances are the following: (1) extension of territorial waters to twelve nautical miles or, in some cases, to

136

200 nautical miles; (2) extension of contiguous-zone competence for health, fiscal, sanitary, and immigration matters beyond twelve miles from the coast (but probably not beyond fifty miles); (3) extension of national jurisdiction over all living and nonliving resources to a distance of 200 nautical miles or more from the coast, including assertion of jurisdiction over the physical continental margin where it extends beyond the fixed distance claimed; (4) assertion of historic water claims to areas in which other legal bases for jurisdiction appear inappropriate; (5) assertions by littoral states of authority to regulate passage through straits used for international navigation; (6) arbitrary establishment of straight baselines in order to generate various types of competence over adjacent ocean areas, including the delimitation of baselines by archipelagic nations utilizing the outermost points of their outermost islands; (7) establishment of zones of peace and security in which naval presence or maneuvering would be prohibited; (8) establishment of mandatory sealanes in areas of navigational congestion; and (9) the initiation of mining of deep-seabed minerals by nations possessing the requisite technology and economic commitment.

(2) *Use of force.* The United States could, in order to avoid the adverse effects of acquiescence, use military force to assert U.S. interests where the regimes established by another nation or group of nations conflict with United States ocean policy objectives.

(3) *Negotiation or purchase.* The United States or its citizens could negotiate for or purchase from other nations or groups of nations the authority to conduct certain activities where a regime established by others conflicts with United States policy objectives. This negotiation or purchase could occur at either the governmental or the private level.

4. *Limited international agreement.* The United States could undertake to create bilateral and multilateral arrangements with affected or like-minded nations to protect its security and economic interests. The objectives of entering into such arrangements would be to solve immediate problems such as boundary or fishery conservation matters, and to serve as models or catalysts for the development of new international law.

(5) *Domestic legislation.* Another alternative would be for the United States to enact domestic legislation designed to protect United States security and economic interests and to enforce those rights against other nations that might challenge their validity.

(6) *Unilateral action.* Finally, and as a variant of the preceding alternative, the United States might simply proceed to make whatever uses of the marine environment it feels are in its interest—for example, it might initiate deep-seabed mining—and determine subsequent courses of action in response to the reactions of other nations.

United States Interests Involved in the Law of the Sea

If a proper assessment of these alternatives to a law of the sea treaty is to be made, it is necessary to know specifically what interests the United States has in the ocean.[6] It can, of course, be fairly said that the United States has an interest in every one of the items and subitems on the agenda for the third conference. However, only a few of these are of sufficient economic or security importance to warrant their consideration in an evaluation of alternatives.

These major interests are: (1) fisheries, recognizing the disparate interests of coastal, distant-water, and anadromous species fishermen; (2) hydrocarbons, including both the development of petroleum and natural gas from the U.S. continental shelf and the activities of American companies engaged in similar operations off the coasts of other nations; (3) the mining of deep-seabed minerals; (4) navigation, taking into account the different problems posed by navigation on the high seas, in economic resource zones, through territorial waters, and through and over straits used for international navigation; (5) military uses of the sea, including navigation and the deployment of antisubmarine warfare tracking and detection devices; (6) scientific research off the coasts of other nations; and (7) pollution of the marine environment, including such issues as the establishment of minimum international standards for activities in economic resource zones and the regulation of vessel source pollution.

Assessment of Alternatives to a Law of the Sea Treaty

This section contains discussion of the principal advantages and disadvantages of each option with respect to selected major U.S. interests in the law of the sea. The assessments are given in general terms, space not being sufficient here to discuss in detail each of 432 "boxes" in a three-dimensional matrix formed by six possible conference outcomes, a dozen national interests, and six alternative courses of action.

Acquiescence in Other Nations' Acts or Agreements. With respect to fisheries interests, acquiescence in other nations' unilaterally established 200-mile (or broader) economic resource zones would tend to validate similar claims by the United States and would reinforce the legal basis for our protecting and managing the nation's coastal fisheries through a broad exclusive fisheries zone. It would

---

[6] For a more detailed discussion of United States interests in the ocean, see H. G. Knight, "United States Oceans Policy," pp. 246-73; L. S. Ratiner, "United States Oceans Policy: An Analysis," *Journal of Maritime Law and Commerce,* vol. 2 (January 1971), pp. 225-66; H. G. Knight, "Special Domestic Interests and United States Oceans Policy" in R. G. Wirsing, ed., *International Relations and the Future of Ocean Space* (Columbia, S.C.: University of South Carolina Press, 1974), pp. 10-43; J. A. Knauss, "Factors Influencing a U.S. Position in a Future Law of the Sea Conference," Occasional Paper No. 10, Law of the Sea Institute, University of Rhode Island, April 1971.

not, however, afford protection for anadromous species because there would presumably exist an area of high seas beyond an economic zone in which the rule of freedom of fishing would still obtain. Acquiescence would imply our acceptance of, for example, a Japanese assertion of high seas fishing rights with respect to Pacific salmon beyond the U.S. fishing zone. Distant-water fishing efforts could be seriously impaired by acquiescence in 200-mile economic resource zones. Access to fishing grounds off the coasts of other nations could be denied at the discretion of the coastal state, because there would be no agreement on a system obligating such states to admit foreign fishermen where the allowable catch of a given species was not taken.[7] Although such a possibility bodes ill for U.S. tuna and shrimp fisheries, it seems more likely that access would be permitted upon compliance with rules and regulations imposed by the coastal state and upon payment of license or other fees appropriate to the activity. Thus, though distant-water fishing might become more expensive, it probably would not be prohibited altogether.

There is little contention about coastal states' exclusive jurisdiction over the hydrocarbon resources of their continental shelves, so that acquiescence on this issue would simply constitute a continued validation of the continental shelf doctrine. The only negative impact would appear to be the absence of a "security of investment" treaty provision that might afford to American companies some measure of protection from illegal or uncompensated expropriation with respect to their operations on other nations' continental shelves.

Should the United States acquiesce in an international agreement adopted by the Group of 77,[8] seabed-mining activities would probably be greatly restricted, with a resultant loss of access to the area and loss of the resources and revenues derived therefrom.[9] If, however, there were no such "unacceptable" agreement, and if the resources were simply left in their present *res nullius* status—pursuant to which any nation or individual is free to mine seabed minerals—then acquiescence would maximize the interests of the United States in securing access to the resources, since it is foremost among those possessing the technology requisite for resource development.

---

[7] The United States has, in the law of the sea negotiations, supported the concept of "preferential" fishing rights (also known under the rubric of "full utilization") pursuant to which coastal states would have an obligation to admit foreign fishing effort where allowable catch of a particular species was not taken by domestic fishermen. Most developing coastal nations favor "exclusive" rights, with no obligation to admit distant-water fishermen.

[8] The "Group of 77," which in fact now numbers over 100 members, consists of the *developing* member states of the United Nations.

[9] This is so because proposals at the conference by the Group of 77 and its members make clear their preference that an international authority possess a monopoly right to exploit seabed resources, that access for companies from technologically advanced nations be granted only on an ad hoc negotiated basis, and that price and production controls be imposed on seabed-mining activities (all of which would probably pose economic risks of a sufficiently high order to discourage the flow of investment capital from the United States).

The most serious impact of acquiescence would probably occur in the realm of navigation. It seems likely that developing coastal states will (1) establish regulatory systems which would affect navigation in their 200-mile economic zones, (2) apply the "innocent passage" standard,[10] or an even more restrictive test, to navigation in their narrower territorial waters, and (3) strictly regulate passage through straits used for international navigation. If this is in fact the case, and if the United States should acquiesce in these regimes, a substantial loss of naval mobility would occur, and additional costs might be imposed upon merchant shipping and fishing vessels. Of course these costs would depend upon the degree of restriction imposed by the coastal state.

It is generally assumed, at least with respect to merchant shipping, that because all people (in developing and developed nations alike) have an interest in maintaining an inexpensive and free flow of commodities by sea, developing coastal nations would not use their legal authority or naked power to interfere with that commerce or to impose additional cost burdens on it. The fallacy of this reasoning is set forth in the following excerpt relating to OPEC oil price rises:

> The real enigma is the behavior of the poor countries that have no oil. After all, the tax that OPEC has imposed on all oil-consumers is hideously regressive and the incidence of suffering very different: Indian peasants are paying exactly as much for their oil as Swiss bankers are, and the man who will no longer be able to afford fertilizer and fuel to grow food for his family is suffering far more than the American who can no longer afford to visit Yellowstone in his eight-cylinder car. And yet, leaders of the poor countries have praised OPEC and given it their support at the United Nations. . . .
>
> . . . The truth is that the voices praising OPEC do not belong to the poor but to those who control their lives—narrow, self-appointed ruling groups (elections have become a rarity in Africa and Asia) fond of shiny black cars and numbered Swiss accounts. Westernizing, yet fiercely anti-Western, these dictatorial elites see in OPEC a force that can humiliate the West, and perhaps even destroy its prosperity. Those who eat three ample meals a day in Dacca or Bamako instruct their nephews serving as delegates to the U.N. to applaud when the Kuwaitis say that the price of oil is low and that the recent 500 percent increase was only fair. It is doubtful whether those who are starving because of the shortage of oil-based fertilizer have been asked for their opinions. Their rulers value the license of unfettered sovereignty and anti-Westernism far more than mere food for hungry people.[11]

---

[10] The current definition of "innocent passage," contained in the Territorial Sea Convention, is passage which is "not prejudicial to the peace, good order or security of the coastal state." In addition to being subjective, the absence of any compulsory dispute settlement mechanism applicable to the convention's provisions means that the coastal state is the sole interpreter of the definition.

[11] Miles Ignotus, "Seizing Arab Oil," *Harper's Magazine*, vol. 250, no. 1498 (March 1975), pp. 46-47.

Thus, acquiescence in coastal state regimes cannot be undertaken with any assurance that commercial navigation, and *a fortiori* naval mobility, will not be impaired.

Military interests would obviously be affected by restrictions on navigation in the economic zone, territorial sea, or straits. There would probably also be a cost associated with nonaccess to the continental shelves of other nations for the implantation of antisubmarine warfare devices since United States acquiescence in those continental shelf regimes would dictate acceptance of their demilitarized status for even passive listening devices.[12]

The impact on scientific research would be similar to that on navigation. Restrictions placed by coastal nations on oceanographic research activities could greatly limit the access of scientists to economic zone areas, even with respect to the atmosphere and water column at great distances from the coast. Thus, acquiescence could substantially limit the acquisition of knowledge about the marine environment.

Finally, acquiescence in extended, unilaterally proclaimed coastal state jurisdictional areas would almost ensure the absence of any international minimum standards concerning pollution for the economic zone. Since developing countries will probably be quite lax in establishing environmental regulations, a threat could be posed to preservation of the quality of the ocean. In addition, arbitrary regulations concerning pollution standards could be applied (for reasons unrelated to protection of the marine environment) to vessels navigating in the economic zone, with attendant imposition of costs or limitations on mobility.

Overall, given the probable unilateral and multilateral actions described above, and given U.S. acquiescence in those actions, the impacts would be quite adverse for U.S. interests in almost all cases, coastal fisheries and outer-continental-shelf oil and gas development being the exceptions. It seems fairly clear, then, that acquiescence in unfavorable unilateral and multilateral regimes would not be an acceptable alternative to a law of the sea treaty.

Use of Force. With respect to virtually all of the issues involved, the use of force is a possible method for pursuing U.S. security and economic objectives where those objectives conflict with the unilaterally or multilaterally established regimes of coastal developing nations. Force could, for instance, be used to secure access to 200-mile fishing zones of other nations for distant-water fishermen on the basis that waters beyond twelve miles were subject to high seas freedom of fishing; force could be used to protect deep-seabed mining operations being conducted contrary

---

[12] See the proposal of Mexico and Kenya made at the Caracas session of the Third Conference which provided that "[n]o State shall be entitled to construct, maintain, deploy or operate on or over the continental shelf of another State any military installations or devices or any other installations for whatever purposes without the consent of the coastal State." UN Doc. A/CONF.62/C.2/L.42/Rev.1 (13 August 1974).

to a Group of 77 seabed treaty; or force could be used to protect merchant shipping in economic zones, territorial waters, or straits. But even if the use of force were effective in securing these objectives, its costs would probably be high.

In the first place, the United States would be put in the position of potentially violating the United Nations Charter proscription of the threat or use of force in the conduct of international relations. The resulting effects on bilateral and multilateral relations could be extremely severe. A good argument can be made, however, that the mere positioning of military vessels on the high seas (for example, to protect a seabed mining site) is a legitimate exercise of freedom of the high seas and of the right of self-defense, and that even escorting a merchant vessel through a strait more than six miles wide in the face of opposition by the littoral state would be a legitimate exercise of freedom of the high seas (or, at worst, would constitute legal retortion or reprisal in response to the implied threat of arrest posed by the coastal state). To use military force to protect *all* interests of the United States in the ocean, however, would require a tremendous increase in military appropriations in order to produce the hardware necessary for enforcement.

Thus, without going into detail on an issue-by-issue basis, it is clear that the use of force is an alternative to a law of the sea treaty that could achieve U.S. security and economic objectives but at a cost which would probably be prohibitive if applied across the board. Used on a limited, ad hoc basis, though, and in conjunction with other alternatives, it should be considered a useful and probably effective method of securing certain objectives. The use of force would probably have the least attendant costs and adverse reactions if used to preserve *existing* rights rather than to assert new ones. Thus, to protect deep-seabed mining operations against threats of physical violence, to ensure free navigation beyond a three-mile limit and innocent passage within a three-mile limit, and to guarantee freedom of fishing beyond twelve miles, would seem to be the most appropriate areas for the threat or application of force.

Negotiation or Purchase. The purpose of this alternative is to secure U.S. policy objectives by ad hoc negotiations or "purchase" arrangements. If any U.S. interests can be accommodated by negotiation without imposition of additional costs, this would seem to be an optimal method, short of a comprehensive and widely accepted international agreement, for achieving desired national goals in the law of the sea. However, it must be borne in mind that ad hoc agreements depend upon the good will of the respective governments and that when governments or their attitudes change, the relationships between the nations involved can change. Obviously, where the rights are purchased (either with hard cash or for trade-offs external to law of the sea matters) the price will be stated in the bargain. As in the case of negotiation, changing governments or changing attitudes within governments can cause fluctuations in the price being paid for the particular access or right, and the situation can deteriorate to an unstable or status quo situation following unsatisfied increased payment demands.

Turning to specific interests, if the United States were to negotiate access rights for distant-water fishing interests in other nations' exclusive fishing zones, there would be concomitant pressure on the United States to permit other nations to fish within its economic zone on the same or similar conditions. Depending upon the particular fisheries' stock in question this could be more or less desirable. Perhaps the best use of the negotiation or purchase alternative would be with respect to anadromous species where, for an appropriate trade-off, the Japanese might be persuaded to abstain from high-seas salmon fishing. Again, the cost would have to be examined to determine whether it was in the overall interest of the nation to pursue such a course of action.

With respect to seabed mining, a revenue-sharing provision might constitute a payoff or purchase fee that could ameliorate the concern of the Group of 77 over continued seabed mining by nationals of technologically developed countries. As long as the United States was specifying the amount to be contributed and thus itself controlled any escalation, this would appear to be a viable method of purchasing a conflict-free environment for deep-seabed mining.

Perhaps the most troublesome area would be navigation and military use of the sea. Here, even though rights were purchased, the situation would still be one of constraint as compared to high-seas freedom of navigation. The purchase rights could turn out to be contingent on a friendly government's remaining in power or on maintenance of particular attitudes within a friendly government. This uncertainty could impose costs in the nature of contingency preparations which would be more burdensome than the utilization of preexisting high-seas freedom of navigation. Similar comments would apply to scientific research.

In general, the negotiation and payment for achievement of U.S. security and economic objectives in the oceans appears to afford some opportunities for success, though it would seem desirable wherever possible to control the costs to be paid in order to prevent their escalation in a situation which would be unfavorable for the United States or which would force a withdrawal of the agreement.

Limited International Agreement. This alternative, as noted above, envisions the United States entering into bilateral or limited multilateral agreements, with a view to both settling specific problems and establishing a precedent for the development of international law. For example, limited bilateral agreements could be useful in coastal fisheries management on the same basis as the two-year ad hoc agreements with the Soviet Union, Poland, and other nations in the past. However, such agreements do not really establish viable international precedents except insofar as they are devices to permit management of high-seas fisheries or access to exclusive fishing zones. More appropriate would be an agreement between, for example, all the nations fishing in the North Atlantic Ocean, to the effect that they would mutually agree to grant access to other contracting parties in instances where the particular stock in question was not being fully utilized even though located entirely within one nation's economic zone. This sort of generalized agreement could then be expanded by accession to include other potentially interested nations and could be emulated in other regions of the world. Ultimately, of course, the U.S. policy objective of preferential (as opposed to exclusive) rights for fishing in an economic zone could evolve as a rule of customary international law based on state practice and on the proliferation of these types of limited agreements.

This alternative has its greatest potential in the area of seabed mining. If all countries presently possessing the requisite technology for mining manganese nodules were able to agree on a single treaty text—perhaps as a counter to a treaty adopted by the Group of 77—the treaty would provide a basis from which mining practice could develop. If the treaty facilitated rational development of the resource, other nations might be persuaded to denounce the restrictive treaty and become party to the more functional treaty in order to participate in the revenue sharing and other benefits accruing to parties. Thus a multilateral treaty originally negotiated by a handful of countries could grow over a period of time into a widely accepted system for seabed mining.

As far as navigation, military issues, scientific research, and pollution are concerned, there would seem to be less potential for limited multilateral agreement, though in particular situations this might be a useful method for developing accommodations among several nations with common interests in particular uses of the sea.

In general, it seems extremely likely that many nations will fall back on regional or limited multilateral agreements to solve specific problems as they arise. It does not seem likely that this type of arrangement would be viewed as an effort to create international law, though to the extent that it was, it would appear to afford a very useful alternative to a comprehensive and widely accepted law of the sea treaty.

Domestic Legislation. The United States could seek to protect its interests in certain areas by enacting domestic legislation and taking appropriate unilateral action pursuant thereto where required. Such legislation might be cast in strictly protectionist terms. On the other hand, the legislation could be viewed as a catalyst for the initiation of new rules of customary international law much as the Truman Proclamation of 1945 was the catalyst for the doctrine of the continental shelf.

144

I have elsewhere presented in some detail suggestions about how U.S. domestic legislation might be developed in the areas of fisheries, seabed mining, deep-water ports, and pollution, so as to have this law-creating effect while still protecting basic U.S. economic and security interests.[13] Only a brief summary will be given here.

Insofar as coastal fisheries are concerned, I would suggest that domestic legislation be preceded by findings of the type specified by the International Court of Justice in its decision in the cases of the *United Kingdom* vs. *Iceland* and the *Federal Republic of Germany* vs. *Iceland*[14] for the establishment of a coastal state's preferential right to adjacent fisheries. The bill should also expressly provide for the maintenance of established fishing rights of other nations and should contain criteria similar to those set forth by the court providing a method by which those established rights could be determined. The bill could also contain an obligation on the Department of State or some other responsible agency to negotiate mutually acceptable catch levels where the unregulated exercise of preferential and established rights would exceed the allowable catch. Finally, the bill could implement a management program designed to elicit the optimal amount of biologic, economic, and other relevant data concerning fisheries off the United States coast with a view to developing a rational management system through the negotiating process where established rights are involved, and through domestic implementation where there is no foreign fishing.

The idea in all of this would be to develop a bill which, if emulated by other coastal nations for their 200-mile economic zones, would adequately protect distant-water fishing interests of the United States. It is, of course, uncertain whether such a far-sighted fishing bill would be copied in the same manner as the Truman Proclamation. Nonetheless, there appears to be little to lose, and a great deal to gain, in taking such an approach as an alternative to a law of the sea treaty.

With respect to deep-seabed mining, provision might be made in domestic legislation for recognition of seabed mining licenses issued by other nations pursuant to identical or similar domestic legislation. This would avoid conflicts over access to mineral resources which might be claimed by two or more competing companies licensed by different states, and it would encourage the establishment of a concordant practice on the part of the nations involved that could lead to the development of new customary international law rules on the subject.[15] The legislation might also contain a provision for a registry or depository of claims made pursuant to domestic legislation in order to facilitate dispute settlement and avoid claim jumping and other actions that produce conflict. The legislation could

---

[13] H. G. Knight, "Treaty and Non-Treaty Approaches to Order in the World Ocean."

[14] Fisheries Jurisdiction Cases, 3 I.C.J. 175 (1974).

[15] See, for example, The Scotia, 81 U.S. (14 Wall.) 170 (1871), where the United States Supreme Court found the existence of a rule of customary international law based on concordant practices by maritime nations.

contain a voluntary revenue-sharing provision in order that a specific percentage of revenues obtained from deep-seabed mining be made available for international community purposes. This might avoid a conflict with General Assembly Resolution 2749 which provides that "the exploration of the area and the exploitation of its resources shall be carried out for the benefit of mankind as a whole, irrespective of the geographical location of states, whether landlocked or coastal, and taking into particular consideration the interests and needs of developing countries." Finally, provision could be made in the legislation for U.S. participation in a registry office or more sophisticated form of seabed authority which could arise out of the consultations of those nations actually involved in deep-seabed mining.

In general, it would appear that domestic legislation designed not only to protect U.S. interests but also to serve as a catalyst for the development of new customary international law provides a very desirable alternative to a law of the sea treaty, at least with respect to coastal fisheries and seabed mining, and perhaps with respect to other issues as well.

Unilateral Action. This final alternative differs from the domestic legislative approach only in that the activity undertaken is pursued without reliance on statutory authorization. For example, U.S. citizens or corporations could proceed (as they are doing) to mine the mineral resources of the deep seabed and to allow the applicable law to develop on a claim-response basis over a period of time. Likewise, distant-water fishermen from the United States could impose themselves on fishing zones beyond twelve miles claimed exclusively by other nations (without military escort, which would be a form of the "use of force" alternative), and permit new rules of customary international law to evolve gradually through the ensuing conflicts.

The efficacy of this approach depends largely on the activity undertaken. With respect to distant-water fishing, it seems likely, in view of the holding of the International Court of Justice in the Fisheries Jurisdiction Cases, that existing coastal states' preferential rights beyond twelve miles will, in the not too distant future, be held to be *exclusive* rights. Thus, to force the issue without other action would probably result in a determination adverse to United States distant-water fishing interests.

Similarly, forcing the International Court of Justice or some other third-party decision maker to resolve the issue of the legitimate maximum breadth of the territorial sea would probably result, at present, in a finding that twelve-mile territorial seas were permissible. This would, of course, gravely restrict the options available to U.S. shipping and naval interests that can now operate under the theory that high-seas areas more than three miles from the coast are subject to freedom of navigation and overflight. The impact on straits passage would be quite serious. Thus, to engage in activities leading to independent decision making on the legitimate breadth of the territorial sea, without taking other initiatives, would appear to be counterproductive.

With respect to seabed mining, however, the initiation of activities would appear to be a viable option. It is extremely unlikely that any court would hold the resources of the deep seabed to be subject to a moratorium pending international agreement.[16] Further, the practices established during the conduct of such operations could form the basis of a workable legal regime. Although domestic legislation may be enacted either to guarantee security of tenure to the mine site at the request of the mining companies, or to ensure appropriate fiscal and environmental regulation at the request of interested sectors of the public, the initiation of mining activities under a freedom-of-the-seas and *res nullius* theory would appear to be legally sound and economically beneficial to the United States.

Conclusion

There appear to be a number of alternatives to a law of the sea treaty which, used in concert and where most appropriate on a subject-matter basis, could provide the framework for a reasonably stable regime in the ocean in the absence of a widely accepted and comprehensive law of the sea treaty. In fact, it would appear that U.S. security and economic interests could be sufficiently protected through a combination of domestic legislation, limited treaties, purchase of rights, unilateral action, and the occasional application of force. This being the case, a strong argument can be made that the United States should not sign or ratify any law of the sea treaty unless the agreement optimizes most of its major policy interests and promises demonstrable beneficial effects on international relations which will inure to the benefit of this nation.

---

[16] Some have urged that resolution 2749, because it declares that the resources of the deep seabed are to be exploited only pursuant to an international agreement to be reached, constitutes a de facto moratorium on all seabed mining activities. This position is unsound because (1) General Assembly resolutions are not binding legal obligations but constitute only indications of nations' general expectations, and (2) resolution 2749 was a compromise agreed to by many nations only to facilitate the progress of the law of the sea negotiations.

COMMENTARY

Northcutt Ely

In the limited time available, I shall take up first what I regard as the most imminent problem that the United States and our negotiators face. On returning to the negotiations at Geneva, they will discover that there is a time bomb ticking away in the American 1970 treaty proposal, which is still on the table. This is a proposal for the international regime. In 1970, you will recall, the American delegation proposed at the Geneva session a comprehensive treaty which included provisions for mineral resources on the continental margin and the deep seabed, fisheries, and navigation; but its novel and outstanding contribution, which troubles me greatly, was its proposal for the international regime, the International Seabed Resource Authority.

If our offer is accepted, this authority will consist of a council of 24 representatives of 24 states, an assembly of representatives of all of the signatories (150 perhaps), a secretariat, three administrative commissions, and a tribunal. This top-heavy structure, which I have called, perhaps unkindly, a "floating Chinese pagoda," is supposed to do what?

It is a floating OPEC which is designed to police the extraction of mineral resources beyond the limits of national jurisdiction. And what is the business it is to transact? At present, zero; ten years from now, perhaps three or four mining ventures; fifteen years from now, perhaps another half-dozen; twenty-five years from now, perhaps hydrocarbon ventures beyond the continental margin.

This, to me, is an appalling prospect. I believe Parkinson's law operates internationally, and I do not believe that if you create this supergovernment and let it float around out there, these bureaucrats are forever going to be deprived of the bureaucrat's natural nourishment—papers to shuffle. Business will be generated; it will not be restricted to the deep seabed, because there is no business there. There is no demand for international lawyers bubbling up out of the deep. Instead, this business will be the control of navigation and of many other items that we do not want to vest in any international government. If we do not like the legislation—and it is legislation that comes out of this legislative body of politicians—we hail into the tribunal.

Now it is difficult to see what the docket of the tribunal is going to be. Where are the deep-seabed controversies that justify keeping an international supreme court supplied with desks, clerks, chambers, and limousines, indefinitely? But there are plenty of other international disputes that can be hailed there by a slight misinterpretation, we would call it, of this charter. I do not believe we are going to stay out of the fly paper of that tribunal any more than we stay out of the fly paper of this international legislature.

Do not create this creature. Why is it in the American international interest to interpose this new obstacle to free access by American consumers to the remaining resources of the world that are not now locked up by governments hostile to the interests of our consumers?

Here in the deep seabed are copper, nickel, cobalt, manganese—items all on the critical list for importation into the United States, which we will greatly need, and which now are there under the existing law of nations for us to take and use, as they are for others.

Free access, to me the common heritage of mankind, is a continuing right of free and nondiscriminatory access, free of price control, free of production control, free of restraints of accommodation and restraint of trade. We are getting exactly the reverse of that if we create this hostile supergovernment. Do not do it. On day one of the resumption of the negotiations, say, "I am very sorry. We neglected to withdraw this 1970 treaty from the table. We are withdrawing it now." Bear in mind that this treaty contained, among its other proposals, the notion that the coastal states, including the United States, would relinquish all rights seaward to the 200-meter isobath, and would take back a trusteeship of the mineral resources between the 200-meter isobath and the edge of the continental margin, to be administered under the treaty and under that law alone. This draft stipulated that the coastal state should have no greater right within the trusteeship zone (the continental margin) than any other state, except to the extent that was conferred by this treaty. In other words, we renounced whatever sovereign rights we might have claimed to the continental margin.

Now let me pause here a minute and say that under existing international law, it is perfectly clear that the coastal state's exclusive jurisdiction over seabed minerals extends to, but is limited by, the continental margin (the prolongation of its land territories) under both customary law and under the Convention on the Continental Shelf. No state claims a right to turn the Pacific Ocean into a national lake. Mexico does not claim the right to go 1,000 miles to sea, going around the French (Iller Tipperton) Islands to get at Mr. Greenwald's manganese nodules out there.[1] This argument is conjured up to justify an international regime that is totally contrary to American interests, so let us not fall for it. On day one, pull that piece of paper back and say, "Sorry fellows, we neglected to cancel this earlier."

---

[1] Editors' footnote: Richard Greenwald, who was attending the conference, is general counsel for Deep Sea Ventures, Inc., one of the more technologically advanced firms interested in ocean mining.

Why do we do this? Why do we offer to create this international regime? It is argued that the offer is part of a great international bargain by which we shall achieve certain other national interests. What are they? One relates to navigation, military and commercial, commonly called "free transit through the straits." Under existing international law, as our nation recognizes it, the three-mile line marks the limit of the territorial sea. If we don't sign a new treaty that records our acquiescence in a twelve-mile zone, we are not bound by it. In the Straits of Gibraltar, to take one horrible example, with a postage stamp of Spanish territory on the African side and Spain on the European side, it is said that Spain could prevent the free transit of our submerged submarines, could interpose restrictions on tankers coming out of the Mediterranean, and could effectively block the Straits of Gibraltar. To dispose of this argument in one word: "nonsense." Does anybody think that Spain is going to drop depth charges on submerged submarines of the United States and of Soviet Russia going through the Straits of Gibraltar? This is a most outrageous proposition—and we create the problem for ourselves.

What would we gain by acquiescing in a 12-mile zone or for that matter, in a 200-mile economic zone? If we don't acquiesce in a 12-mile zone, why do we pay any price at all to get it modified? We could easily keep the 3-mile zone we have. If there is pressure on us to acquiesce in a 12-mile zone, we can say, "All right, what will you give us in return? Free overflight? Free transit through straits? If you won't, sorry fellows, your conference ended yesterday."

I am not saying that it is wrong to reach a reasonable compromise, but what we are being offered is not any reasonable compromise. Look at the resolution of the Group of 77 on the type of deep-sea regime they want—control of production, control of prices, a new barrier to our access to these resources.

As to fisheries, I do not purport to know very much, but I can say that I am as confused by the present American offer, which came out of Caracas, as I was by the 1970 offer. I do not know what this offer means. Does the present American proposal mean that New England fishermen can kick out and keep out the Russian deep-sea fleet? Does it mean that our tuna fleet can or cannot fish within the 200-mile zone off Latin American countries? I am not going to argue these points. What I do say is: do not let this time bomb, the international regime, tick any more. Get rid of it. As the American Bar Association wisely said in the House of Delegates Resolution in 1968, "We do not need supergovernment in the deep sea. We need agreements on self-restraint that we will not harm our neighbors; they shall not harm us. We will not poach; they will not poach. We will abide as good neighbors under ordinary norms of conduct."

My neighbors and I can agree that our children can cross each other's gardens to get to school. But we observe self-imposed restraints. We are not going to trample each other's flowers—and we do not have to bring a policeman into the spare bedroom to make sure of that. Don't create an international police force to do a job that does not exist.

Kenneth W. Dam

As a commentator, I am in a difficult position this afternoon because I have nothing particularly critical to say about the two papers on which I am to comment. I shall, however, have some comments on the general perspectives of those papers, and I shall also have some comments on the perspectives taken in the papers delivered this morning.

I am convinced, as a result of the discussion today, that it is the consensus of this meeting that no agreement at all would be preferable to the worst-case agreement that might come out of the law of the sea conference. I also believe that it is generally accepted here today, though this is obviously more controversial, that no agreement would be preferable to what the United States initially proposed.

One can conceive of a feasible, partial agreement that would be preferable to no agreement. It obviously would be desirable to have an agreement on the protection of freedom of navigation through straits. It would be desirable to negotiate access for our distant-water fisheries, and so forth.

What I miss in the papers is any road map of how we get from where we are now to where we want to be. But that is not a criticism of the papers. The speakers were not asked to provide such a road map. What they were asked to do, they did very well. On the other hand, how the United States should proceed now is the most important question, particularly for those who are convinced by the direction of the papers that we have read and listened to.

We can identify two primary, overall perspectives, particularly in the papers given this morning. One was the perspective of the U.S. national interest. Willett and Johnson gave us a convincing explanation of what the U.S. economic national interest is. Professor Nye's points on the political side were well taken, and I shall mention the political dimensions later.

A second perspective was provided more by the commentators than in the papers. This second perspective has to do with what would be a desirable solution for the world, viewing the world as a polity. This world perspective, as opposed to a U.S. national-interest perspective, seemed to be implicit in the thrust of many of the comments about the distribution of income. A variation on this second perspective was to be found in the discussion of what the true interests of many less-developed countries are with respect to having low prices for the resources they buy.

A third perspective is worth considering. It is not, however, an alternative to either of the two perspectives just described and can be discussed under either heading. This third perspective has to do with the question of the importance of the international law aspects of the issues we have been discussing.

I am driven to look at this third perspective by the realization that if, instead of being at the American Enterprise Institute, I were at the American Society of International Law, law of the sea questions would be discussed in extraordinarily different terms.

In our discussions here at the American Enterprise Institute there has been a certain tendency to dismiss the question of whether order and stability, if achievable, would be of importance. There has been a tendency to caricature the proponents of order and stability by saying, "They're predicting anarchy if the conference fails." Anarchy will not result from a failure of the conference.

One reason that economists ignore what I shall call the international law viewpoint is that it is very hard to quantify the values of order and stability. But order and stability are important. After all, even though it cannot be shown, particularly ex post, to have been rational for the parties involved, we have had a number of wars recently; we certainly have experienced a good deal of terrorism. I would assume that wars and terrorism are bad, if for no other reason than that they reduce the gross national product.

Moreover, there is the question of what value, if any, existing international law would have in protecting existing rights if the conference were to fail and, particularly, if it were to fail in the wrong way. It may be that the situation would be much worse following an inconclusive conference than it was to start with. My conclusion is simply that any overall evaluation of either the U.S. national interest or the world's interest would have to take greater account of the values of order and stability than we have taken here. On the other hand, I readily concede that in some quarters those values have been taken entirely too seriously.

Most of my comments will be addressed to a somewhat different question, and that question is suggested by Ann Hollick's earlier inquiry: can the United States as a government ever agree on what its national interest is? I should like to view the law of the sea negotiations as a problem of U.S. public policy formation. The procedural aspects of public policy are extremely important and too often overlooked. Let us find out how we arrived *here,* before we worry about how we are going to get *there.* In other words, let us ask how U.S. policy was formed.

The foundations of U.S. policy were formed in the National Security Council procedure that led to the 1970 presidential decision. The most important actors were the Navy and the Department of State. The Navy's interest is quite clear, and I do not propose to describe it, because I have little time. It has been adequately described by others.

The Department of State might have many interests, and certainly, the regional bureaus would look at the issues from a perspective different from that of the Economic Bureau. However, the issue was captured by the Legal Advisor's Office, and in that office it was in the hands of a man who had a strong commitment to public international law, to order and stability, and who devoted more time to that issue than any legal advisor, I suspect, has ever devoted to any single issue in the past. The values of order and stability were very well represented.

The Interior Department was a participant, largely on behalf of petroleum interests and to a certain extent on behalf of hard mineral interests. Also, the Department of Commerce became involved with respect to fisheries. But the economic issues that we have been discussing, it is fair to say, did not play any significant role in the formation of the U.S. policy.

The people who were at that time involved on behalf of the four departments that I have mentioned will undoubtedly deny that assertion. They will say, "Well, after all, Interior and Commerce were there. They were the ones that were interested in economics."

I do not think that hypothetical response is correct, because Interior and Commerce were not interested in the economic questions that we have been talking about today. That response reflects an advocacy attitude toward public policy formation that I understand, but that, on the whole, I deplore.

Let us look at what some of the economic policy issues were. One was the question of how we should spend a stream of income that will amount to—according to estimates for 1985—$2 billion to $5 billion per year. We have had a great deal of discussion today as to whether $2 billion is a large or small figure, but it certainly would have been considered substantial by what was then the Bureau of the Budget (now the Office of Management and Budget), but they were not involved in an active way.

One way of looking at the question whether $2 to $5 billion is a large or small sum of money is to ask the following question: If one assumes that the reason that the United States is offering revenue sharing is to ensure freedom of navigation for the U.S. Navy, how much would the U.S. Navy be willing to pay for the piece of paper that they hope to get out of the conference? Would they be willing, for example, to give up the Trident program? Would that piece of paper contribute more to U.S. national security than the Trident program? The dollar sums are reasonably similar. Would the Navy be willing to give up two to five Polaris submarines a year, and for how many years? Such questions give us a way of looking at the question of whether the sum is large or small.

Revenue sharing might, of course, be a way of giving aid, and one would have to take that possibility into account. The analysis would quickly become very complex. These questions give us more of a feel for what is involved than

154

either the absolute dollar figures or a comparison with the gross national product of the United States.

The revenue-sharing proposal and, to a large extent, the seabed proposal were tax measures, but the Treasury was not significantly involved in 1970. Moreover, the U.S. proposals raised fundamental issues about the allocation of economic resources, yet the Council of Economic Advisers was not significantly involved. One cannot fairly blame the Navy and the State Department. It was the myopia of the officials involved in economic policy at that time that led to their failure to participate.

But I can say that, after the 1970 decision and the creation of the Law of the Sea Task Force within the U.S. government, it became very difficult, even when economic policy officials perceived the importance of the issues, for them to be able to participate. By that time a technocratic group—and I do not use that term in a pejorative sense—was in charge of policy. That group had everything to lose bureaucratically and nothing to gain by expanding the group of players. And I believe that that is to some extent still the situation, although I am not close to the internal U.S. government discussions.

Given that bureaucratic situation, what can one say about the direction in which we should move now or about the probable outcome of the negotiations? Since the Navy treats its position in the negotiations as a free good for which it does not have to pay, it naturally is acting very much like a veto group. If it had to pay in some way for its position, it might change its posture somewhat. One can go on to analyze the other positions in the same way, including those of the economic policy makers, who are surely not sufficiently sensitive to the possible political costs of changing positions at this point.

I find it difficult to answer Ann Hollick's question—whether the United States can ever agree on what its interest is. Even if agreement is possible, the U.S. government would encounter some difficulties in carrying out whatever negotiating policy its agreement on national interest might imply.

To begin with, it seems to be a basic premise of international negotiations that it is impossible for the U.S. government to develop a fallback position, unless it wants to fall back to it before it arrives at the conference. Even the SALT negotiation fallback position was published in the *New York Times* shortly after it was arrived at, and in the law of the sea situation, with so much domestic consultation necessarily involved, it is impossible to come to the conference with an agreed fallback position. The U.S. negotiators have to go into the conference proclaiming essentially what it is that they have agreed they want to come out of the conference with. In any event, they certainly cannot have a Machiavellian position—such as, an intention of causing the conference to fail.

Coupled with those negotiating limitations, there is the natural tendency, whenever negotiations become very sticky, for people to fear failure itself as

155

somehow compromising their diplomatic manhood. I therefore predict that we shall have an agreement. I predict that it will not be optimal from the point of view of any of the U.S. agencies involved. It will not even be optimal from the standpoint of any agreement that we might hypothetically reach on what the U.S. national interest is.

My concluding observation is that we ought to think about these kinds of policy-formation problems before we move into this kind of international arena in the future, especially with respect to any future problem that raises, as do these negotiations, all of the fundamental interests of the entire U.S. government—its military interests, its diplomatic interests, and its economic interests.

Myres S. McDougal

I might say that I am at some disadvantage here. I do not enjoy these occasions unless I can attack. Unhappily, I find myself in almost complete agreement with our two principal speakers in their conclusions that the conference is likely to fail and that no agreement is better than a bad agreement.

Maybe Professor Dam is correct in saying that we should not announce a deliberate policy of trying to scuttle the conference. We might, however, let nature take its course without raising too much of a hand.

I think I profited by all of the papers by our economist friends. However, I think that our economists abstract much too much from context. Many of the values at stake in these problems cannot be quantified. Economists make the mistake, as systems people more generally do, of trying to work with too few variables and too few values. If they can make so few variables work, God bless them, but I am in the paradoxical situation of liking some of their conclusions except on straits, while wishing to give better reasons for such conclusions.

With respect to Professor Hollick's paper, I do not think that she or any of the other speakers or commentators—except perhaps Professor Dam—emphasized enough the inclusive interest that the United States shares with all other states in the aggregate production of values from the oceans. It is not merely wealth, but all values, and a multiplier effect with respect to all values, which is at stake in the exploitation of the oceans. This aggregate at stake is what is known as the common interest, and what I am sure our friend Dr. Pardo meant when he first spoke of "the common heritage of mankind." Unfortunately, Dr. Pardo's nice label has been utterly perverted and, by "double-speak," converted into its exact opposite. It has become a fraud used to justify the extension of the most monopolistic and destructive claims that the world has ever observed.

I disagree with Professor Knight only on one minor point. I think that when he suggests that the United Nations Charter might preclude us from using force in defense of our rights, he misreads the charter. The later reference to defensive rights may qualify the first proposition. I see nothing in the charter to preclude our use of force, if this appears to be advisable, to protect our existing rights.

The most useful contribution that I can make in the brief time that our selfish chairman will allow me is, hence, to try to put this problem in its broader context.

Very little has been said here today about differentiating between kinds of resources. What we have in the oceans is a great reservoir of potential values—what historically has been regarded as a sharable resource of the highest degree. The economists, if they would make their fullest contribution to policy, should be developing the notion of what they sometimes call a multiplier effect. With a few simple rules of the road, this great sharable resource of the oceans can be used by many people, with many initiatives, with many skills, for the almost infinite production of new values for all the peoples of the world.

One of the papers—I believe it was the Johnson paper—emphasized the global benefits to be obtained from shared use. The land masses are less sharable, though even these are organized in a global economy. In recent days, I have been working a little upon the law of the environment—international environmental problems. I began teaching as a land lawyer, working with drainage basins within our own country, and was struck with the interdependencies within a single drainage basin. Morris Llewellyn Corke called these the physical and utilization unities. You cannot do anything in a single drainage basin that does not affect everything else done in that basin. It has occurred to many observers that this same interdependence is true of the whole globe.

One cannot realistically talk of the law of the sea, or of the law of the oceans, apart from the law of the land masses. Eighty-five percent of ocean pollution comes from the land masses. The atmosphere that is over Tokyo today will be over New York thirty days from now. The whole globe, in a broad sense that we cannot ignore, is, in terms of interdependencies, one great sharable resource.

Though we may not have to negotiate about all of the problems, about all of our interdependencies at any one time—our economists have something to say about what is convenient to negotiate at any given moment—we cannot neglect any of these problems in the long run, if we are to continue to serve our own exclusive interests or this broader inclusive interest that we share with other states. Hence, I would begin, if I had the time, by spelling out in detail these global interdependencies, of which the oceans are only a part.

The next thing to observe would be these arrogant new claims to exclusive control over the great sharable resources of the oceans. We are confronted by a megalomania of unilateral claims of special interest. I have been doing a history of the rise and fall of inclusive and exclusive claims to resources over a very long period of time, and have found that these claims come and go in cycles. We would now appear to be in a phase of claims as nationalistic and arrogant as history has ever known. These claims are coming at a time when the resources of the oceans are being despoiled, when they are being exhausted, and when some of the truths that we accepted in the past are disappearing.

Grotius based his plea for freedom of access for this multiplier effect on the grounds that the resource could not be occupied or exhausted. On the contrary, we have learned that it can be occupied, and it can be exhausted, but the multiplier effect is still achievable. The oceans are still sharable, and shared use is even more indispensable for common security interests than ever before. This is the fundamental point that many of the statesmen of the new countries do not see.

Let us now turn to the legal process that responds to all of these claims, both inclusive and exclusive, about the uses of the oceans and associated resources. International law is a far more complicated process than has appeared in our discussion here so far. Professor McKean said it would be a sad state of affairs if we had fifty separate sovereignties in the United States, and had to negotiate about every value and every resource all the time. The suggestion was that we do not have on a global scale anything comparable to the U.S. Constitution. Well, the fact is that we do.

No constitution of any importance is written. The British have a constitution, even though it is not written. We do have a global constitutive process, by which law is made and applied in very much the same way that it is made in any mature national community. Most of the law that is made in the global context is made in processes of cooperation, by people acting together for shared interests. The sanction derives from their perceptions of common interests and of what has to be done to preserve their common interests.

Law always has had some potential coercive force behind it. Law requires not only expectations of authority but also expectations of control. Both sets of expectations are created by informed, customary interaction. If I had time, I would go into greater detail on this process; it offers much more hope than has been suggested here today.

We will not have anarchy if this sea conference breaks up in confusion. We will still have perceptions of common interest, potentialities for reciprocity and retaliation, and a tremendous amount of cooperation on the global scale. The United States, Russia, and Western Europe have enough control to put effective power behind the expectations of shared enjoyment if they have any will to do so.

From this identification of the problem let us turn next to the basic policies at stake. All law serves the function of protecting, clarifying, and securing the common interests of the people who have effective power in a community. Hence, we cannot in the long run make and secure any claims that we cannot relate to the common interest of the other peoples of the world. Some people are now making claims that they cannot relate to the common interest. Eventually they are

158

bound to be defeated, and to have to resort to naked power. If naked power is resorted to, as Professor Hollick suggests, we are in a relatively good position.

No state has any monopoly of independence, any great complete freedom of choice today. But we, like other states, have our own exclusive interests to protect. These interests begin with our internal security, freedom from military attack. In addition, we have our own exclusive economic interests—the expansion of our own economy, the free functioning of our own society, the protection of every basic value we seek. These are our own unique exclusive interests, but every state has comparable interests.

Beyond this, however, there is an inclusive global interest that is not emphasized in any of these papers. Every state in the world has these same unique exclusive interests. All states also have a shared interest in using the great sharable resource constituted by the oceans and all the associated resources for the greatest production and widest sharing of all values—not simply wealth, but security, health, enlightenment, communication, and so on. The first concern must be the creation of the largest possible aggregate of values for all to share. The oceans have been used to promote every value that man demands. All these values must be fed into your computer, if you are to try to quantify costs and benefits.

If we look to past trends in the pursuit of these basic policies, both Professor Knight and Professor Dam have rightly emphasized that for 200 years we have had a pretty good international law of the sea. It has sought to protect freedom of access for all by giving everyone who can acquire the technological capabilities and skills the right to catch fish, move ships, fly, communicate by cables, and so forth. The details of this William Burke and I spelled out in the first chapter of our book, *The Public Order of the Oceans*. This freedom has redounded to the benefit of every human being on the globe. Our economists rightly stress this global net production. The law of the sea has worked very well without any great central organization and with only a few simple rules of the road. Unhappily, in modern times we have never before had quite the breakdown of this process or the failure to understand it that we have today.

Let us examine the factors that have conditioned the success of the law of the sea. I think we owe its successes not simply to the fact that Britannia once ruled the waves or had a lot of effective power, but to a broad perception of common interests that the peoples of the world have shared. This, as we have already observed, is the most fundamental sanction for law in any community.

When people fail to perceive a common interest and take to violence, law breaks up. Why have we failed on the law of the sea? Why have we met with all these exaggerated demands from special interests? Our failure is, I think, a failure in intelligence, a failure in understanding, a failure in communication. I do not think our government has adequately prepared for these conferences.

159

I do not think our scholars have written the books they should have been writing for the last twenty-five years.

If we had properly clarified our own position here, and the stake of all people in shared enjoyment, we might not be in as bad a situation as that in which we find ourselves. On a deeper level, the difficulties go back to the fight between totalitarian and nontotalitarian conceptions of public order. They reflect also on the growing struggle between the north and the south. Some people are hungry and some are overfed. These are some of the conditions under which we will have to operate in the future.

If we look toward the future, we can see two different kinds of constructs. The more pessimistic is that the demands of special interests will grow and accumulate and accelerate. Dr. Pardo was just saying to me that there was no assurance that our own government, our own country, would not be making extravagant demands for vast territorial waters or thousands of miles of the seabed. And, of course, when I read some of the bills introduced into the Congress I have to agree with him. There is no assurance that even our own people, our own senators, will sufficiently understand the conditions under which the peoples of the world can continue to achieve this long-term aggregate common interest. The claims of special interests are claims against the community: "I want this no matter what happens to others."

The more optimistic construct is that people will again begin to perceive their common interest in preserving the goose that lays the golden egg, in obtaining the multiplier effect in the enjoyment of the oceans, in acting to take into account all the interdependencies that affect the global environment and production from the oceans and the land masses. You see, even the economy on the land masses is dependent on the economy of the oceans, the air space, and other resources. Our best hope is that we will perceive this, that we will make our own demands in accord with this interest, and that we will be able to persuade others to act similarly.

We come now to the final question, what are the alternatives before us? I think the two principal speakers have explored these with admirable comprehensiveness and clarity. The sum of what they advise is, if you cannot do anything that moves you in the direction of your long-term common interests with other peoples, then do nothing. This is a model of action that most of us follow in our private lives: if we do not see a rational course of action, then we refrain from action.

I think the most urgent task upon us is to increase our own understanding of these problems and to communicate this understanding to others. These new countries cannot themselves gain in the long run by new assertions of monopoly. It is just fantastic that they propose by 200- or 500-mile claims to cut off scientific research; they lack even the technology for ordinary enjoyment of the areas they are demanding.

160

One of my friends has written a paper to show that the states cannot possibly make effective these monopoly claims. If we can bring them to see this, that they've got more to gain in the long run, as some of the economists' papers here point out, by cooperative action and shared enjoyment which produce this multiplier effect, maybe we can serve the aggregate common interest.

Others of my friends propose, as has been suggested here, that the United States adopt a model statute, which could be copied by other states, that would express something of this conception of common interest and the modalities by which it can be secured on the whole range of problems, from access to resource exploitation and control.

I think this proposal has something to commend it. The principal point I would emphasize is that those of you who have social science skills and economic skills can contribute much to the people, lawyers and others, who do have to make policy on these problems. You should ask what you can contribute to this multiplier notion; what are all the values at stake here, and how can they be preserved? I have just seen a paper on ocean problems by Professor Richard Cooper of Yale, which is a superb contribution to the sort of thing that I am talking about.

You should not, however, try to incorporate all the tasks and skills of other specialists. Government is a very complicated thing. It does require, as Professor Nye was saying, a great many different functions and kinds of understanding. Information has to guide rational decision making. People have to take the initiative and promote activities. There has to be some procedure for declaring what the authoritative community policy is.

All kinds of procedures are necessary for the invocation of this policy and for its application in particular instances. The market notion may bring clarity to many of these steps, but there have to be highly institutionalized structures to perform these different tasks. The market alone is hopelessly inadequate. The market alone cannot perform the intelligence function. There are so many externalities here that you cannot possibly internalize them all without more complicated (political) structures. This does not mean that I am not in agreement with many of your specific proposals. I think I share Mr. Ely's aversion to an international organization that would monopolize the deep seabed. It is not necessary to have that kind of structure, but it is necessary to have more than some of you implied in your papers.

Arvid Pardo

I find myself in some difficulty because I largely agree with both papers presented. However, I shall comment briefly on Professor Gary Knight's excellent paper.

Some of the points made in this paper may be a little optimistic. For instance, Professor Knight may be overly optimistic in hoping that ultimately the U.S.

policy objective of preferential rights for fishing in the exclusive economic zone could evolve because it appears more likely that in the long run the United States will accept the concept of exclusive rights rather than that of preferential rights.

I agree that stability of expectations should be the basic goal of ocean policy. I would only comment that a legal regime must be viable in order to be stable; to be viable, a regime must take into account the implications of technological advance and must be accepted as equitable by the great majority of states.

The stated goal of the law of the sea conference, as expressed in United Nations General Assembly Resolution 3067 (XXVIII), is to adopt a treaty dealing with all matters relating to the law of the sea, bearing in mind that the problems of ocean space are closely interrelated and need to be considered as a whole. I agree with Professor Knight in believing that this official goal will not be achieved unless present trends are drastically reversed. It is unrealistic to expect a comprehensive treaty dealing with all matters related to the law of the sea, not only because of time constraints for the conclusion of a treaty or because of the characteristics of the negotiating process but also because of the narrowly sectoral approach of states to law of the sea questions.

I agree that all the alternatives to a law of the sea treaty mentioned in Professor Knight's paper are possible. There is also the possibility that there may be a combination of outcomes; thus, we could envisage the conference adopting a resolution or declaration of principles together with a treaty covering some issues.

It may be useful in this connection to bear in mind the true purpose of the law of the sea conference as distinguished from its stated purpose. I believe that, at least for the majority of the conference, that is, for coastal states, the true purpose of the conference is to achieve international recognition of perceived national interests in the seas without much regard either to international equity, to the maintenance of international order, or to the long-term viability of the treaty. Within this framework, which reflects rather closely the great majority of the proposals made by states at Caracas, we may expect international recognition of a vast expansion of coastal state jurisdiction over ocean space. This will take place both directly and indirectly: directly through the adoption of some version of the archipelago concept, through the adoption of the concept of a 200-nautical mile exclusive economic zone under comprehensive coastal state control, and through redefinition of the continental shelf concept to include at least the continental margin.

Expansion of coastal state jurisdiction will take place indirectly through the adoption of very imprecise criteria for drawing straight baselines, through the adoption of an imprecise definition of the continental margin, and through the adoption of articles recognizing coastal state interests—perhaps even jurisdiction—for certain purposes beyond both an imprecisely defined continental margin and the 200-nautical-mile exclusive economic zone.

Perhaps this outcome may not be very satisfactory. In any event, it is necessary to make two fundamental points with regard to present events in the oceans. First, traditional law of the sea is moribund, whatever the outcome of the present conference. Hence it is unrealistic to suggest that free access to ocean resources will continue to be recognized for much longer. Free access will be replaced by regulated access; the choice will be between regulated access under national sovereignty or comprehensive jurisdiction to all ocean resources, or regulated access under national sovereignty to some ocean resources and under an international regime to other ocean resources.

Second, the oceans are perceived by all countries as increasingly vital to national interests. Conflicts relating to the oceans, their uses and their resources, will consequently become more difficult to solve because the interests at stake will be greater. Since it is virtually certain that there will not be a comprehensive and equitable treaty, we may expect the conference to be followed by a period of instability marked by frequent unilateral actions by states. States, however, will find it advantageous to coordinate their claims and actions in the seas, and this could lead to the growth of regional regimes for the seas largely replacing traditional law of the sea. This process will be imperfectly and unsatisfactorily coordinated through existing international organizations, such as the Intergovernmental Maritime Consultative Organization and Intergovernmental Oceanographic Commission and perhaps the future seabed authority.

I agree, in general, with Professor Knight's discussion of the principal advantages and disadvantages of the policy options he examined. However, I wonder whether all the options he mentions are real options. On what legal basis, for example, could the United States contemplate using force? Could force be legally used, for instance, if a state, taking advantage of the straight-baseline provisions of the 1958 Territorial Sea Convention and of the even more vague provisions of the future treaty, closes an international strait by changing its baselines? International straits connect two parts of the high seas or one part of the high seas and the territorial sea of a state; now, however, through the exercise of its rights under international law, a state converts a body of water that was previously territorial sea or high seas into internal waters over which it is well established that a state has unrestricted sovereignty.

Fisheries are another example. On what basis could the use of force be justified to prevent states from exercising exclusive jurisdiction over fishery resources in a wide zone adjacent to their territorial sea, when in all probability the United States itself will adopt legislation asserting similar claims?

The question of the continental shelf is yet another example. As we all know, the outer limit of the legal continental shelf under the 1958 treaty is highly controversial; in recent years states have tended to give increasingly expansive unilateral interpretations to the ambiguous definition of the continental shelf

163

contained in Article I of the 1958 convention; furthermore the United States in the Outer Continental Shelf Act established no clear limit to its own continental shelf. In these circumstances it is difficult to see on what basis the United States could threaten the use of force if some coastal state decided to claim that its legal continental shelf extended far into the sea, perhaps 600 miles or more, in order to claim sovereign rights to manganese nodule deposits.

In short, in the present vague state of the law of the sea, the use of force hardly seems a realistic option.

Other options mentioned by Professor Knight are: (1) acquiescence in other nations' acts, (2) negotiation or purchase, (3) limited international agreement, and (4) domestic legislation. These are all realistic options, but they all also have serious drawbacks. Acquiescence to other nations' acts could have serious adverse impact on some U.S. interests, as Professor Knight has noted. Negotiation or purchase is certainly a viable method of securing some U.S. policy objectives for limited periods of time, but, as Professor Knight notes, political situations can change and negotiated prices can increase.

Limited international agreements, either bilateral or multilateral, deserve serious consideration and could be useful both to settle specific problems, for instance in the area of fisheries, and to assist in the further development of international law—but in areas where the security of states is directly involved they are likely to be less useful. Also—I am only repeating in slightly different words what Professor Knight has written—limited agreements concluded by the United States could be a factor in accelerating the conclusion by other nations of regional or limited multilateral agreements. This could rapidly lead to the final disappearance of a universally recognized law of the sea.

Domestic legislation, either cast in protectionist terms or designed as a catalyst for the initiation of new rules of customary international law, is the last policy option mentioned by Professor Knight as a possible alternative to the conclusion of a comprehensive law of the sea treaty. Bearing in mind competing internal pressures, the legislative and political processes in this country, and precedents going back to the Truman Declaration, I must admit that I am a little skeptical of the possibility that legislation on significant matters can be adopted which could serve as a catalyst for the initiation of new universal rules of customary international law. It is more probable, in my view, that any domestic legislation adopted would either reflect a narrowly protectionist attitude or would be designed primarily to protect the interests of industrialized coastal states. Such legislation could be a source of conflict.

In conclusion, it does not appear that any of the alternatives to a law of the sea treaty enumerated by Professor Knight is entirely satisfactory. Used wisely and in combination, however, they would appear to provide not "a framework for a reasonably stable regime in the oceans," but a reasonable opportunity to protect important American interests in ocean space over the medium term, at the cost, however, of the disappearance of a universally recognized law of the sea, of the increasing probability of conflict with groups of states having different interests, and of the lack of any credible prospect for limiting the rapid expansion of national claims and jurisdiction in ocean space. These prospects can be accepted only with great reluctance. In my view the long-term interests of the United States clearly require the achievement of a widely accepted law of the sea treaty which will precisely define the outer limits of coastal state jurisdiction for all purposes and clearly establish the rights and duties of states both within and outside national jurisdiction. I would even suggest that the United States has an interest in reasonable and equitably balanced international management, not merely of the seabed, but of all ocean space beyond national jurisdiction.

I base my views, among other things, on the following considerations: first, the power and influence of the United States in the world is declining; in these circumstances the United States may find it advantageous to see some, at least, of its interests protected by a universally accepted law of the sea. Second, the United States has experimented over the past fifty years with almost all the alternatives to a law of the sea treaty mentioned by Professor Knight. Indeed the present state of the law of the sea is largely the result of actions taken by the United States. I doubt whether anyone would maintain that the results have been an undiluted success. The launching of the legal continental-shelf concept, for instance, has enabled the United States to obtain exclusive control of vast mineral resources; it has, however, also given rise to developments that threaten very important U.S. interests in a number of other ocean-related fields.

There is a further factor which, perhaps, merits consideration. As we all know, developing countries have been putting forward far-reaching demands with regard to the regulation of activities, particularly mining, on the seabed beyond national jurisdiction. Many developing countries would also wish to see regulation of all major activities conducted in ocean space beyond national jurisdiction through an international organization. The reasons for these attitudes are obvious. As formulated, the demands are unreasonable, yet it might be in the interests of the United States to reassess some of its fundamental positions in the light of these demands. Are the freedoms of the high seas really sustainable in the contemporary world? Are we not moving unavoidably toward a regulated use of ocean space, whether within or outside national jurisdiction? Is not reasonable international regulation preferable to unlimited expansion of national legislation? Given a situation in which the United States may soon no longer be the most powerful, is not reasonable international regulation providing stability of expectations preferable to the present freedom?

If such a fundamental reassessment were undertaken—and I recognize that this may be impractical at the present stage of negotiations—the United States, instead of being perpetually in a defensive posture, might rapidly acquire conference leadership and sufficient prestige with the majority of developing countries to obtain their acquiescence to a balance of power within a future international authority for the oceans which would safeguard U.S. interests.

John Norton Moore

Some of the titles of the papers of this afternoon's session make me feel a little bit like Churchill when he learned that his obituary notice had been published in the newspaper. He said he thought it was a little premature to discuss his death. I think it is a little premature to discuss alternatives to the law of the sea treaty at this point, when we are heading toward the most important of the substantive negotiating sessions of the conference. Caracas was basically a transition from the smaller Seabed Committee and its style of negotiation toward a conference of 140 to 150 different states.

I do see some very stark choices. I think the fundamental choice facing the world today is whether we are going to go forward toward an agreement which will benefit essentially all nations, or whether we are going to slide off the razor's edge in the other direction toward what I firmly believe to be conflict and chaos in the ocean. That does not mean that the United States, or indeed any other nation, has an interest in a treaty at any price. We do not. We have an interest in a treaty which protects fundamental U.S. interests and leads toward order and stability in the oceans. I am optimistic that such a treaty can be achieved.

I will keep the word "cautious" in front of my optimism, but I can see a consensus developing. That consensus is continuing to develop during the Evensen group discussions that we have held in the interim period since Caracas and my own feeling is that there is a substantial likelihood that the fundamental portion of the political compromise will fall into place at Geneva.

If Geneva is a failure in the sense that substantial progress is not made in the negotiations, then the United States, as well as a number of other countries, is going to have to consider alternatives that protect some of its more urgent interests, which I think we all know and which the panel has discussed.

Even then I would not see the pursuit of these alternatives as implying the definitive failure of the negotiations. It is a question of looking around at what one's urgent interests are and what other alternatives there are in the interim period for trying to protect those interests during a more protracted negotiation.

Obviously, it has to be a good treaty. It has to be one that is acceptable not only in terms of fundamental U.S. interests, but also in terms of the fundamental interests of the other major maritime powers and of the major groupings of states. It is always uncertain in a large negotiation such as this whether that is fully perceived by the members of all groups. There are many indications that the conference leaders from all regional groups do perceive that and do not see it as a zero-sum game in which the developing countries, for example, get everything and the maritime states achieve nothing in the treaty. I think it is understood that that would be merely an academic exercise and would not result in a successful law of the sea treaty.

Some ask why do we need a treaty in the first place? Why is it useful to be exploring a treaty and what are the risks of the treaty process?

There is no question that the United States is delighted with the three-mile territorial sea, but most nations of the world (I think they number more than fifty today) recognize a twelve-mile territorial sea. If the United States can, by an international agreement, clearly achieve recognition of guarantees of transit through and over straits used for international navigation, as we must to sign a treaty, it will be helpful to our interests, and those of the international community as a whole, in the future of the law of the sea. My own feeling is that we are going to achieve such guarantees in a successful law of the sea treaty.

With respect to our coastal resource interests—our own coastal species of fish, for example, and our own continental-margin minerals—there is essentially no risk with or without a law of the sea treaty. Without a law of the sea treaty, customary international law will evolve, I think, in the direction of broad claims, as is indeed already the case under the continental-shelf convention.

On the other hand, I think there are some advantages to both of our coastal resource interests, from the standpoint of a definite outer boundary to the continental margin, which would enable greater stability of expectations for the investments that are going to be necessary, and ease of acceptance of the 200-mile economic zone vis-à-vis the principal distant-water fishing nations. The latter have never accepted bilaterally U.S. coastal fisheries' jurisdiction, but in an overall law of the sea treaty where they have other interests at stake they may be willing to accept a 200-mile economic zone. Therefore, I think there are substantial advantages in going the treaty route with respect to even our coastal resource interests.

With respect to marine scientific research and freedom of navigation generally in the economic zone, the trend through time in the absence of a treaty is toward a 200-mile territorial sea, with very broad restrictions on navigation. With a law of the sea treaty of which the fundamental political compromise provides for expanded coastal state resource jurisdiction, protection of navigational freedom of movement in general, and a good environmental regime to protect the marine environment, we are going to be much better off than we would be under the customary international law that would otherwise emerge.

Regarding freedom of marine scientific research, the pattern of claims is likely to lead to consent regime out to 200 miles, if a good treaty is not achieved. On the other hand, by a treaty process we have a good chance of placing reasonable restraints on the exercise of coastal state jurisdiction and preserving reasonable freedom of marine scientific research in the ocean in the interest of all nations.

With respect to dispute settlement and conflict avoidance and conflict management problems in general international relations, again, the United States shares a host of bilateral oceans problems with many countries. We spend a great deal of energy on those bilateral problems. We are much better off if they can be resolved fundamentally within the context of an overall law of the sea treaty. And by the way, we can do a lot more in the law of the sea context in terms of negotiation than we can in bilateral agreements, because we have more flexibility. Among other reasons for this a nation can accept broader jurisdictional arrangements when it is receiving quid pro quos in other areas of a treaty.

Do we really want a chaotic pattern of ocean law that takes years to develop through the slow customary international legal process of claim and counterclaim, interspersed in many cases by cod wars or the other problems that are currently arising? I think the answer is no. We are much better off if we have stability of expectations for the investment and business decisions that are going to be needed in the oceans.

With respect to deep-seabed mining, once again we have a dispute concerning the existing international law. It is the U.S. view that in the absence of a successful law of the sea treaty freedom of the high seas prevails. It is the view of many other nations of the world that mining the resources of the deep seabed is not permitted in the absence of a treaty specifically providing a framework for this. The question is, if the treaty fails, what will be the cost to the United States of going forward with deep-seabed mining?

Now, on all of this I would like to again make it very clear that the United States will not simply sign any treaty, although we strongly feel that a treaty is a non-zero-sum game, in the sense that essentially every player is going to benefit in the process. Nevertheless, the United States has to protect a whole variety of vital interests, and there is a point at which a law of the sea treaty is less protective than the slow customary international law process.

We must have unimpeded transit through and over straits used for international navigation. We must have guaranteed access to deep-seabed minerals under reasonable conditions for mining, and we must have a variety of other points spelled out in the treaty which are going to protect U.S. vital interests. But I think the real choice is between on the one hand going forward in a difficult and extremely complex process, but nevertheless a process that is making progress, and on the other hand prematurely searching for other alternatives. As far as I am concerned, until we are convinced that it is not possible to have this kind of overall negotiated settlement, we must persevere in seeking a good comprehensive ocean law treaty in the interest of all nations.

DISCUSSION

PROFESSOR KNIGHT: I have one comment in response to Dr. Pardo's point about the use of force. First of all, Professor McDougal was entirely right in saying that there is nothing in the UN Charter which proscribes the use of force in self-defense or in the preservation of an existing right. If I did not say that, I should have.

Dr. Pardo has asked on what basis we would use force if, in fact, pursuant to treaty, a nation or group of nations used arbitrary straight baselines to convert an area that was either territorial waters (subject to innocent passage) or high seas (subject to freedom of navigation) into internal waters subject to the absolute right of prohibition of navigation. The answer, I think, is fairly straightforward. One, if we were not a party to that treaty, then it would not bind us. If the area were high seas, it would remain high seas until either (1) there arose a new rule of customary international law supplanting it, which would take a long time, or (2) we acquiesced in that regime, either by a statement or acts, or by becoming a party to that treaty. If the closure were done by a unilateral act not pursuant to a treaty, *a fortiori* the area would remain high seas and we would have the right to navigate there.

To use force to preserve an existing right, then, is not contrary to the UN Charter and is, as I have advocated in my paper, a viable method for preserving U.S. navigation rights.

EDITOR'S NOTE: Knight's closing response produced an exchange between Louis Sohn and Myres McDougal concerning the Charter of the United Nations. Sohn argued that the UN Charter forbids resorting to war or to military acts of force to defend a right, except to protect oneself from an armed attack. McDougal argued that this is a very limited minority view of the UN Charter and that practice differs with it. The floor was then opened to comments and questions.

Basil Petrou asked McDougal, Sohn, and Knight if they felt that an unsuccessful or partially successful law of the sea conference would establish any precedents that would be used by the International Court of Justice or other international legal forums. Myres McDougal felt that the International Court would turn to the conference records, but that if the records are as confused and contradictory as his colleagues find them, they would be of little use. Louis Sohn offered a different view, arguing that the 1930 conference is a good example of such precedent setting. No conclusions were reached in 1930, but from 1930 until 1958 writers used the 1930 conference as the best evidence of what many states thought international law should be. Sohn thought the present conference proceedings would be used in the same manner. Gary Knight took the position that customary international law will take longer to evolve and that a judicial decision maker will not look to a conference position simply because 80 percent of the nations favored it.

Joseph Nye returned to the earlier discussion on the use of force and argued that discussion of this as a legal question misses the point. He argued that the politics and maneuvering of a given situation is as important as the legal question. He cited the maneuvering in the cod war off Iceland as an example. In the cod war each side used force with restraint in the attempt to have the other side appear to be the aggressor.

Nye then asked each member of the panel to discuss his or her view of the costs and benefits of ending the Geneva session with either a resolution encompassing five or six major principles and points, a very brief framework treaty, or with a decision postponing action to yet another year, another round, or declaring total failure. Arvid Pardo thought there was a possibility that such a resolution might be adopted, but he doubted that it would address itself in a meaningful manner to what he considers essential points: conflict avoidance, management of ocean resources, and dispute settlement. Louis Sohn stated that he would be quite happy with a declaration of five to seven principles. Northcutt Ely strongly disagreed, arguing that the group is heavily weighted against the interests of the United States. Ely felt the worst outcome in Geneva would be adoption of the 1970 U.S. draft treaty; this will not happen, he felt, because it is emphatically rejected by the coastal states. Ely thought that it was difficult to see anything coming out of Geneva that would not be a detriment to our present position in the law of the sea. Ely then asked John Norton Moore if the United States were still advocating the international regime spelled out in the 1970 draft treaty. Moore responded that the delegation has never altered its fundamental position and that the proposal includes the administrative machinery that Ely had objected to so strongly.

Richard Greenwald asked if there were any way the defense interests that had been discussed in both sessions could be quantified. Myres

McDougal *responded that they could, but that one cannot make precise calculations and come up with an exact number. He argued that if one fails to protect security interests, nothing else matters.*

Ross Eckert asked John Norton Moore what other generous proposals, in addition to the 1970 draft treaty, were likely to be placed on the table by the U.S. delegation. John Moore responded that the delegation is going to Geneva to negotiate a treaty to protect our interests as well as the interests of others. He felt it would be possible to reach a reasonable agreement that satisfies both sides.

Roland McKean wanted to clarify the statement he made in the morning session regarding the term "anarchy," which may have been misunderstood by some of the political scientists and lawyers present. He was arguing as an economist using the definition of anarchy common in economics literature, and he wanted to point out that in his view of the ocean situation one can achieve a good deal of coordination without central direction.

John Moore was asked if he felt Committee One in Geneva would arrive at some definition of what area is beyond national jurisdiction and if there were a discrepancy here with the work of Committee Two. Moore replied that the trend in the negotiation is to a broad-margin solution, subject to a reasonable-objectives definition of the outer edge and probably subject to revenue sharing beginning at 200 miles. He stated that the political understanding of the conference was that this issue of the limits of national jurisdiction would be settled in Committee Two and then referred to Committee One. This would present no problem, because the same countries are participating in both committees.

The conference ended with an observation from Dennis Logue that Moore had come in late and had missed many of the conferees' comments. Logue thought Moore's comments suggested that there was no reason to despair, because there is a good likelihood of reaching agreement on a treaty—while in fact a good number of the participants were despairing for precisely that reason.

PART THREE

EPILOGUE

GENEVA UPDATE

James L. Johnston

The spring of 1975 saw the completion of the second substantive session of the Third United Nations Conference on the Law of the Sea (UNCLOS). The first substantive session was held during the preceding summer in Caracas. These two sessions, eight and ten weeks in duration respectively, were preceded by six years of preparation. But that was not the beginning of the attempt to write a new law of the sea. Two UN conferences preceded this third attempt. The first was concluded in 1958 with only minor contributions recorded, and the second, held in 1960, failed to reach any agreement.

Substantive agreement continues to elude the negotiators at the third law of the sea conference. The only agreement thus far relates to the functioning of the conference and not to the substantive issues it is addressing. Even here, the inventory of achievement is pitifully small. The officers of the conference have been elected, the rules of procedure have been adopted, and subsequent sessions have been scheduled. The United States holds two of the vice-presidential offices, and it has agreed to a set of procedural rules which give voting control to the Group of 77, the block of developing countries that now numbers more than 100.[1] As for the scheduling of the substantive sessions, the conference has resisted holding another during 1975 and has expressed itself strongly against meeting in a cold climate.[2]

This description is drawn exclusively from unclassified sources and represents the personal views of the author, who was the senior representative of the Department of the Treasury to the UN Conference on the Law of the Sea. Consequently, this is only part of the story on the law of the sea. However, it is a part that has hitherto not been told.

The text has benefited greatly from comments by Ross Eckert and my Treasury colleagues, Ryan Amacher, Bruce Malachevich, Basil Petrou, Richard Sweeney, and Thomas Willett (who also provided the encouragement), along with Northcutt Ely, Richard Greenwald, and Cecil Olmstead. Errors which remain are, of course, my exclusive responsibility.

[1] Despite firm pronouncements that the United States was insisting upon adoption by two-thirds of the conference participants, it subsequently agreed to the rule of adoption by two-thirds of those present and voting. Interestingly, the United States relented on the voting rules for agreement, yet it was prepared to walk out if it did not obtain two vice-presidencies.

[2] In a meeting of the General Committee on 2 May 1975, the conference president, H. S. Amerasingbe, said that holding the conference where the climate was frozen would cause delegates and the talks to be frozen; while meeting in a temperate climate would make the delegates and the negotiations temperate.

The Geneva session did see the issuance of "informal single negotiating texts," [3] and these have been acclaimed widely as indications of conference progress. These texts will be examined in some detail later in this discussion, but it should be made clear here that they are the personal product of the three main committee chairmen and cannot in any sense be considered a recording of agreements. Indeed, if the provisions of the informal single negotiation texts were incorporated unchanged into a new treaty on the law of the sea, it would be in the opinion of many observers an absolute, complete, and unmitigated disaster for the interests of the United States and the rest of the world as well. There are those, however, who see many satisfactory provisions in the texts. In my view, this is akin to characterizing World War II solely in terms of bringing the industrialized world out of a depression.

In comparing the Geneva session with the previous Caracas session, John Norton Moore, deputy chairman of the U.S. delegation, reported to the Senate Foreign Relations Committee that "the Geneva session made progress and, in some respects, substantial progress. Most significantly, the will to negotiate, which had been largely missing at Caracas, was in greater, if not universal evidence." [4] Moore goes far beyond most observers in his estimate of progress and cites the fact that (1) negotiations took place in small, often secret groups, and (2) that informal single negotiating texts were produced. However, because the "negotiations" were closed to all but a small group of delegates representing a minority of participating delegates, and because of the lack of obvious connection between the "negotiators" and the single texts in many respects, the assertions by Moore and others are virtually impossible to corroborate or refute.

The Informal Single Negotiating Texts

Conflicting claims are made (often by the same observer) for the significance of the informal single negotiating texts. Clearly, it would be undesirable for a government's representative to assert that the single texts are in any sense negotiated instruments. Besides complicating the process of amending the parts that are inconsistent with the country's interests, there is a danger that endorsement of parts of the texts would contribute to the formation of customary international law which could be cited against the country's interests in judicial forums. This could occur despite the fact that the country's stand on one issue was contingent upon agreement on another, and even when the treaty does not come into force.

On the other hand, the UN conference negotiations face competition from alternative methods of accommodating national interests. Domestic legislation,

---

[3] *Informal Single Negotiating Text,* A/CONF. 62/WP.8/Part I, Part II and Part III (Geneva: UN Conference on the Law of the Sea, 7 May 1975).

[4] Statement by the Honorable John Norton Moore before the Senate Foreign Relations Committee, Subcommittee on Oceans and International Environment, 22 May 1975.

unilateral action, bilateral and small multilateral negotiations, and even the threat of force are some of the alternatives. Because these alternatives exist, the treaty negotiators have a tendency to put the best light possible on the international negotiations in order for the negotiations to be allowed to proceed.

In spite of the difficulty, indeed the undesirability, of identifying which parts of the single texts represent consensus and which do not, these texts deserve examination. First, they provide a convenient structure for a report on the Geneva session, and second, they offer an insight into the U.S. negotiators' performance. Senator Lee Metcalf has observed that "the single text may not be a negotiated document. But it is a measure of sorts of the effectiveness of our negotiators in getting our point of view prominently displayed before the Conference." [5]

The remainder of the discussion will therefore address the most important provisions in the single texts. It does not compare each provision with the U.S. delegation's instructions, however. Such an exercise, besides divulging those instructions, would entail a lengthy explanation of how the United States, with its conflicting ocean interests, arrived at its present policy. Interesting though it would be, this story might help other delegations thwart the United States in its objectives. But a general discussion of the single texts would seem to be useful in identifying which U.S. international interests are likely to be affected by the eventual law of the sea treaty and to offer some predictions about the outcome of the negotiations. This is necessarily a personal assessment.

The First Committee: Deep Seabed

The First Committee of the law of the sea conference dealt with a unified subject—the regime and machinery that will govern the seabed beyond national jurisdictions. The specific resource involved is the manganese nodules which blanket, in varying degrees of concentration, the deep seabed under international waters. These nodules contain nickel, copper, and cobalt, which are commercially attractive now, and manganese and fifteen or so other minerals, which are potentially attractive.

The United States is a net importer of copper and is almost entirely dependent on imports for nickel, cobalt, manganese, and many of the trace metals found in manganese nodules. Underlying the major division of opinion in the negotiations on this subject is the fact that a number of developing countries are land-based producers of these minerals and their substitutes and are anxious to protect their export earnings by restricting the supply of manganese nodules.

[5] Statement of Senator Lee Metcalf of Montana introducing hearings of the U.S. Senate, Commerce Committee, National Oceans Policy Study, on the status of the Law of the Sea Conference, 4 June 1975, p. 3.

The interests of these developing countries were manifested at the Caracas session [6] and emerged fully developed at the Geneva session. Marked by an explicit reference to the "new international economic order" by the drafter of the single text for the First Committee in his introduction,[7] and reflected throughout the text itself, are extensive provisions for the "direct and effective control" of recovery and related operations within a regime that coordinates *worldwide* mineral production to protect the export earnings of land-based producers. The short-term success of the OPEC cartel has not been lost on the rest of the Group of 77. It is a model that exporters of other raw materials are striving to emulate in the belief that it quickly and effectively accomplishes the transfer of wealth from industrialized countries to developing countries.

Of course there are some flaws in this reasoning, which in time will tend to erode support for the "new international economic order" in the law of the sea conference. For example, the major land-based producers of the minerals found in manganese nodules are industrialized countries, not developing countries.[8] Thus, measures to harmonize mineral production will largely benefit producers in countries which have already developed economically. Developing countries, meanwhile, are becoming the hardest hit by higher prices for the raw materials they consume. One measure of this trend is the increase in their oil-based balance of trade deficit, reflected in their reserve losses since October 1973.[9] However, until the Group of 77 stops regarding the international authority as a base for the formation of mineral cartels, or until the seabed producer countries assert themselves more forcefully in the First Committee's negotiations, the tendency will be to give the international authority complete and effective control over seabed recovery operations and a pervasive coordination role in land-based production planning.

These are the necessary conditions for an effective cartel. It is a forlorn hope to expect the authority to be satisfied with control over just half of the seabed or to tolerate voting protection for seabed producer countries in the authority's council— though these hopes are often held out by parties interested in going on with negotiations. Such concessions on the part of the Group of 77 would imply that members had abandoned their cartel formulation objective. It was not surprising, therefore, that the Group of 77 totally rejected efforts to negotiate these provisions, which incidentally might not be sufficient protection for consumer and seabed

[6] See the statement by James L. Johnston to the Marine Technology Society, 26 September 1974. Reprinted in "Law of the Sea Briefing," Occasional Paper No. 24 (Kingston, R.I.: Law of the Sea Institute, December 1974), pp. 7-10.

[7] Paul Bambela Engo, "Introduction to Single Text Relating to the Mandate of the First Committee," A/CONF.62/WP.8, Part I (Geneva: UN Conference on the Law of the Sea, 9 May 1975), p. 2.

[8] *United States: Working Paper on the Economic Effects of the Deep Seabed Exploitation,* A/CONF.62/C-1/L.5 (Caracas: UN Conference on the Law of the Sea, 8 August 1974).

[9] See the *New York Times,* 3 August 1974, for a vivid description of the effect of higher petroleum prices on the agriculture of India.

producer interests. One representative of the U.S. nodule-mining industry has indicated that under such an arrangement "there would be little or no margin of safety." [10]

This same mining industry official characterized the single text for the First Committee as an "unmitigated disaster." For all our negotiators' efforts, even a quick reading of the single text makes it obvious that, as Senator Lee Metcalf put it, "the international community owns, and runs, everything beyond 200 miles and can hand the bill to U.S. taxpayers and consumers." [11]

There has been considerable discussion in post-Geneva congressional hearings of another single text for the First Committee. Written by the committee's working group chairman, it is often referred to as the Pinto text. This text, some U.S. negotiators have argued, is also unacceptable, but it is a better basis for future negotiations.[12] The industry representative cited above called the Pinto text a "mitigated disaster" by contrast with the official single text, which he considered an "unmitigated disaster." [13] A comparison of the two texts reveals that in many important respects the wording is identical or achieves the same effect. Both texts want direct and effective control by the authority, the protection of land-based producers' export earnings, discrimination in favor of developing countries, transfer of technology from its owners to developing countries, state contributions and profit sharing from operations to support the authority financially, and exemption of the authority's assets and income from national taxation. Several of the provisions in the Pinto text, however, are *less* desirable than those in the official text. For example, the Pinto text provides that the authority would have the discretion to decide which areas would be open for commercial recovery operations. No such provision appears in the official, sometimes called the Engo, text. The one important provision for which the Pinto text is supposedly superior concerns voting protection in the authority's council. Under the Pinto text a three-fourths rather than a two-thirds majority would be required for the council to act—but at best seabed producers would have only one-fourth of the votes. It would seem that under either arrangement seabed producer countries would always be defeated in votes, albeit by a smaller margin under the Pinto text.

The negotiations in the First Committee have essentially collapsed. The gulf between the two main protagonists—the land-based mineral producers and the

---

[10] Statement of Marne A. Dubs before the U.S. House Merchant Marine and Fisheries Committee, Oceanography Subcommittee, 16 May 1975 (Washington, D.C.: U.S. Government Printing Office, 1975), pp. 37-74.

[11] Metcalf, statement introducing law of the sea hearings.

[12] Leigh S. Ratiner in response to questions on 16 May 1975 before the Oceanography Subcommittee of the House Merchant Marine and Fisheries Committee. For a report, see "Failure in Geneva Becomes Preamble to Spring in New York," *Ocean Science News,* vol. 17 (16 May 1975), pp. 1-2.

[13] Statement of Marne A. Dubs before the U.S. Senate, Commerce Committee, National Oceans Policy Study, 4 June 1975, p. 9.

potential seabed producers—is too great to be bridged by concessions. Their objectives are diametrically opposed. One group, the seabed producers, wants to begin recovery operations. The other group, composed of the land-based producers and their ideological brethren, will permit seabed production only if it fits their plans for a worldwide mineral cartel. Between such objectives there is no basis for accommodation except capitulation by one of the interests.

The Second Committee: Coastal Areas under National Jurisdiction

Since more than two-thirds of the delegations are from coastal states, interest in the law of the sea conference centers on the Second Committee. At the Geneva session the countries that are landlocked or "geographically disadvantaged" formed a bloc to push their objectives—access to the oceans and participation in neighboring fisheries on some as yet undefined priority basis. The emergence of this group, which except in international negotiations would lack a strong stake in the law of the sea, is effectively delaying the process of reaching agreement. This is an important factor in the inability of the law of the sea conference to meet the UN timetable for adopting a convention in 1975.

The formation of a bloc of landlocked and geographically disadvantaged states (GDS) caused a particular problem for the Group of 77. The newly independent African countries in the geographically disadvantaged bloc saw the opportunity to achieve some negotiating leverage in bilateral consultations with their neighbors over access to the ocean. In addition, some of the countries in this bloc with longer histories of independence saw that they could improve the terms under which they now have access to the sea. Severe criticism was leveled against this bloc by coastal state members of the Group of 77 who repeatedly emphasized that many members of the geographically disadvantaged bloc could in no way be considered disadvantaged. They cited, in particular, Austria, Czechoslovakia, and Switzerland. However, the bloc remained a cohesive group throughout the Geneva session.

The Group of 77 would undoubtedly gain the upper hand if, by virtue of its numbers, it could construct a package deal and present it to the conference for an all-or-nothing decision. A carefully designed package might force maximum concessions from the other countries, certainly more than they would be willing to make if they could consider the issues individually.[14] Since the Group of 77's voting potential is absolutely necessary for the approval of an all-or-nothing package, and since the landlocked and disadvantaged countries are necessary for a two-thirds majority, one could conclude that agreement within the Group of 77 will have to precede serious negotiations for a treaty and that provisions in the

---

[14] For an analysis of this principle with respect to economic choice, see Milton Friedman, *Price Theory* (Chicago: Aldine, 1962), pp. 12-16. For further applications of choice theory to negotiating problems, see the Tollison and Willett paper in this volume.

single text which are now satisfactory to maritime countries might be subject to radical alteration after the landlocked and geographically disadvantaged countries are realigned with the Group of 77.

The Continental Margin. The single-text provisions for the continental margin reflect the strong presence of states with sedimentary rock formations extending more than 200 miles from shore. (The United States could be classified as a broad-margin state, but it has not acted as assertively to secure its margins as some other such nations have.) First, the text uses the definition of the continental margin beyond 200 miles that brings the greatest area under the jurisdiction of broad-margin states. While petroleum geologists believe that the probability of finding hydrocarbons in sedimentary columns decreases as one goes seaward from the land mass, certain geological structures containing down-faulted blocks do have hydrocarbon potential, and the broad-margin states near these structures have insisted upon the safer, more extensive definition of the margin. Given the present state of geologic knowledge, a reasonable delimitator would be the seaward edge of the continental slope, with perhaps some margin for measurement error. The single text goes far beyond this method of delimitation.

The second problem has to do with the sharing of revenues from the continental margin. The single text provides for a royalty of x percent to be shared from the continental margin, but *only* where the margin extends beyond 200 miles. The supporters of royalty provisions such as this argue that a quid pro quo is implied by revenue sharing in exchange for clear national jurisdiction over the continental margin beyond 200 miles. However, as the National Petroleum Council has shown,[15] the economic viability of recovery installations becomes increasingly tenuous as operations move away from the shore and into deeper water. Thus, under the provisions of the single text, a broad-margin state could effectively lose the economic potential from the outer edge of the continental margin if the royalty became a rate significantly greater than zero.

The third problem is the single-text provision that allows the international authority to negotiate the extent to which revenues will be contributed by developing countries. If the international authority is dominated by the Group of 77, as many observers expect it to be, there is little doubt about who will contribute revenues and who will not.

A fourth problem has to do with the international authority's being the recipient of the funds instead of an international organization that specializes in economic assistance to developing countries. If the single text from the First Committee is any guide, the authority's income will be used first to support its administrative expenses and then for various price stabilization schemes, such as buffer stocks of raw materials.

---

[15] National Petroleum Council, *Ocean Petroleum Resources,* Washington, D.C., March 1975.

In spite of these fundamental problems with the single text for the continental margin, this portion of the negotiations is developing for the benefit of the broad-margin states. Between the Caracas and Geneva sessions, all mention of revenue sharing within the 200-mile zone disappeared and the opposition to coastal state jurisdiction over the resources of the continental margin beyond 200 miles from shore decreased markedly. The sole remaining source of resistance has been black African states. However, the emergence of the bloc of landlocked and geographically disadvantaged nations, which includes many African members, had tempered this resistance. One explanation for the Organization of African Unity's initial opposition to a broad-margin solution was its attempt at accommodation with the African landlocked states. Apparently the coastal states in the Organization of African Unity reasoned that moderation on their part concerning the extent of coastal state jurisdiction would be met by similar moderation on the part of their landlocked neighbors over sharing in the coastal fisheries of the region. Clearly this has not developed, and it would seem that it is just a matter of time until the broad-margin states of Africa join similar states from other regions in support of a broad-margin solution, perhaps without any revenue sharing at all.

Straits. A great deal has been made of the proposed expansion of territorial seas from three to twelve miles and its effect on navigation through straits. It is often claimed that the waters of over 100 straits will overlap if territorial seas become twelve miles in width. The problem arises with the so-called regime of innocent passage that exists within territorial seas. At present, this concept is only vaguely defined. It reflects the coastal states' security concern with ships that approach their shores. As Osgood has observed, only a handful of straits are affected, and as military technology advances, the importance of straits passage decreases.[16]

The critics of one twelve-mile territorial sea and the innocent passage regime assume that countries with the ability to restrict passage through straits and other areas will in fact stringently restrict passage through straits. There are several reasons to question this result. First, a coastal state accrues costs by restricting navigation, both the direct costs of detecting violations by ships or aircraft, patroling and enforcing the restrictions, administering the penalties, and collecting the fees, and the indirect costs of distinguishing among ships so that the prices of imports and exports are not raised to the straits states and their allies, and coping with animosity and possible retaliation from maritime powers on whom these states otherwise depend.

The most important straits are bordered by more than one country. Thus, for the straits states to close an important strait would be equivalent to their

---

[16] See the paper by Robert Osgood and the floor discussion in this volume.

forming a viable monopoly—always a costly business. To enjoy whatever monopoly rents would accrue from restricting passage, it would be necessary for several states to act in concert. This arrangement contains an inherent destabilizing factor, however, since it would be in the interest of any one of the states bordering on the strait to reduce prices enough to draw for more than its share of the monopoly rent. In the limit, this behavior would reduce the monopoly rents to zero. This would be the expected result if the countries bordering on the strait were generally on friendly terms. The same result would come much more quickly if the states were not on friendly terms, like Spain and Morocco which border the Strait of Gibraltar.

Another moderating influence is the existence of substitutes for passage through straits. In some instances, going the longer way around is a viable substitute, given the relatively low cost per mile of ocean transportation. In other situations overland hauling is a way of bypassing a strait; a pipeline across the Thailand isthmus, for example, is an alternative to tanker passage through the Strait of Malacca. The actual or *potential* existence of these and other substitutes reduces the potential long-term gain from straits monopolies.

One might conclude from the high direct and indirect costs and the availability of substitutes for passage through many of the straits that there is not a large gain to be realized from restricting transit. This coupled with the fact that states bordering on straits are themselves often important maritime powers that depend upon unimpeded, lower-priced transit to support the demand for vessel construction and operating services which they provide, suggests that the straits states may not have powerful incentives to commit themselves to a program of restricting passage.

Thus, the rather reasonable provisions for straits passage, and indeed innocent passage within territorial seas that appear in the single text, were to be expected. The straits states and others as well simply do not have much to gain from restricting navigation in waters under their jurisdiction.

The Economic Zone. The creation of an economic zone extending 200 miles from shore is largely a response to technological developments which now permit the harvesting of resources from that area. As it turns out, both the living and mineral resources tend to be concentrated within 200 miles from shore, and coastal states are, understandably, hoping to obtain jurisdiction over them.

The large amount of space in the single text devoted to the economic zone and directly related issues underscores its importance to the coastal state delegations, the largest group at the conference. A careful reading of the single text suggests that obtaining jurisdiction over the economic resources of the zone is the primary focus. The provisions relating to "residual rights," such as freedom of navigation, overflight, laying pipelines, and so on, to the conservation of living resources, and to scientific research would seem at first glance to suggest the contrary. However, it can be argued that they too are consistent with the notion of maximization of economic welfare rather than with the idea of harassing navigation or protecting coastal states from military threats by maritime powers.

Article 47 on residual rights must be read in conjunction with Article 45 and the rest of Part III to see that the emphasis is on the resources. Article 47 itself exempts communications and navigation from coastal state jurisdiction in the economic zone. The possible assignment, then, of some of the residual rights to the coastal state would seem to be more consistent with the idea of resource jurisdiction over some yet-to-be-developed raw material, than with a political move to restrict a threat to its security. Recasting the residual rights provisions to focus exclusively on resources would seem to be an exercise on which no state would have to expend much negotiating capital.

The conservation of living resources is another potentially misleading objective cited in the single text. One might impute to those provisions a concern with solving the so-called common-pool problem. The management provisions in Article 51, however, do not solve the problem. Indeed, it can be argued that they aggravate it.[17] On the other hand, coastal states that want to preserve their fisheries until they have the technology, or so that they can sell the exclusive rights to the foreign fisherman, are served very well by the economic zone provisions. Having exclusive jurisdiction with a vaguely defined obligation to allow foreigners into the fishery, where the foreign catch limit is determined solely by the coastal state, makes the assignment of property rights very clear. It is this provision that lays the more effective groundwork for an eventual solution to the common-pool problem.

Concern with scientific research in the single text is another possible source of misunderstanding. While scientific research in the economic zone is made subject to the consent of the coastal state in the single text, it is not clear that it is a response to espionage action disguised as research such as Project Jennifer, the recent attempt to raise the Russian submarine, or any security concern on the part of coastal states.

A more plausible explanation for the consent regime is that there is no framework in which an inventory of a developing coastal state's marine resources can be initiated. Scientists have often uncovered natural resources of considerable value in the oceans. This history of discovery, of course, has a more specific relevance to a coastal state than the promise of research increasing the general welfare of mankind by advancing scientific knowledge. Developing countries, in an attempt to influence the selection of research projects and to channel these efforts into searches for undiscovered marine resources in their economic zones,

---

[17] Douglass C. North and Roger L. Miller, *The Economics of Public Issues* (New York: Harper and Row, 1973), pp. 108-12.

have adopted the only technique that is readily available—requiring consent for research. By exercising this admittedly negative control they can reject research unrelated to resource discovery in the hope of sparking a reallocation of funding that corresponds with their research priorities.

Doubtless, a better course would be the development of a positive system where resource-related research could be proposed by coastal states. This would have the effect of redirecting research efforts to the more applied categories, but might also prevent an overall contraction of marine research activity.

Obstacles to Agreement in the Second Committee. If, as the above discussion suggests, these three areas do not pose serious problems, and no problems arise out of misunderstanding of the underlying economic considerations, then one might ask whether there are impediments to reaching agreement in the Second Committee. The answer is, most certainly, yes. One problem is direct and obvious, the other is subtle.

The obvious difficulty in the Second Committee negotiations is the emergence of the bloc of landlocked and geographically disadvantaged states referred to earlier. This bloc has as its objective access to the sea and priority participation in nearby coastal fisheries. The problem arises only because countries that do not have a primary interest in the law of the sea were included in the negotiations. Because of the parliamentary nature of the conference, the votes of these countries have equal value with those of nations that do have a primary interest. Consequently, the geographically disadvantaged bloc must be accommodated to some extent. It will take time not only to work out the details of the accommodation at the *regional* level, but also to gather information on the specific coastal resources to be shared with landlocked countries so that the involved states understand clearly the value of what they are acquiring or handing over.

However, a paradox is emerging. Although the demands of the landlocked and geographically disadvantaged nations can only be met on a *regional* basis, the concessions that this bloc has to offer in exchange can only be made at the *overall* conference level. It is not clear that such an accommodation can be drafted at the law of the sea conference. This suggests that a successful conclusion to the conference, if possible at all, might take several years. The coastal states, for the most part, are not terribly eager to resolve the issues at once. The evidence suggests that time is on their side. The development of recovery technology is a slow process, and as the value of coastal resources increases, jurisdiction can be accommodated in national legislation and customary international law.

Another trend is the increase in the ranks of the coastal states. Several states which, in the past, considered their interests to be mainly maritime are undergoing a metamorphosis into states with important coastal interests. The United Kingdom, Norway, and Greece are notable examples because of recent reassessments of their continental shelf resources. This is not to say that the navigational interests of maritime powers are vulnerable under the customary international law that is developing outside the law of the sea conference, though the treaty alternative provides a more definitive regime. But if the choice is between the uncertain and slow development of customary international law and a definite but less than perfect treaty protecting navigational freedoms, it is not clear that chaos and conflict would be brought about only by the former. At this point, however, it is important to note that the continuation of the law of the sea conference without the resolution of all the issues in the package, *itself* contributes to customary international law. To continue too long in the conference discussions is to risk the worst of both alternatives—a more rapid development of customary international law which limits navigational freedoms.[18]

A more subtle problem, but no less serious, has to do with the opportunity to develop a more stable climate in the economic zone. Many developing countries in recent years have given the extractive industries reason for pause because of their frequent unilateral abrogations of contracts. The industries' caution, understandably, would equally affect their dealings with countries that do not have histories of revoking contracts but that might have valuable marine resources in their economic zones. In this instance, an international agreement establishing compulsory dispute settlement machinery, which would be effective in insuring a stable investment climate in the face of transitory political problems, could speed the development of recovery operations. Resolution of this issue would seem to be much more important for less-developed countries, which are really hurt by this fear, than for developed countries, which now have little to lose. A fair assessment of conference concerns would place the resolution of this issue very low on a list of priorities for most delegations.

In the light of this situation, one must observe that this missing provision from the single text eliminates an important motivation for reaching agreement on the treaty. If a stable investment climate is lacking, the resources of the economic zone are less valuable than otherwise. This postpones recovery operations and whatever new income they might bring to the coastal state and delays the day when the overall law of the sea package has a positive value sufficiently large to offset the costs of negotiating the treaty.

The Third Committee: Science and Pollution

Most of the provisions relating to scientific research and protecting the marine environment are contained in the single text for the Third Committee. However, because the Third Committee is an offspring of the Second Committee, there are

---

18 Thanks are due to Basil Petrou for pointing this out to me.

186

traces of the science and pollution issues in the Second Committee's work and, indeed, elsewhere.

Protecting the Marine Environment. There are several aspects of the pollution issue. From the perspective of the environmentalist, the provisions of the single text give little assurance that pollution in the oceans will be abated. Richard A. Frank, a lawyer with the Center for Law and Social Policy, has said, "If the environment provisions in the single negotiating texts emanating from Geneva were now before the Senate for advice and consent to ratification, the environmental groups would be recommending that the Senate not approve those provisions." [19] The brutal truth is that most delegations to the conference are unconcerned with the quality of the marine environment, except in the negative sense that they wish to be sure that protective measures will not inhibit their economic development. But neither are they anxious to use environmental measures to harrass navigation in either territorial seas or economic zones.

The committee was faced with three alternatives for dealing with vessel-source pollution: offshore pollution zones with coastal states both setting and enforcing standards; flag-state enforcement of international standards; or a compromise between these two alternatives, port-state enforcement of international standards. Generally speaking, "the single negotiating text adopts a system of primary enforcement and standard-setting responsibility by flag states." [20] The outcome clearly underscores many delegations' belief that protecting the environment is relatively unimportant, since port states would not be expected to enforce regulations as vigorously as coastal states.

The conference's eagerness to shield economic development from international environmental provisions is also evident in the absence of articles dealing with land-based pollution. The single text simply obliges states to conform to generally accepted international standards. These, it should be noted, are not yet established, and apparently "considerable discretion [is left] to states to determine which international measures they must accept." [21] Nor are there liability provisions for environmental damage, except damage caused by scientific research. Further, a double standard established in Articles 3 and 4 permits special consideration to developing nations in meeting their environmental duties. All of these points underscore the low regard in which environmental protection is held by many delegations.

The single text of the Second Committee permits coastal states to establish regulations for environmental preservation in the territorial sea, but only in the context of innocent passage. It also exempts military ships from regulation and

---

[19] Richard A. Frank, Testimony before the U.S. Senate, Commerce Committee, National Oceans Policy Study, 4 June 1975, p. 5.

[20] Ibid., p. 6.

[21] Ibid., p. 21.

adopts no coastal state cognizance in the economic zone. All these factors reveal the reluctance of many states to accept navigational restrictions that would adversely affect maritime interests and increase the costs of commercial shipping.

The thread that seems to recur in all of the pollution provisions is the dual notion that neither economic development nor navigation should be restricted by environmental provisions. To the extent that these provisions represent the views of delegations, it would appear that economic concerns are paramount and environmental ones secondary. This situation has led one environmentalist to conclude that

> [t]he United States, desiring to prevent degradation of its magnificent coastal areas, and wanting to do its share to foreclose damage to international marine areas, will simply have to legislate unilaterally [and] . . . such unilateralism will not be inconsistent with a law of the sea treaty; it will supplement the treaty.[22]

Scientific Research. The consent regime established in Article 49 of the single text for the Second Committee, which is discussed above, is echoed in only slightly modified form in the single text for the Third Committee. The essential elements of coastal state consent for research conducted in the territorial sea, the economic zone, and the continental margin beyond the 200-mile limit are strongly implied. Extensive participation in research by the coastal state and release of research results as soon as feasible to the coastal state are explicitly provided for.

The coastal state's often-expressed desire to participate during all phases of research seems to reflect two objectives: first, the transfer of research skills to the coastal state, and second, the publication of any results of economic significance after their communication to the coastal state. Both of these motivations are essentially economic and reflect the view held, rightly or wrongly, by many delegations, that scientific research should be directed toward their development goals. The requirement that research findings be made public, in particular, effectively separates scientific research from military research and proprietary research conducted for the exclusive benefit of the extractive industries.

Until now, scientists have insisted upon the freedom to control their own research and the conditions of publication. Thus, they are pessimistic about the fate of scientific research under a law of the sea treaty. However, at least one scientist has even more misgivings about the emerging wave of *national* legislation establishing fishing zones than about an international regime.[23] Apparently, the concern is that the extension of national jurisdiction over fisheries will take a variety of forms and will be unevenly applied to scientific research. It is not clear

---

22 Ibid., pp. 28-29.

23 John A. Knauss, Provost for Marine Affairs, University of Rhode Island, in testimony prepared for the U.S. Senate, Commerce Committee, National Oceans Policy Study on the Geneva Session of the Third Law of the Sea Conference, 4 June 1975, p. 5.

why a degree of nonuniformity in the national regulations affecting scientific research is not preferable to a treaty that is very likely to control scientific research both in the economic zone and in the international area, but the latter seems to be the preference of the scientists.

Some Miscellaneous Issues

The conference is also dealing with other issues which are not as controversial as those addressed above. This is not to say that they are unimportant. For the states directly affected, they involve major policy objectives. However, their resolution does not seem to be in doubt. Here too, the desire of nations to maximize their economic interests seems to be a major determinant of their policy positions.

Islands. As it is developing, the coastal regime for island states will not be essentially different from that of other coastal states. The one special provision governing islands denies them the right to claim an economic zone or continental shelf for rocks that cannot sustain human life. At first glance, this would seem to erode some coastal states' claim to an expanded continental margin. However, on closer inspection, the delimitation referred to in the continental margin provisions turns out to be independent of the existence of offshore rocks, the outer boundary being determined instead on the basis of the "natural prolongation" of the continent.

This definition of the continental margin is designed to incorporate continentally derived sedimentary rock under coastal state jurisdiction. Lone standing rocks are often of volcanic origin, and thus are not petroleum-bearing sedimentary rock. Furthermore, rocks such as the famous islet, Rockall, located northwest of Ireland, are associated with faulted terraces which tend to fall within the "natural prolongation" definition of the continental margin. Consequently, the habitation qualification for rocks does not appear to be a significant impediment to access to offshore resources by coastal states, and it is additional evidence that potential restrictions on navigational freedom are avoided whenever there are no offsetting marine resource considerations.

Archipelagos. The major contribution of the single text when it comes to archipelagos is a definition. Without going into the details, this definition establishes the following as archipelago states: [24] Cape Verdes (if and when independent),

---

[24] The list of states qualifying as archipelagos under the single text is a first cut estimate made by the geographer of the U.S. Department of State, Robert Hodgson, on 18 June 1975. The question of including the Bahamas turns on the manner in which atolls are treated in a revised draft of the single text.

Grenada, Fiji, Indonesia, Jamaica, Maldives, Papua-New Guinea, the Philippines, and perhaps the Bahamas. The states that probably do *not* qualify include: Canada, Cuba, Cyprus, Dominican Republic, Haiti, Iceland, Ireland, Japan, Malagasy Republic, Malta, Mauritius, Micronesia, Nauru, Tonga, United Kingdom, and Western Samoa.

Like many of the other single-text provisions, this definition of the archipelago accommodates two principles: it permits some island states to bring valuable resources under their jurisdiction (in this case, mainly fisheries), yet it proscribes unrestrained grabs for large ocean areas, ostensibly to avoid political interference with navigational freedoms.

Fisheries on the High Seas. Articles 103 to 107 of the single text for the Second Committee must be read in conjunction with those outlining the rights of coastal states in their economic zones. All the encouraging words in the former articles about conserving living resources are effectively offset by the latter which permit coastal states to treat highly migratory species (mainly tuna) essentially as they please whenever these fish are inside their economic zones. Of course, the conservation techniques for coping with the so-called common-pool problem which are referred to in the articles are based upon maintaining constant stocks, that is, maximum sustainable yield. Many experts have pointed out that this criterion does not lead to the optimal yield in the broad economic sense.[25]

The only certain effect of these two sets of articles will be an increase in the cost of harvesting highly migratory species due to coastal state behavior and failure to conserve these species on the high seas. This in turn means that in the future there will be higher market prices and reduced output for these fish, which are among the most valuable species harvested.

Lateral and Opposite Delimitation. This issue is mentioned here not because of its inclusion in the single text, but because of its omission. The question of delimitation between and among states is properly recognized as an issue better left to bilateral or small multilateral negotiations among the states directly involved. Its omission clearly facilitates the progress of the conference.

It is regrettable that certain other issues were not omitted for the same reason. Only the few countries that possess the technology to recover manganese nodules, for example, need be involved in the deep-seabed negotiations. On the matter of the economic zone, the landlocked and geographically disadvantaged group is blocking what would be relatively easy negotiations if coastal states alone were participating.[26]

---

[25] See, for example, Richard J. Sweeney, *Second Best in Fishing Regulation,* paper prepared for the Office of the Assistant Secretary of Treasury for International Affairs, 1975.
[26] See Tollison and Willett paper in this volume for further development of this point.

Dispute Settlement. The single texts of the First, Second, and Third committees refer to the subject of dispute settlement without, however, composing draft articles on this subject. In fact, the three committees left the important question of dispute settlement to an informal ad hoc working group with a peak participation of about sixty delegations. This group produced a document which includes three major options and three suboptions and which, ipso facto, cannot be characterized as a *single* text. Even so, not all of the delegations that "took part in the work of the informal group . . . accepted the basic assumptions on which the group proceeded and some continued to oppose to the very end several important provisions contained in the informal working paper by the co-chairman of the group." [27]

Unlike the omission of lateral delimitation between states, the failure of the law of the sea conference to produce an official single text on dispute settlement is a serious matter. One might argue that delay in arriving at a single text on dispute settlement must assuredly mean delay in agreeing on a final treaty, for dispute settlement is the *sine qua non* of any body of law.

Summary

The axiom that nations act in their own interests, especially their economic interests, is reflected in all of the issues embodied in the law of the sea. It must be granted, of course, that not all negotiators are of equal skill, nor are the negotiators' motivations always perfectly aligned with interests they nominally represent. However, there is probably a kind of evolutionary theory at work where only those legal institutions survive which fill an important role for the producers and consumers. In a sense there is competition not only among interests of nations, but also among legal institutions. Should negotiators miscalculate (or misbehave), the convention they create does not survive and a strong motivation develops among the interests directly affected to circumvent the institution. This does not mean that proponents of interests are less than diligent in securing their interests. They are as evidenced in the several negotiations of the law of the sea conference. Developments in the technology of recovering offshore resources give rise to extensions of jurisdiction by coastal states eager to capture the benefits from the resources. Land-based producers of some minerals are leading the Group of 77 to adopt protectionist measures to help maintain the mineral export earnings of producers in less-developed countries. To achieve this national interest, they urge the adoption of a regime restricting the recovery of manganese nodules and perhaps consolidating much of the world's production of nickel, copper, cobalt, and manganese to cartels patterned on the model of the Organization of Petroleum Exporting Countries.

---

[27] Prepared Statement of Professor Louis B. Sohn to the U.S. Senate, Committee on Commerce, National Oceans Policy Study, 4 June 1975, p. 8.

In the final analysis, *the treaty must represent a mutually beneficial arrangement* which reflects the relative strengths of the interests being negotiated. Failure to achieve this leads directly to a search for alternative institutions and the coincident demise of the treaty.

The informal single negotiating text, while not a negotiated instrument, is a measure of the negotiators' success in obtaining prominent display for their viewpoints. The correlation between the provisions of the single text and the main trends in the discussions may not be close, but the successful negotiators of the single text do reflect the basic will to secure the economic interests of their countries.

Another attitude underlying the single text is an unwillingness to restrict navigation and other high-seas freedoms for political advantage. Rather than a single zone to which all dimensions of sovereignty would relate, the conference is defining many coastal belts, each of which seems to coincide with the range of a particular resource. The continental shelf is related to petroleum. The economic zone is associated with the range of coastal species of living resources. The contiguous zone and the territorial sea are related to the use of the sea, as for example, dump for pollutants. In each instance, national jurisdiction is expanded only to the extent of the economic resource, and not so far as to impede navigation. This restraint in extending jurisdiction makes one hopeful that within economic zones nations will behave rationally and hinder navigation only to the extent required for more valuable resource exploitation. To do so would clearly be consistent with the national interest since it would reduce the likelihood of increasing transportation costs.

The fact that it has taken six years to arrive at a single text is one indication that agreement on a treaty will not be reached soon. Whether and when a widely accepted treaty can be negotiated is most difficult to estimate. The deputy special representative for the United States has reported, "It is now clear that the negotiations cannot be completed before mid-1976 at the earliest and at this time it is not clear whether or not a treaty can be completed during 1976.[28]

One explanation for the delay, which is consistent with the single text, is that most countries do not yet have the technology to recover marine resources and few have been successful in attracting foreigners to operate off their shores *on their terms*. This situation will change eventually, but for the present, most states evidently do not feel pressured to arrive at a quick solution. They probably also sense that the trends in customary international law are in the desired direction. Consequently, the costs of waiting are not high. Indeed, there may be positive rewards for waiting. Should a country be overanxious for a treaty, it might be tempted to make concessions in hopes of speeding the pace of the nego-

---

[28] Statement of John Norton Moore before the U.S. Senate, Commerce Committee, National Oceans Policy Study, 3 June 1975, p. 2.

tiations. Of course, this would be a short-sighted view since such concessions are more likely to encourage delay by prompting countries to hold out for further concessions. Clearly, one important consequence of delay is the possibility that the countries that now have technological advantages or depletable resources might lose them.

The sheer number of important issues and of delegations is one of the factors slowing down the negotiations, but it has another important implication that is less obvious. The law of the sea negotiations are not a zero-sum game. That is, a concession by one country will not necessarily equal in magnitude the gain by another. Failure to recognize this situation could lead to negotiating mistakes, such as excessive generosity in making concessions and insistence upon too much protection for an interest. These mistakes further delay agreement.

It is by no means clear that failure to reach agreement in the near term will result in "anarchy and chaos," as is often claimed.[29] The legal regime for the oceans during all of recorded history has been characterized by a general lack of law. Indeed, most human endeavor remains unregulated by the sort of detailed international law discussed in this third UN conference. To characterize the relatively unregulated conduct of human endeavors in general, and use of the oceans in particular, as being chaotic would seem to be an exaggeration.

One might also question the ability of law to reduce conflict and eliminate chaos in all cases. There is a real danger, in fact, that a badly drafted treaty produced in haste might restrain appropriate activities and thus make the treaty itself a source of conflict and chaos. Economic analyses reveal many instances of legal restrictions on activities leading to misallocation of resources. When this happens, it becomes positively advantageous for someone to evade or overturn the restrictions. If the cost of doing this is less than the gain, conflict ensues, the rule of law is weakened, and the stage is set in the more extreme instances for social, economic, and international confrontation.

Another factor working for a more deliberate pace in the development of a law of the sea treaty is the advantage that could accrue to the Group of 77 if it should arrive at a consensus within its own ranks on a package deal to be presented to the other delegations. It might obtain maximum concessions from the rest of the conference by offering the package on an all-or-nothing basis. Formulating this package is taking an inordinate amount of time. The principal stumbling block has been the emergence in Geneva of the bloc of the landlocked and geographically disadvantaged states which is seeking access to the sea and priority participation in nearby fisheries. An interesting indication of their hopes of achieving these goals is their endorsement of the idea that some of the residual

---

[29] See especially the speech by U.S. Secretary of State Henry A. Kissinger before the American Bar Association convention, 11 August 1975, in Montreal, Canada. Also see the speech by U.S. Under Secretary of State Carlyle E. Maw before the International and Comparative Law Center of the Southwestern Legal Foundation, 18 June 1975, in Dallas, Texas.

rights in the economic zone should accrue to the coastal state.[30] If the landlocked and geographically disadvantaged bloc did not aspire to sharing in the resources of the nearby economic zones, it would have an interest in reserving these residual rights to the international community and thereby avoiding any possible increase, however slight, in the costs of ocean transportation. It goes without saying that the coastal states are most reluctant to grant an open-ended right to landlocked and geographically disadvantaged states to participate in their fisheries on a priority basis. For the time being, then, there is an impasse in accommodating the forty-five or so landlocked and geographically disadvantaged states who make up almost one third of the conference participants.

According to some African delegates who are members of the Group of 77, this situation is responsible for the group's lack of responsiveness to the concessions offered by developed countries in the deep-seabed negotiations of the First Committee. They say that there will be no resolution of the deep-seabed issues in the First Committee, where the Group of 77 is pretty much of one mind, until an accommodation is worked out with the landlocked countries on the Second Committee issue of their participation in the fisheries of coastal states. (It is worth noting that many of these forty-five or so states are land-based mineral producers and are, consequently, in the mainstream of Group of 77 thought in the First Committee.)

This suggests that it is the negotiation in the Second Committee that is pacing the progress in the first, not the reverse. If this conclusion is correct, then developed-nation concessions in the deep-seabed negotiations will not promote their objectives in the Second Committee, such as free passage through straits, since the impasse is ultimately conflict among less-developed states.

The overall conclusion that this observer reaches is that it may take years, if not another decade, for a widely adhered-to treaty to be negotiated, and even then the treaty is likely to be quite unfavorable to the developing nations' interests. During this time, customary international law will be developing at a slower pace, but toward a generally satisfactory resolution of the issues, by virtue of state actions. The choice that states face is whether to place their future fates in the hands of a law of the sea conference that, whether or not ultimately "successful," itself contributes to customary international law in perhaps a very undesirable way, or whether states, singly and in small groups united by common primary interests, will affect the course of a new oceans law by their own actions. An increasing number of states are choosing to chart their own course in the law of the sea.

---

[30] The representative of Singapore speaking on behalf of the landlocked and geographically disadvantaged states to the formal session of the Second Committee, 23 April 1975.

LIST OF PARTICIPANTS

Alexander, Lewis M., *Law of the Sea Institute, University of Rhode Island*
Amacher, Ryan, *Office of Research and Planning, Department of the Treasury, and Department of Economics, Arizona State University*
Barcella, Mary, *American Petroleum Institute*
Barton, John, *United Press International*
Blaney, Harry C., *Policy Planning Staff, Department of State*
Brown, Seyom, *The Brookings Institution*
Carlson, Eugene, *United Press International*
Christie, Francis T., Jr., *Resources for the Future*
Clarkson, Kenneth, *Department of Economics, University of Virginia*
Cline, William, *The Brookings Institution*
Coase, Ronald H., *University of Chicago Law School*
Coler, Mark, *Office of Raw Materials and Oceans Policy, Department of the Treasury*
Cook, Charles F., Jr., *American Mining Congress*
Cornell, Nina, *The Brookings Institution*
Dam, Kenneth W., *University of Chicago Law School*
De Soto, Alvaro, *Permanent Mission of Peru to the United Nations*
Dubs, Marne A., *Ocean Resources Department, Kennecott Copper Corporation*
Dugger, John, *International Energy Affairs, Federal Energy Administration*
Dykstra, Jacob J., *Point Judith Fishermen's Cooperative Association, Rhode Island*
Eckert, Ross D., *The Hoover Institution*
Ely, Northcutt, *Attorney, Washington, D. C.*
Englund, Merrill, *Office of Senator Lee Metcalf*
Finger, Michael, *Office of Research and Planning, Department of the Treasury*
Fisher, Anthony, *Department of Economics, University of Maryland*
George, James, *Subcommittee on Budgeting, U.S. Senate*
Greenwald, Richard, *Deepsea Ventures, Inc., Gloucester Point, Virginia*
Haight, G. Winthrop, *Forsyth, Decker and Murray, New York, New York*
Hollick, Ann L., *Johns Hopkins School for Advanced International Studies*
Hollander, Edward, *Council on International Economic Policy*
Hussey, John, *National Oceans Policy Study, U.S. Senate*
Johnson, David B., *Department of Economics, Louisiana State University*

195

Johnston, James L., *Office of Raw Materials and Oceans Policy, Department of the Treasury*

Kilmarx, Robert A., *Center for Strategic and International Studies*

Klock, David, *Office of Research and Planning, Department of the Treasury*

Knight, H. Gary, *Sea Grant Legal Program, Louisiana State University*

Landauer, Jerry, *Wall Street Journal*

Logue, Dennis E., *Amos Tuck School of Business Administration, Dartmouth College*

Miller, James C., III, *Staff, Council of Economic Advisers*

Mitchell, Edward J., *National Energy Project, American Enterprise Institute*

Moore, John Norton, *U.S. Law of the Sea Task Force*

McDougal, Myres S., *Yale Law School*

McGuire, Martin, *Department of Economics, University of Maryland*

McKean, Roland, *Department of Economics, University of Virginia*

McKeogh, Kay, *Office of Raw Materials and Oceans Policy, Department of the Treasury*

McKnight, Maxwell, *National Petroleum Council*

McWethy, John F., *U.S. News & World Report*

Niehaus, John, *Council on International Economic Policy*

Nye, Joseph S., *Department of Government, Harvard University*

Osgood, Robert E., *Johns Hopkins School for Advanced International Studies*

Pardo, Arvid, *Woodrow Wilson International Center for Scholars*

Paulsen, Walter E., *Ocean Policy Staff, U.S. Coast Guard*

Petrou, Basil, *Office of Raw Materials and Oceans Policy, Department of the Treasury*

Pulsipher, Allan G., *Staff, Council of Economic Advisers*

Ranson, R. David, *Office of the Secretary, Department of the Treasury*

Rooney, James, *Council on International Economic Policy*

Seevers, Gary L., *Council of Economic Advisers*

Sohn, Louis B., *Harvard Law School*

Somers, Edwin, *U.S. News & World Report*

Sweeney, Richard, *Office of Research and Planning, Department of the Treasury*

Tollison, Robert D., *Department of Economics, Texas A&M University*

Tosini, Peter C., *Office of Energy Economics, Department of the Treasury*

Usnick, Michael, *Office of Management and Budget*

Vega, Ramon, *Office of Research and Planning, Department of the Treasury*

Volpe, Michael, *Business Publishers, Inc.*

Walsh, Captain Don, *U.S. Navy (ret.), Annandale, Virginia*

Walsh, James P., *Commerce Committee, U.S. Senate*

Whitehurst, Clinton H., *General Accounting Office*

Willett, Thomas D., *Office of Research and Planning, Department of the Treasury*

Winter, Ralph K., *Yale Law School*

Zecher, Richard, *Staff, Council of Economic Advisers*

Cover and book design: Pat Taylor